T0319714

The Entrepreneurial Society

This book is a compilation of research contributions that have been presented at the conference Entrepreneurship, Culture, Finance and Economic Development that was held in Caen in June 2008.

The Entrepreneurial Society

How to Fill the Gap Between Knowledge and Innovation

Edited by

Jean Bonnet

Assistant Professor of Economics, University of Caen, France

Domingo García Pérez De Lema

Accounting Professor, Faculty of Business Studies, Technical University of Cartagena, Spain

Howard Van Auken

University Professor, College of Business, Iowa State University, USA

Edward Elgar

Cheltenham, UK • Northampton, MA, USA

Published by
Edward Elgar Publishing Limited
The Lypiatts
15 Lansdown Road
Cheltenham
Glos GL50 2JA
UK

Edward Elgar Publishing, Inc.
William Pratt House
9 Dewey Court
Northampton
Massachusetts 01060
USA

A catalogue record for this book
is available from the British Library

Library of Congress Control Number: 2009941250

Mixed Sources
Product group from well-managed
forests and other controlled sources
www.fsc.org Cert no. SA-COC-1565
© 1996 Forest Stewardship Council

ISBN 978 1 84844 891 9

Printed and bound by MPG Books Group, UK

Contents

Contributors

Abdesselam, Rafik Laboratoire ERIC EA 3038, University Lumière Lyon 2, France.

Aragón Sánchez, Antonio Department for Business Organization and Finance, Faculty for Economy and Business, Murcia University, Spain.

Bailly, Franck CARE EA 2260, Equipe Mondialisatie et Regulation, University of Rouen, France.

Bögenhold, Dieter School of Economics and Management, Free University of Bolzano, Italy.

Bonnet, Jean Faculty of Economics and Business Administration, CREM UMR CNRS 6211, University of Caen, France.

Chapelle, Karine CARE EA 2260, Equipe Mondialisatie et Regulation, University of Le Havre, France.

Cieply, Sylvie IUP banque assurance, CREM UMR CNRS 6211, University of Caen, France.

Cussy, Pascal Faculty of Economics and Business Administration, CREM UMR CNRS 6211, University of Caen, France.

Deák, Csaba Faculty of Economics, University of Miskolc, Hungary.

Dejardin, Marcus ERIM, Erasmus University Rotterdam and CERPE, FUNDP, University of Namur, Belgium.

Duréndez, Antonio Faculty of Business, Technical University of Cartagena, Spain.

Fachinger, Uwe Economics and Demography, Centre for Research on Ageing and Society, University of Vechta, Germany.

García Pérez De Lema, Domingo Faculty of Business, Technical University of Cartagena, Spain.

Hernández-Cánovas, Ginés Faculty of Business, Technical University of Cartagena, Spain.

Le Nadant, Anne-Laure Faculty of Economics and Business Administration, CREM UMR CNRS 6211, University of Caen, France.

Le Pape, Nicolas Faculty of Economics and Business Administration, GAINS-TEPP and CREM, University of Le Mans, France.

Madrid-Guijarro, Antonia Faculty of Business, Technical University of Cartagena, Spain.

Rubio Bañón, Alicia Department for Business Organization and Finance, Faculty for Economy and Business, Murcia University, Spain.

Sastre Vivaracho, Paula Department for Business Organization and Finance, Faculty for Economy and Business, Murcia University, Spain.

Testa, Stefania University of Genoa, Italy.

Van Auken, Howard College of Business, Iowa State University, USA.

van Stel, André EIM Business and Policy Research, Zoetermeer, the Netherlands.

Verheul, Ingrid Rotterdam School of Management, Erasmus University, Center for Entrepreneurship, the Netherlands.

Introduction

Jean Bonnet, Domingo García Pérez De Lema and Howard Van Auken

In recent years entrepreneurship has re-emerged as an important component underlying economic growth in Europe and North America. The restructuring of the US economy from an industrial-based economy to an entrepreneurial-based economy is well under way. Entrepreneurial firms (young and innovative firms) are an integral part of the transition process and have been the engine of economic growth for over a decade. The vast majority of all businesses in the USA are small, and a record number of new firms are started each year. Small firms make a significant contribution to private sector output, employment, net new jobs creation and innovations. Many of the new firms are the creators and leaders of new industries. Most job-creating firms are fast-growing and generating a disproportionate amount of innovations, patents and new technologies. Evidence indicates that the trend toward an entrepreneurial society is accelerating (Wong et al., 2005).

Small businesses are important to economy vibrancy, employment growth and wealth creation for almost all world economies (Craig et al, 2003). Europe is in this respect certainly more entrepreneurial than in the 1960s and 1970s. However European economies remain considerably less entrepreneurial than other world economies. In fact, the world economy has generally become more entrepreneurial than European economies (Audrestch, 2006; surveys of Global Entrepreneurship Monitor, GEM). According to Erkki Liikanen (2003) (Member of the European Commission, responsible for Enterprise and the Society Information), 'Europe suffers from an entrepreneurship deficit in comparison to the US'. Strong recent economic growth in the US economy is partly due to the entrepreneurial activity associated with the creation of knowledge-based companies. European economies may benefit from developing a similar economic strategy that is based on greater entrepreneurial intensity, especially in the innovation sectors. The lack of entrepreneurship capital leads to the European paradox; a high level of knowledge investment with poor results in terms of growth and reduction of unemployment (Audretsch,

2007b). Moreover the gap in productivity between Europe and the USA is deepening. In addition, some prospective studies predict that the European contribution to world production will decline due to the catching-up effect of the Asian emergent economies (IFRI, 2002). By stimulating the spirit of entrepreneurship, Europe might reinforce its economic position.

Many macroeconomic and institutional causes can explain differences in entrepreneurial intensity between countries and areas. These include economic growth, level of development, unemployment rate, development and operation of the financial system, intensity of administrative barriers, specificities of the labor market, self-employment taxation, legal consequences of firm failure, entrepreneurial spirit and collective perception of firm failure. As Audrestch (2007b, p. 69) observes: 'Barriers to entrepreneurship can impede knowledge spillover entrepreneurship. Such barriers range from legal restrictions and impediments to the existence and availability of early stage finance, or to social and institutional tradition discouraging entrepreneurship and a stigma associated with failed attempts as entrepreneurship. The capacity of an economy to generate entrepreneurial behaviour is shaped by the extent of its underlying entrepreneurship capital'. This set of causes, which affects entrepreneurship capital, has to do with what Baumol refers to in a 1990 article as the rules of the game, that is, the structure of reward in the economy (Baumol, 1990). He notes that certain societies historically favored rather adverse structures of reward to the development of entrepreneurship. These structures divert national or local elites from the exercise of the entrepreneurial function and prove indirectly harmful to the diffusion of technical progress (ancient Rome with the valorization of the political office, medieval China with the mandarin system and so on). Over the recent period, these structures enable us to understand the 'unhooking' of certain European countries relative to the difference between an entrepreneurial society which embraces private initiative and a wage society which increases the opportunity cost associated with undertaking new ventures.

The decision to become an entrepreneur is mainly a decision of allocation of one's human capital balancing an entrepreneurship opportunity cost with a reward (financial, symbolic – social status –, indeed psychological) prospect. The microeconomic decision to get into entrepreneurship allows approaching entrepreneurship in terms of occupational choice. From a labor market perspective the decision to set up a new firm can be viewed as a self-employment choice, that is, an alternative to a salaried or unemployed position. In an entrepreneurial society wage earners are not guaranteed job security or economic stability because of employers' latitude to reduce labor costs through lay-offs. On the other hand, a flexible labor market can encourage individuals to undertake new ventures because of the positive signal for future employers even if the company fails. Too rigid a labor market and the stigmatization of entrepreneurial failure discourages some qualified and experienced employees to value their human capital as entrepreneurs. In most European countries unemployed people are very much overrepresented in the population of new entrepreneurs. The share of unemployed new entrepreneurs is high because of the low propensity to launch a firm when employed or enrolled as a student. If we compare France, the UK and the USA we can notice that France has a low entrepreneurial activity, the UK a medium one and the USA a high entrepreneurial activity. This gap reflects the traditional opposition between a salaried society and an entrepreneurial society which encourages employment through entrepreneurship. If we consider the 2000–03 period, the average total entrepreneurial activity (TEA) varies from 4.35 per cent for France to 6.6 per cent for the UK and 12.7 per cent for the USA (GEM, 2004).

The first part of the book, comprising three contributions, is entitled: Contextualizing the link between factors and effects of new firm's formation.

Why would it be desirable to have more entrepreneurs? Taking into account structural changes, diversity of motives and new regulation in the labor market, a proportion of entrepreneurs (mainly self-employed) may not be considered as innovators in the Schumpeterian sense.

Yet, according to Ingrid Verheul and André Van Stel (Chapter 1), three positive effects can be found in the economic literature. The selection effect that accounts for the survival of the fittest; the breadth effect that stresses the diversity of the products ensuring opportunities for incremental innovations and new offers of products (spillovers) and the complementary effect that allows a direct positive welfare effect through a better match between the supply of goods with an increasing demand for variety. One may wonder whether all entrepreneurs fare the same in this respect. Differentiating among firms according to the criteria of age, education and gender and taking into account the level of development of the country, interesting patterns emerge. In developing countries older and more highly educated entrepreneurs are particularly important for stimulating economic growth, while younger entrepreneurs are more important in developed countries.

In the same vein, according to Jean Bonnet and Pascal Cussy (Chapter 2), the insufficient involvement of younger educated people and especially French elites – for instance, graduate students from 'Grandes Ecoles' – in entrepreneurship is critical for economic growth in the case of France. This insufficient involvement may be explained by the existence of sunk costs[1] for this type of population and contributes greatly to the inadequacy of entrepreneurial capital described by Audretsch. The best talents apply for comfortable positions as executives as civil servants or working in public firms with attractive wage trajectories. 'Better paid (members of the five main state bodies) and more highly regarded than other civil servants, the members keep this advantage until the end of their career' (Lebègue and Walter, 2008). And, as innovative projects require a long time to finalize, they also imply the risk of a greater depreciation of the human capital when the project fails. In that case there exists a greater sunk cost for graduate individuals who have experimented with entrepreneurship failure that reduces the propensity to launch a project for this type of population.

Dieter Bögenhold and Uwe Fachinger (Chapter 3) question the solo self-employment in Germany. Does it serve as a valve of a pressing labor market or must it be regarded more positively as a new option in the classic division of labor by which an increasing number of people find new self-reliance and job stability? They identify structural changes but also changes in labor market regulation and changes in welfare state regulations that 'make it easier for firms to outsource jobs and to do business with the same people as freelancers'. Nevertheless the category of self-employment also reflects structural changes within an economy and society and the emergence of new innovative professions which can operate also through freelance activities or micro-firms. Self-employment is heterogeneous and mono-causal explanations do not match, especially at the regional level since regional differences can be regarded as different levels of historically grounded specific socio-economic differences. Regional differences must be taken as elements and variables of a holistic entrepreneurship research.

Once the importance of innovative entrepreneurship is acknowledged, one may think about the factors that enhance or rather constrain entrepreneurial firms to emerge or to develop. The science-technology-firm system, formed by the association of universities, research centers, scientific parks, incubators, public administration, business organizations and firms, develops, supports and improves research, technological development and innovation. In this context, Markman et al. (2005) highlight the role of University Technology Transfer Offices (UTTOs) in the success of business incubators and technology parks in university settings. This link is justified by the fact that research-orientated institutions are identified as the modern seedbeds for technological innovation. However, the scarcity of collaboration among the agents included in the science-technology-firm system often constrains potential profitability. Analysing this system to establish a better match between supply and demand of resources and knowledge could increase collaboration, synergies and incentives that improve the regional research and development effort. Therefore, universities should be considered as critical agents in economic growth and development (Chrisman et al., 1995). Some authors put forward access to financial capital as a prerequisite for any entrepreneurial and especially any innovative commitment. A set of theoretical articles show that new entrepreneurs are financially constrained (Jaffee and Russell, 1976; Stiglitz and Weiss, 1981). However, there is no empirical consensus on the existence of credit rationing. For instance, Evans and Jovanovic (1989), Evans and Leighton (1989), Holtz-Eakin et al. (1994) show a significant positive relationship between individuals' wealth and their probability to become self-employed. They conclude that start-ups suffer from capital gap. Nevertheless financial capital could be correlated with unobservable factors such as managerial skills, or more generally human capital of the entrepreneur. Hence the introduction in some work (Blanchflower and Oswald, 1998; Lindh and Ohlsson, 1996) of exogenous events such as inheritances, gifts or incomes from the lottery confirms the positive influence of wealth on the entrepreneurial commitment. Financial constraints would exist and would tend to exclude those who have insufficient funds. According to Parker (2004) this leads to the endogeinity problem: 'Whereby the self-employed are wealthy because of previous success in self-employment'. Parker sheds light on several alternative explanations also consistent with the previous results on financial constraints. Cressy (1996), for his part, finds, using British data, 'that human capital is the true determinant of survival of new firms and that the correlation between financial capital and survival is spurious'. 'Provision of finance is demand – driven, with banks supplying funds elastically and business request governing take-up. Firms self-select for funds on the basis of the human capital endowments of the proprietors with "better" business more likely to borrow. A reason why others have seemingly identified start-up debt-gaps may be the failure to test a sufficiently rich empirical model' (Cressy, 1996, p. 1253). In a recent report the OECD (2006) supports the idea that 'in a number of high income OECD countries, there is little evidence of an overall scarcity of financing for SMEs' (p. 11). Although there is no empirical consensus on the existence of credit rationing, it is acknowledged that one of the main weaknesses for the development of European incubators is the lack and underdevelopment of seed financing and business angel networks (Aernoudt, 2004). This situation is in contrast with the USA where a financial system supporting business formation and growth has been created (Acs and Szerb, 2007).

The second part of the book is entitled: Understanding the importance of access to finance and to available support systems. Four contributions deal with access to resources for new entrepreneurs, highlighting access to finance. Access to an adequate supply of resources is indeed crucial for firms to be able to operate and survive.

In the first contribution Ginés Hernández-Cánovas, Antonia Madrid-Guijarro and Howard Van Auken (Chapter 4) investigate the role of qualitative factors (for example, personality/experience of the entrepreneur, characteristics of the firm's product/services and firm's strategy/organization) for commercial banks when assessing applications for funding by technology-based firms in Spain. Capital acquisition among technology-based firms is difficult because of a number of factors, including, for example, the high perceived risk associated with lack of collaterals, limited stream of revenues and lack of understanding of technology commercialization among traditional providers of capital. Lenders assess funding requests using both qualitative and quantitative information. The study by Hernández-Cánovas, Madrid-Guijarro and Van Auken shows that qualitative factors are as important as quantitative information to assess the creditworthiness of technology-based firms. The study finds that qualitative factors related to the personality and experience of the entrepreneur, characteristics of the product and services offered by the firm, and the strategy and organization of the firm are taken into account in addition to the traditional quantitative factors. The value of soft information together with a high rotation of loan officers can help explain why financial institutions incentivize the use of more complete credit files where this information can be stored.

Sylvie Cieply and Marcus Dejardin (Chapter 5) study financial constraints that new French firms experienced during the mid-1990s when the role of banks was predominant. Financial constraints affecting new firms are some of the factors most cited for impeding entrepreneurial dynamics from flourishing. In fact, financing is one of the primary reasons for distress and failure among new firms. Obstacles to capital acquisition among new firms are due to a number of reasons that include, for example, a high risk of default and inadequate collaterals (especially for firms introducing innovation). The inability to provide well-established track records to bankers leads to information asymmetry which, in turn, commonly acts as a constraint to capital acquisition through credit rationing. Three types of credit rationing are distinguished: the well-known strong and weak credit rationing cases and a self-constraint case induced by the discouragement of entrepreneurs on the credit market. Cieply and Dejardin find that many new firms (more than half of their sample) are not, in fact, credit constrained. Also strong rationing and self-constraint rationing are higher for innovative firms, which supports the idea that the proportion of discouraged borrowers is higher in innovative sectors than in non-innovative sectors. Other means of financing, like venture capital, business angels and trade credit, played a minor role in the financing of new French firms during the mid-1990s.

Antonio Aragón Sánchez, Alicia Rubio Bañón and Paula Sastre Vivaracho (Chapter 6) explore the context of entrepreneurship in Spain, focusing on regional environment factors assessed by a pool of experts disseminated in all the 17 Spanish regions (plus Ceuta and Melilla). The data were collected as part of the Global Entrepreneurship Monitor initiative. A central focus of their study is to better understand differences in entrepreneurial orientation among regions. This type of study is important as governments try to develop policies supporting entrepreneurial firms that can effectively compete in world markets. Greater access to capital from private investors and an active venture capital market were two of the differences between regions with relatively high and low entrepreneurial activity. Other factors explaining differences in entrepreneurial activity included availability of scientific parks/incubators, support for science and technology, economic support for engineers and access to physical infrastructure. Financial support for infrastructure is a prerequisite underlying all of these additional factors.

The importance of private equity is examined by Rafik Abdesselam, Sylvie Cieply and Anne-Laure Le Nadant (Chapter 7). Their chapter uses differences in financial and legal systems to explain the differences in the role of private equity in the financing of transfers of shares in five European countries (France, Germany, Italy, Spain and the UK) that have different corporate governance systems. Similarities and dissimilarities in the financing of transfers of shares are compared between the countries. Their study finds differences between the UK, which is a pure market-based economy, and the other countries, which are rather bank-centered economies. Private equity firms are very important in the financing of transfers of shares in bank-centered economies, and in the financing of transfers of shares in civil law countries. Their results suggests the need for financial intermediaries providing equity financing in the economies with a lower investor protection, lower quality of accounting standards and a lower quality of law enforcement. Differences between France and the UK in terms of deals' financing suggest that convergence towards the Anglo-US corporate governance system is not completed yet.

Education and culture play an important role in entrepreneurship. Examining diversified populations and their attitude towards entrepreneurship is a way to extend research at the micro-level while also considering macro-level implications. For example, Hofstede (2001) notices that uncertainty-avoidance is not equally distributed among cultures. The different populations may be, for example, ethnic populations, which raises the question of whether ethnic entrepreneurship exists and, if so, is a response to labor market discrimination or driven by specialization or market niches and network supports. The object of analysis may also be countries where entrepreneurship was not permitted for a long time (Eastern countries). How does the entrepreneurial commitment take place in this context and what kind of support does it need? Education and experience may also have an impact on the commitment of the individual and the strategies pursued that facilitate firm success. Part of literature in management has identified what has been named the entrepreneurial orientation (EO) of entrepreneurs: 'An entrepreneurial firm is ones that engages in product market innovation, undertakes somewhat risky ventures and is first to come up with proactive innovations, beating competitors to the punch' (Miller, 1983). Lumpkin and Dess (1996) have identified five variables to specify the definition of the concept of entrepreneurial orientation (proactiveness, competitive aggressiveness, willingness to take risk, autonomy and innovativeness). Proactiveness is characterized by the anticipation of opportunities, the detection of future trends in the market and a high responsiveness to market signals that allows the firm to benefit from first mover advantages. The firm acts in advance to less responsive rivals, thus enabling it to be in a good position to seize market shares and to show superior performance over rivals. A proactive firm tends to shape its environment in its favor (Frese et al., 1996). It acts in anticipating future problems, needs or changes. Competitive aggressiveness is measured by the intensity of a firm to outperform its industry rivals: deliberate action/reactive action. To be aggressive requires adopting tactics towards competitors in order to weaken them or to benefit from their weaknesses. It also has to do with a reactive behavior, that is, the capacity to respond to threats, to trends and demands that already exist in the marketplace (Lumpkin and Dess, 1997). In the case of new firms the aggressiveness posture is a means to establish a position, a kind of legitimacy.

The third part of the book is entitled: Accounting for the interplay between the individual and the organizational levels and the firm's behavior and performance.

In the first chapter Domingo García Pérez De Lema and Antonio Duréndez (Chapter 8) focus the research on young SMEs, identifying organizational culture and assessing the relationship between organizational culture, particularly regarding innovative culture, management control systems (MCS) use, and their effects on performance. The development and evolution of young firms is a central issue in entrepreneurship research. The outcome in terms of firms' performance, particularly growth, has received considerable empirical and theoretical consideration, but the simultaneous pattern of growth and profit performance evolution of young firms has received relatively little empirical attention. Using a sample of 89 young Spanish SMEs, they find that innovative culture and use of management control systems have a positive effect on firms' performance. The empirical evidence confirms that an innovative culture (a mixture of clan and adhocracy) affects positively young firms' global performance, while a hierarchical culture negatively influences the internal process model of performance. Additionally, their findings show that management control systems allow the young firms to achieve higher organizational performance. Thus they verify that management control systems are an essential factor for young firms, since they provide essential information for decision-making processes. Young entrepreneurs should be made aware of benefits resulting from the implementation of an innovative culture and the use of management control systems. They should understand that an innovative attitude implies the adoption of new ideas and values that are not threats but strengths, in order to gain competitiveness and ensure the future of the firm. The best strategy might be to focus on exploratory learning and innovation.

Jean Bonnet and Nicolas Le Pape (Chapter 9) show that post-entry strategies of new entrepreneurs have some implications on the duration of the new firm. The survival of the new firm depends not only on the entrepreneur's characteristics, the founding and environmental conditions of entrepreneurship, but also on the development policy that the new entrepreneur adopts and has the capacity to implement (Covin and Covin, 1990). Besides financial variables often cited in the economic literature, the real behavior of the firm and of its owner play an important role in the explanation of the survival of the firm. Entrepreneurial behavior that includes all activities or attitudes aimed at overcoming rivals increases the life span of the firm. A proactive posture then constitutes an efficient strategy for the survival and the development of the new firm. Proactiveness could result from a specific entrepreneurial spirit, from a lower aversion to risk or from entrepreneurial abilities that some individuals are endowed with. The intriguing connections between this 'entrepreneurial human capital' and the implementation of successful aggressive policies must be explored in further detail.

Csaba Deák and Stephania Testa (Chapter 10) use the concept of intellectual capital, the ability to utilize knowledge resources, in two dimensions, regional and organizational. Intellectual capital is a key element for the development of dynamic core competencies in firms. In SMEs the regional cognitive and intangible resources are especially important due to the scarcity of resources experienced by this kind of firm. In this chapter the authors deal with the factors that determine the participation of SMEs in regional and organizational intellectual capital exchange. Deák and Testa classify firms in different groups: (1) companies that play an essential role in knowledge generation and diffusion (give and take subgroup); (2) companies that operate in egoistic terms (take subgroup); and (3) companies that remain isolated (no give-no take subgroup). As previous literature is devoted to knowledge-intensive sectors, this research is focused on non-knowledge-intensive sectors (food industries in Northwest Italy and North Hungary) in order to fill the gap. This research confirms that different firms' behaviors in relation to the intellectual capital exchange exist among SMEs, and that heterogeneity depends on individual-level entrepreneurial characteristics, and not only on a firm's knowledge base or position within networks.

Franck Bailly and Karine Chapelle (Chapter 11) explore the non-profit entrepreneurship in the French region of High-Normandy. Non-profit organizations are important in the economy due to their contribution to the GDP growth and employment. The type of entrepreneurship embodied in non-profit organizations is different from the one identified in for-profit organizations. The specificity is based on a high social motivation, as entrepreneurs or CEOs of non-profit organizations are more sensitive to social and ideological considerations. However, this specificity is at least somehow controversial, and several authors are cautious about it. In this sense, the decline of public funds may lead to non-profit organizations seeking commercial private funding; this fact could change the initial social goal of the company. The authors investigate the presence or absence of social motivations in non-profit organizations, and if this kind of firms has easier access to finance (public and private funds) than their for-profit counterparts. Better access to funds at non-profit organizations could be justified by the non-profit-distribution constraint and the social motivations. Bailly and Chapelle conduct an original survey on established organizations, and find that social motivations of non-profit organizations exist and are reflected in the target groups of firms' actions. However, the results about access to finance are not so clear. Although financial entities and public institutions favor the non-profit status, through larger loans and government subsidies, this treatment could be justified by the larger number of founders in non-profit organizations, and by the provision of stronger guarantees.

NOTE

1. In industrial organization, sunk costs refers to irreversible investments when the firm decides to enter an activity. Here the sunk costs refer to the depreciation of part of the human capital of the 'Grandes Ecoles' students when they decide to become entrepreneurs due to the loss of the Grand Ecoles networks.

BIBLIOGRAPHY

Acs, Z.J. and L. Szerb (2007), 'Entrepreneurship, economic growth and public policy', *Small Business Economics*, **28**, 109–22.

Aernoudt, R. (2004), 'Incubators: tool for entrepreneurship?', *Small Business Economics*, **23** (2), 127–35.

Agarwal, A. (2006), 'Engaging the inventor: exploring licensing strategies for university inventions and the role of latent knowledge', *Strategic Management Journal*, **27** (1), 63–79.

Albert P. (2009), 'Le high-tech, grande illusion du décideur', *l'Expansion Entrepreneuriat, Innover, Développer, Grandir*, January, 14–19.

Audretsch, D. (1995), *Innovation and Industry Evolution*, Cambridge, MA: MIT Press.

Audretsch, D. (2006), 'L'émergence de l'économie entrepreneuriale', *Reflets et Perspectives de la vie économique*, **XLV** (1), 43–70.

Audretsch, D. (2007a), *The Entrepreneurial Society*, New York: Oxford University Press.

Audretsch, D. (2007b), 'Entrepreneurship capital and economic growth', *Oxford Review of Economic Policy*, **23** (1), 63–78.

Baumol, W.J. (1990), 'Entrepreneurship, productive, unproductive and destructive', *Journal of Political Economy*, **98**, October, 893–921.

Baumol, W.J. (2004), 'Education for innovation: breakthroughs vs. corporate incremental improvements', *NBER Papers*, no. 5, April.

Bhattacharjee, A., J. Bonnet, N. Le Pape and R. Renault (2008), 'Entrepreneurial motives and performance: why might better educated entrepreneurs be less successful?', University of Cergy-Pontoise working paper du THema.

Blanchflower, D.G. and A.J. Oswald (1998), 'What makes an entrepreneur?', *Journal of Labor Economics*, **16** (1), 26–60.

Bonnet J., S. Cieply and M. Dejardin (2005), 'Financial constraints on new firms: looking for regional disparities', *Brussels Economic Review*, **3**, Autumn, 217–46.

Carree, M.A. and A.R. Thurik (2003), 'The impact of entrepreneurship on economic growth', in Z.J. Acs and D.B. Audretsch (eds), *Handbook of Entrepreneurial Research*. Boston, MA: Kluwer Academic Publishers, pp. 437–71.

Chrisman, J.J., T. Hynes and S. Fraser (1995), 'Faculty entrepreneurship and economic development: the case of the University of Calgary', *Journal of Business Venturing*, **10**, 267–81.

Commission Européenne (2003), 'Rapport sur la compétitivité européenne', Document de Travail SEC no. 1299.

Commission of the European Communities (2003), 'Entrepreneurship in Europe', green paper, Brussels, 21 January, document based on COM(2003) 27 final.

Covin, J.G. and D.P. Slevin (1989), 'Strategic management of small firms in hostile and benign environments', *Strategic Management Journal*, **10**, 75–87.

Covin, J.G. and D.P. Slevin (1991), 'A conceptual model of entrepreneurship as firm behaviour', *Entrepreneurship Theory and Practice*, **16** (1), Fall, 7–25.

Covin, J.G. and T.J. Covin (1990), 'Competitive aggressiveness, environmental context, and small firm performance', *Entrepreneurship Theory and Practice*, **15** (2), 35–50.

Craig, B., W. Jackson and J. Thomson (2003), 'On SBA-guaranteed lending and economic growth', Federal Reserve Bank of Cleveland working paper, April.

Cressy, R. (1996), 'Are business start-ups debt-rationed?', *Economic Journal*, **438**, 1253–70.

Duflo, E. (2008), 'Too many bankers?', 'Research-based policy analysis and commentary from leading economists', accessed 8 October 2009 at www.voxeu.org/.

Evans, D.S. and B. Jovanovic (1989), 'An estimated model of entrepreneurial choice under liquidity constraints', *Journal of Political Economy*, **97** (4), 808–27.

Evans, D.S., and L. Leighton (1989), 'Some empirical aspects of entrepreneurship', *American Economic Review*, **79** (3), 519–35.

Fairlie, R.W. (2004), 'Does business ownership provide a source of upward mobility for blacks and Hispanics?', in D. Holtz-Eakin (ed.), *Entrepreneurship and Public Policy*, Cambridge, MA: MIT Press, pp. 153–80.

Fairlie, R.W. and A. Robb (2006), 'Families, human capital, and small business: evidence from the characteristics of business owners survey', in Mirjam Van Praag (ed.), *Entrepreneurship and Human Capital*, Amsterdam, Netherlands: Amsterdam Center for Entrepreneurship, Faculty of Economics and Business, University of Amsterdam, July, pp. 5–11.

Florio, M. (1996), 'Large firms, entrepreneurship and regional development policy: "growth poles" in the Mezzogiorno over 40 years', *Entrepreneurship and Regional Development*, **8**, 263–95.

Fonseca, R., P. Lopez-Garcia and C.A. Pissarides (2001), 'Entrepreneurship, start-up costs and employment', *European Economic Review*, **45** (4–6), May, 692–705.

Fosfuri, A. and M.S. Giarratana (2004), 'Product strategies and startups' survival in turbulent industries: evidence from the security software industry', Universidad Carlos III Departamento de Economía de la Empresa business economics working papers wb044816.

Frese, M., W. Kring, A. Soose and J. Zempel (1996), 'Personal initiative at work: differences between East and West Germany', *Academy of Management Journal*, **39** (1), 37–63.

Frese, M., M. Van Gelderen and M. Ombach (2000), 'How to plan as a small scale business owner: psychological processes characteristics of action strategies and success', *Journal of Small Business Management*, **38** (2), 1–18.

GEM (Global Entrepreneurship Monitor) (2004), 'Executive report', Z.J. Acs, P. Arenus, P. Hay and M. Minniti, Babson College and London Business School.

GEM (Global Entrepreneurship Monitor) (2006), 'Summary results', N. Bosma and R. Harding, Babson College and London Business School.

Gilson, R. (1999), 'The legal infrastructure of high technology industrial district: Silicon Valley, Route 128, and covenants not to compete', *New York University Law Review*, **3**, 575–629.

Hofstede, G. (2001), *Cultures' Consequences*, 2nd edn, Thousand Oaks, CA: Sage.

Holcombe, R.G. (2003), 'The origins of entrepreneurial opportunities', *Review of Austrian Economics*, **16**, 25–43.

Holtz-Eakin, D. and C. Kao (2003), 'Entrepreneurship and economic growth: the proof is in the productivity', Syracuse University Maxwell School Center for Policy Research working paper no. 50.

Holtz-Eakin, D., D. Joulfaian and H.S. Rosen (1994), 'Sticking it out:

entrepreneurial survival and liquidity constraints', *Journal of Political Economy*, **102** (1), 53–75.

Institut Français des Relations Internationales (IFRI) (2002), *Le commerce mondial au XXIème siècle*, report, October.

Jaffee, D.W. and T. Russell (1976), 'Imperfect information, uncertainty and credit rationing', *Quaterly Journal of Economics*, **90** (4), November, 651–66.

Johansson, E. (2000), 'Self-employment and liquidity constraints: evidence from Finland', *Scandinavian Journal of Economics*, **102** (1), 123–34.

Jovanovic, C.B. (1982), 'Selection and the evolution of industry', *Econometrica*, **50**, May, 649–70.

Keh, H.T., T.T.M. Nguyen and H.P. Ng (2007), 'The effects of entrepreneurial orientation and marketing information on the performance of SMEs', *Journal of Business Venturing*, **22**, 592–611.

Kirzner, I.M. (1979), *Perception, Opportunity and Profit*, Chicago, IL: University of Chicago Press.

Kirzner, I.M. (1985), *Discovery and the Capitalist Process*, Chicago, IL: University of Chicago Press.

Kirzner, I.M. (2009), 'The alert and creative entrepreneur: a clarification', *Small Business Economics*, **32** (2), February, 145–52.

Klepper, S. and S. Sleeper (2005), 'Entry by spinoffs', *Management Science*, **51** (8), 1291–306.

Krabel, S. and P. Mueller (2008), 'Academic entrepreneurship – what drives scientists to start their company', paper presented at the 25th Celebration Conference 2008 on 'Entrepreneurship and Innovation – Organizations, Institutions, Systems and Regions', Copenhagen, Denmark, 17-20 June.

Lazear, E.P. and R. McNabb (2004), *Personnel Economics, Concepts*, vol 1, *Performance*, vol 2, The International Library of Critical Writings in Economics, series editor Mark Blaug, Cheltenham, UK and Northampton, MA, USA: Edward Elgar.

Lèbegue, T. and E. Walter (2008), Grandes Ecoles: la fin d'une exception française, Paris: Calman Lévy.

Liikanen, E. (2003), 'Entrepreneurship in Europe', Conference on Entrepreneurship/SME Package, Brussels, 22 January.

Lindh, T and H. Ohlsson (1996), 'Self-employment and windfall gains: evidence from the Swedish lottery', *Economic Journal*, **106**, November, 1515–26.

Lucas, R.E. (1978), 'On the size distribution of business firms', *Bell Journal of Economics*, **9** Autumn, 508–23.

Lumpkin, G.T. and G.G. Dess (1996), 'Clarifying the entrepreneurial orientation construct and linking it to performance', *Academy of Management Review*, **21**, 135–72.

Lumpkin, G.T. and G.G. Dess (1997), 'Proactiveness versus competitive aggressiveness: teasing apart key dimensions of an entrepreneurial orientation', in P.D. Reynolds, W. Bygrave, N. Carter et al. (eds), *Frontiers of Entrepreneurship Research*, Babson Park, MA: Babson College, pp. 47–58.

Lumpkin, G.T. and G.G. Dess (2001), 'Linking two dimensions of entrepreneurial orientation to firm performance: the moderating role of environment and industry life cycle', *Journal of Business Venturing*, **16**, 429–51.

Markman, G.D., P.H. Phan, D.B. Balkin and P.T. Gianiodis (2005), 'Entrepreneurship and university-based technology transfer', *Journal of Business Venturing*, **20**, 241–63.

McClelland, D.C. (1961), '"Entrepreneurship behavior" and "Characteristics of entrepreneurs"', in D.C. McClelland, *The Achieving Society*, Princeton, NJ: D. Van Nostrand, pp. 205–58, 259–300.

McClelland, D.C. (1965), 'Achievement and entrepreneurship: a longitudinal study', *Journal of Personality and Social Psychology*, **1** (2), 389–92.

Miller, D. (1983), 'The correlates of entrepreneurship in three types of firms', *Management Science*, **29**, 770–91.

Moreau, R. (2008), 'La spirale du succès entrepreneurial', grand prix 2007 de la réflexion impertinente sur le développement durable, l'entrepreneuriat, et le développement des territoires, *Population & Avenir*, no. 687, March–April.

Moreno, A.M. and J.C. Casillas (2008), 'Entrepreneurial orientation and growth of SMEs: a causal model', *Entreprenership Theory and Practice*, 32, 507–28.

OECD (Organisation for Economic Co-operation and Development) (2006), *The SME Financing Gap: Theory and Evidence*, vol. I, Paris: OECD.

Parker, S.C. (2004), *The Economics of Self-employment and Entrepreneurship*, Cambridge: Cambridge University Press.

Philippon, T. and A. Reshef (2007), 'Skill biased financial development: education, wages and occupations in the U.S. finance sector', New York University Stern Business School mimeograph, September.

Rotter, J.B. (1966), 'General expectancies for internal versus external control of reinforcement', *Psychology Monographs*, **80**, (609).

Rotter, J.B. (1971), 'External control and internal control', *Psychology Today*, **5**, 37–42, 58–9.

Shapero, A. (1975), 'The displaced, uncomfortable entrepreneur', *Psychology Today*, **9** (6), 83–8.

Shapero, A. and L. Sokol (1982), *The Social Dimensions of Entrepreneurship, Encyclopedia of Entrepreneurship*, Englewood Cliffs, NJ: Prentice Hall, pp. 72–90.

Schramm, C. (2009), 'Our role in the evolution of capitalism', in *Kauffman Thoughtbook*, Kansas City, MO: Kaufman Foundation, pp. 8–14.

Smilor, R. (1997), 'Entrepreneurship reflexions on a subversive activity', *Journal of Business Venturing*, **12**, 341–6.

Smith, K.G., W.J. Ferrier and C.M. Grimm (2001), 'King of the hill: dethroning the industry leader', *The Academy of Management Executive*, **15** (2), 59–70.

Stam, W. and T. Elfring (2008), 'Entrepreneurial orientation and new venture performance: the moderating role of intra- and extraindustry social capital', *Academy of Management Journal*, **51**, 97–111.

Stein, J. (2002, 'Information production and capital allocation: decentralized vs. hierarchical firms', *Journal of Finance*, **57**, 1891–921.

Stiglitz, J. and A. Weiss (1981), 'Credit rationing in markets of imperfect information', *American Economic Review*, **71**, June, 393–410.

Whetten, D.A. and K.S. Cameron (1998), *Developing Management Skills*, Reading, MA: Addison-Wesley.

Wiklund, J. and D. Shepherd (2005), 'Entrepreneurial orientation and small business performance: a configurational approach', *Journal of Business Venturing*, **20**, 71–91.

Wong, P., Y. Ho and E. Autio (2005), 'Entrepreneurship, innovation and economic growth: evidence from the GEM data', *Small Business Economics*, **24**, 335–50.

PART I

Contextualizing the link between factors and effects of new firms' formation

Figures of the Global Entrepreneurship Monitor (GEM) show that in low income countries the total entrepreneurial activity is more widespread than in high income countries. Individuals may be pushed into self-employment because of low opportunities of well-paid wage jobs. In line with Lucas's argument this is especially the case for developing countries (Lucas, 1978), where the actual wage is low and a great proportion of individuals are self-employed because they cannot find a salaried position providing them with better earnings. Entrepreneurship there is mainly induced by push motives. It is then important to take into account the interplay between the level of development of the country and the diversity of its entrepreneurs to measure the impact of entrepreneurship on economic growth.

In a finer analysis the GEM survey allows for differentiation according to the motives for setting up the firm. In France and also Germany the necessity motives are particularly important. 'In the GEM framework, individuals start a business for two main reasons: They want to exploit a perceived business opportunity (opportunity entrepreneurs). They are pushed into entrepreneurship because all other options for work are either absent or unsatisfactory (necessity entrepreneurs)' (GEM, 2006, p. 5). A theoretical foundation of this view can be found in Fonseca et al.'s model (2001). They consider a problem of job allocation in a process of search and matching. They show a negative impact of the start-up costs on the employment level: higher start-up costs lead to fewer entrepreneurs and so to a growing number of workers competing for a smaller number of jobs.

Ingrid Verheul and André Van Stel (Chapter 1) show that older and more highly educated entrepreneurs are particularly important for stimulating economic growth in less developed countries while younger entrepreneurs are more important in developed countries.

For Jean Bonnet and Pascal Cussy (Chapter 2) the insufficient involvement of younger educated people and especially French elites – for instance, graduate students from 'Grandes Ecoles' – in entrepreneurship is critical for economic growth in the case of France.

Dieter Bögenhold and Uwe Fachinger (Chapter 3) identify structural changes but also changes in labor market regulation and changes in welfare state regulations that 'make it easier for firms to outsource jobs and to do business with the same people as freelancers'.

REFERENCES

Fonseca, R., P. Lopez-Garcia and C.A. Pissarides (2001), 'Entrepreneurship, start-up costs and employment', *European Economic Review*, **45** (4–6), May, 692–705.

GEM (Global Entrepreneurship Monitor) (2006), 'Summary results', Niels Bosma and Rebecca Harding, Babson College and London Business School.

Lucas, R.E. (1978), 'On the size distribution of business firms', *Bell Journal of Economics*, **9**, Autumn, 508–23.

1. Entrepreneurial diversity and economic growth

Ingrid Verheul and André van Stel

1.1 INTRODUCTION

Several studies have discussed and empirically investigated the link between entrepreneurial activity and economic performance at the level of cities, regions and nations (Audretsch and Keilbach, 2004; Carree et al., 2002; Iyigun and Owen, 1999). In these studies entrepreneurs are often treated as a homogeneous group. However, in the 1980s Gartner (1985, p. 696) argued that: 'The diversity among entrepreneurs and their ventures may be larger than the differences between entrepreneurs and non-entrepreneurs and between entrepreneurial firms and non-entrepreneurial firms'. In practice we see extensive variation between entrepreneurs, for example, in terms of motivations, human capital, goals and so on. Notwithstanding the importance of the number of small firms for economic performance, this (pure) diversity within the small business population may also play a role over and above the sheer quantity effect. It should be noted, however, that a higher number of enterprises 'an sich' also implies higher diversity.[1]

The importance of diversity in entrepreneurship can be better understood in the context of an increasing diversity in demand. Indeed, market demand has become more diverse, induced by an increase in prosperity (Jackson, 1984) and reinforced by the processes of individualization and globalization. Hence, for achieving high rates of economic growth it is important that there is a diverse supply of goods and services to match this demand for variety. A greater diversity of the entrepreneurial population – in terms of characteristics of entrepreneurs and their firms – will contribute to this supply variation.

Cohen and Malerba (2001) distinguish between three important effects of diversity on technological performance within industries, including a selection effect, a breadth effect and a complementarity effect. Here we apply these effects within the context of national economic performance. The selection effect can be traced back to evolutionary economic thought, referring to competition between diverse firms where the best performing ones survive, leading to higher quality of products and services offered.[2] According to Cohen and Malerba (2001) a higher diversity of the firm population leads to a higher expected quality per unit cost of the selected variant. The breadth effect refers to the importance of the availability of a broad range of products at the industry level for the vitality of the industry, offering opportunities for (incremental) innovations and the introduction of other (related) products in the market. The complementarity effect refers to a more complete supply of goods and services available to consumers, which can be seen as a direct welfare effect.

In the present study we try to empirically establish the relative importance of these different effects of entrepreneurial diversity. In particular, we will use measures for the size of a country's entrepreneurial population and the composition of this population (in terms of the shares of certain groups within the entrepreneurial population with specific socio-demographic characteristics), and investigate their relative impact on national economic growth. Because a greater size of the entrepreneurial population (that is, more entrepreneurs) implies stronger competition, we will refer to the competition effect when describing the effect of the size variable on national economic performance. By and large, the competition effect corresponds to the selection effect as identified by Cohen and Malerba (2001). Because the composition variables measure the importance of specific groups of entrepreneurs within the entrepreneurial population (independent of the size of this population), we will refer to the pure diversity effect when describing the impact of these composition variables. By and large, the composition variables capture the breadth effect and the complementarity effect as proposed by Cohen and Malerba (2001).

Concerning the impact of entrepreneurial diversity, the literature suggests that firm outcomes are conditional upon the type of diversity (Pelled, 1996). In this study we focus on particular groups of entrepreneurs, including women, older and higher educated individuals. This means that entrepreneurial diversity is investigated in terms of gender, age and education. We use these socio-demographic proxies for diversity as they have been found important in determining the decision to become self-employed (Blanchflower et al., 2001; Delmar and Davidsson, 2000; Grilo and Irigoyen, 2006) and entrepreneurial performance (Cliff, 1998; Parker and van Praag, 2006; Sapienza and Grimm, 1997). Also, these groups of entrepreneurs have become more important (in terms of numbers) in recent years due to social developments such as the process of gender mainstreaming, the ageing society combined with a higher retirement age to support the welfare system, and the rise of the knowledge-based economy. Nevertheless, these groups are still underrepresented in the entrepreneurial population.[3] Therefore, an increase in the share of these particular groups of entrepreneurs automatically leads to an increase in diversity. We will empirically explore the influence of the various socio-economic entrepreneurial groups on macro-economic performance.

To test for the effect of entrepreneurial diversity on national economic performance, we use data from the Global Entrepreneurship Monitor (GEM). Using a cross-country data sample we investigate the impact of both the size and the composition (in terms of gender, age or education) of a country's entrepreneurial population on GDP growth, while controlling for a range of relevant determinants. The chapter is structured as follows. In Section 1.2 we discuss the concept of diversity and how it is dealt with in different theories. We will also pay attention to the role of entrepreneurship in economic performance and the linkages between entrepreneurship and diversity. Section 1.3 discusses the data sample, the variables included in the study and the research model. Descriptive statistics are also presented of the entrepreneurship variables. In Section 1.4 the results are presented and discussed and Section 1.5 concludes.

1.2 DIVERSITY, PERFORMANCE AND ENTREPRENEURSHIP

1.2.1 Diversity and Performance

The concept of diversity has been studied from different perspectives. From a social perspective diversity has been discussed, for example, in terms of the presence in the population of a variety of cultures, ethnic groups, socio-economic backgrounds, opinions, religions and gender identities.[4] Within a business context one often refers to the so-called 'business case for diversity'. Many research studies have explored the link between (workforce) diversity and firm performance (Kilduff et al., 2000; Richard, 2000; Simons et al., 1999). Workforce diversity often refers to gender and ethnic diversity,[5] but also broader perspectives on diversity are proposed such as diversity in terms of knowledge and (cognitive) capabilities relevant to the job. Indeed, Simons et al. (1999) distinguish between more and less job-related types of diversity, and their (diverging) effects on performance. Several reasons have been proposed as to why it is important to stimulate workforce diversity, including lower employee turnover, lower absenteeism rates, access to a broader pool of talent, new ideas and improved innovation, and confidence of customers (Robinson and Dechant, 1997; Salomon and Schork, 2003).

From a more aggregate economic perspective, diversity of economic actors has been identified as an important driver of economic progress at the level of cities, regions and national economies (Broda and Weinstein, 2006; Florida, 2002; Jacobs, 1984; Saviotti, 1996). Several mechanisms linking diversity and (economic) performance have been proposed. Florida (2002) argues that the influence of diversity on economic performance runs through human capital, where a high share of creative individuals in a certain city or region attracts high-tech and innovative industries.[6] Cohen and Malerba (2001) distinguish between the selection, the breadth and the complementarity effect of diversity in the firm population. The selection effect runs through increased competition, induced by an increased number of (diverse) firms. Nelson and Winter (1982) argue that diversity is an important input in the selection process where the best performing firms survive ('survival of the fittest'), leading to a higher quality of supplied products. The breadth effect of diversity works through available future opportunities for new and related products, where a wide range of products within an industry opens up new avenues for (incremental) innovation, thereby securing the longevity or long-term survival of the industry. The complementarity effect refers to the fact that a varied supply of products and services enables consumers to fulfill their diverse needs.

1.2.2 Diversity in Entrepreneurship: Gender, Education and Age

Given the alleged importance of diversity for economic performance, it is worthwhile to study the variation in entrepreneurship. Within the entrepreneurship literature attention has been paid to different types of diversity, for example, investigating differences between female and male entrepreneurs (gender diversity). Here we focus on differences between female and male, old and young, and higher and lower educated individuals. The factors age, gender and education are found to play an important role in explaining participation in entrepreneurship.

Generally, women are less likely to participate in entrepreneurship than men (Blanchflower et al., 2001, Grilo and Irigoyen, 2006; Minniti et al., 2005; Reynolds et al., 2002) and most business owners are between 25 and 45 years old (Reynolds et al., 1999; Storey, 1994). In terms of education level there is contradicting evidence concerning the relationship with entrepreneurship participation. Some studies find that people with a higher level of education are more likely to become an entrepreneur (Blanchflower et al., 2001; Davidsson and Honig, 2003; Delmar and Davidsson, 2000; Grilo and Irigoyen, 2006), whereas others find a non-linear relationship (Evans and Leighton, 1989; Reynolds, 1997) or even a negative one (Grilo and Thurik, 2005; Uhlaner and Thurik, 2007).

Although a higher level of education may reduce the choice to become self-employed, it may still improve the performance of those individuals who become self-employed. A study by Burke et al. (2000) shows that, combining the negative choice effect and the positive performance effect, education has a positive net effect on job creation. Congregado et al. (2005) find that the probability of hiring employees is higher for self-employed individuals with university studies than for those with lower levels of education. Several studies find evidence for a positive relationship between high education of the founder or owner and venture performance (Bosma et al. 2004; Burke et al., 2000; Colombo et al., 2004; Gimeno et al., 1997; Mata, 1996; Parker and van Praag, 2006). Colombo and Delmastro (2001) find that new technology-based firms tend to have business founders and owners with relatively high education levels. These studies lead us to believe that entrepreneurs with a higher level of education are more successful in terms of performance or innovation than less educated entrepreneurs.

Although female entrepreneurs generally perform less well than male entrepreneurs in terms of number of employees or financial indicators, such as profits and revenues, growth and innovation (Cliff, 1998; Watson, 2002),[7] there may still be learning effects that lead to a higher aggregate level of economic performance (Verheul and Thurik, 2001). For example, women are often said to emphasize the quality rather than the quantity of output (Chaganti and Parasuraman, 1996; Rosa et al., 1996; Verheul et al., 2002). In terms of age, *The Economist* (1999) reports that new ventures of people in the age category of 20 to 25 years old showed a three-year survival rate of 30 percent, as compared to a 70 percent rate for people between 50 and 55 years old in the UK. This indicates that older entrepreneurs, though still a minority group, can have an important contribution to economic performance and job creation. The success factors of older entrepreneurs are said to include experience levels, superior networks, a stronger financial situation and higher self-efficacy levels (Blackburn et al., 1998; Peña, 2002; Schutjens and Wever, 2000; Singh and DeNoble, 2003; Weber and Schaper, 2003). Nevertheless, older entrepreneurs may also experience lower energy levels, part-time involvement and a lower inclination to pursue firm growth (Snel and Bruins, 2004).

1.3   DATA AND RESEARCH METHOD

In the present study we investigate whether, next to the size of a country's entrepreneurial population, the composition of the entrepreneurial population influences national economic growth. The size of a country's entrepreneurship population is measured by the Total early-stage Entrepreneurial

Activity (TEA) index: the percentage of the adult population that is either actively involved in starting a new venture or is the owner/manager of a business that is less than 42 months old. The TEA index is taken from the Global Entrepreneurship Monitor database. The composition of the entrepreneurial population is measured in terms of three aspects of diversity: age, education and gender. Our empirical analysis builds on van Stel et al. (2005). They investigate whether TEA influences GDP growth for a sample of 36 countries. The authors find that the TEA index affects economic growth, but that its influence depends on the level of economic development. The economic contribution of entrepreneurial activity is found to be stronger for highly developed countries than for less developed countries. This may be explained by the lower human capital levels of entrepreneurs in less developed countries.

In this study we perform a similar regression analysis but, in addition to the TEA index, we include selected diversity indices and investigate whether these indices provide additional explanatory power to the model. We use a sample of 36 countries participating in the Global Entrepreneurship Monitor (GEM) in 2002. Seven variables are included in our model: TEA; age composition of entrepreneurship; education composition of entrepreneurship; gender composition of entrepreneurship; GDP growth; per capita income; and the growth competitiveness index (GCI). The sources and definitions of these variables are described below.

1. Total early-stage Entrepreneurial Activity (TEA)
    TEA is defined as the percentage of the adult population that is either actively involved in starting a new venture or is the owner/manager of a business that is less than 42 months old. Data on total entrepreneurial activity are taken from the GEM Adult Population Survey for 2002.
2. Age composition of entrepreneurship
    For this category we construct three age category variables including the share in the total number of entrepreneurs that is relatively young (18-24 years), middle-aged (25-44) or relatively old (45-64).
3. Education composition of entrepreneurship
    We construct three education category variables: the share in the total number of entrepreneurs that has a low level of education (none, primary or some secondary education), a middle level of education (secondary education) or a high level of education (university level or post-graduate education).[8]
4. Gender composition of entrepreneurship
    The gender composition of entrepreneurship is measured using the share of female entrepreneurs in a country's total number of entrepreneurs.

5. Growth of GDP (ΔGDP)
    Real GDP growth rates are taken from the IMF World Economic Outlook database of the International Monetary Fund, version September 2005.
6. Per capita income (GNIC)
    Gross national income per capita 2001 is expressed in (thousands of) purchasing power parities per US$, and these data are taken from the 2002 World Development Indicators database of the World Bank.
7. Growth Competitiveness Index (GCI)
    Data on the Growth Competitiveness Index 2001 are taken from *The Global Competitiveness Report 2001–2002* (p. 32). The GCI is constituted of the following three main factors assessing a country's potential for economic growth: the quality of the macro-economic environment, the state of the public institutions and the level of technology. For further details about this index see McArthur and Sachs (2002).

We investigate whether, next to the other variables, entrepreneurship influences economic growth. As both entrepreneurship and the factors underlying the GCI are assumed to be structural characteristics of an economy, we aim to explain growth in the medium term rather than in the short term. Therefore we choose average annual growth over a period of four years (2002–05) as the dependent variable in this study. Following van Stel et al. (2005) we use (the log of) the initial income level of countries to correct for catch-up effects. In contrast to van Stel et al. (2005), we do not use lagged GDP growth since we are able to measure TEA in a year (2002) preceding the period over which we measure economic growth. Nevertheless, we will include the lagged growth variable in robustness tests.

Following van Stel et al. (2005) we allow for different effects for more and less developed countries.[9] Indeed, TEA rates may include different types of entrepreneurs in countries with different levels of development, suggesting different impacts on growth in these countries. We test for this divergence in effects by defining separate TEA variables for more and less developed countries.

Our model is represented by Equations (1.1) to (1.3). These equations are estimated separately using OLS regressions. The hypothesis of a larger positive effect for the more developed countries corresponds to a situation where $b > c$. In each of the three equations a different aspect of entrepreneurial diversity is investigated. In Equation (1.1) the shares of relatively young and old entrepreneurs are included in the analysis, with the share of entrepreneurs in the middle age class as a reference group to avoid multicollinearity. Similarly, in Equation (1.2) the shares of low and higher educated entrepreneurs are included in the regression (with the group of middle-educated entrepreneurs as the reference group). Finally, in Equation (1.3) we use the share of female entrepreneurs (with male entrepreneurs as the reference group). We also run variants of this model where the impact of these three different aspects of diversity is allowed to differ between more and less developed countries (here denoted as rich and poor countries).

$$\Delta GDP_{it} = a + b\ TEA^{rich}_{i,t-1} + c\ TEA^{poor}_{i,t-1} + d\log(GNIC_{i,t-1}) + e\ GCI_{i,t-1}$$
$$+ f_1\ share\ young\ E + f_2\ share\ old\ E + \varepsilon_{it} \qquad (1.1)$$

$$\Delta GDP_{it} = a + b\ TEA^{rich}_{i,t-1} + c\ TEA^{poor}_{i,t-1} + d\log(GNIC_{i,t-1}) + e\ GCI_{i,t-1}$$
$$+ f_1\ share\ low\ educ\ E + f_2\ share\ high\ educ\ E + \varepsilon_{it} \qquad (1.2)$$

$$\Delta GDP_{it} = a + b\ TEA^{rich}_{i,t-1} + c\ TEA^{poor}_{i,t-1} + d\log(GNIC_{i,t-1}) + e\ GCI_{i,t-1}$$
$$+ f_1\ share\ female\ E + \varepsilon_{it} \qquad (1.3)$$

Table 1.1 provides descriptive statistics of the entrepreneurship indicators. The average TEA index is 8.1 with TEA rates varying between 1.8 for Japan and 18.9 for Thailand. Japan also has extreme low scores in terms of the percentage of young entrepreneurs (0.0) and the share of female entrepreneurs (17.6 percent). With respect to age we see that on average the highest share of entrepreneurs (60.6 percent) can be found in the mid-age group (that is, 25–44), which corresponds with the literature (Reynolds et al., 1999; Storey, 1994). Furthermore, we see that the three education groups – on average – are fairly evenly distributed.[10] The maximum share of low-educated entrepreneurs (74.7 percent) can be found in India whereas Denmark has the highest share of high-educated entrepreneurs (83.3 percent). For female entrepreneurship we see that the average percentage in 2002 is 34 percent with a minimum of 17.6 percent for Japan and a maximum of 49.5 percent for Thailand. From the standard deviations we can see that there is quite some variation between the countries with respect to the entrepreneurial diversity variables. In the next section we investigate whether these variations influence national economic growth.

1.4   RESULTS

The results of our empirical analyses are presented in Tables 1.2–1.4. All tables include the impact of entrepreneurial activity in general (variable TEA). The results for this variable confirm earlier findings by van Stel et

Table 1.1   Descriptive statistics entrepreneurship variables

	Mean	Standard deviation	Minimum	Maximum	Observations (countries)
Size of entrepreneurship population					
TEA (% of adult					
population)	8.1	4.6	1.8	18.9	36
Age composition of entrepreneurship					
Share young					
entrepreneurs (%)	12.9	7.1	0.0	34.1	36
Share mid-age					
entrepreneurs (%)	60.6	7.8	37.2	74.3	36
Share old					
entrepreneurs (%)	26.4	8.4	15.9	62.8	36
Education composition of entrepreneurship					
Share low-educated					
entrepreneurs (%)	22.4	21.7	0.0	74.7	33
Share middle-educated					
entrepreneurs (%)	38.9	16.9	7.1	76.6	33
Share high-educated					
entrepreneurs (%)	38.6	17.6	8.5	83.3	33
Gender composition of entrepreneurship					
Share of female					
entrepreneurs (%)	34.0	6.8	17.6	49.5	36
Share of male					
entrepreneurs (%)	66.0	6.8	50.5	82.4	36

al. (2005) who find that for more developed countries the impact of entrepreneurial activity is significantly larger than for less developed countries. In addition to general entrepreneurial activity, Tables 1.2–1.4 each focus on a different aspect of entrepreneurial diversity. Table 1.2 focuses on entrepreneurial diversity in terms of age. Here we have included the share of young entrepreneurs (18-24 years) and the share of older entrepreneurs (45-64 years). Coefficients for these two variables should be interpreted relative to the reference group (25-44 years). From the results of Models 1 and 2 we see that the age variables do not add to the explanation of economic growth (t-values are below unity). In Model 3 we test whether, like TEA, the impact of the two age groups differs for more and less developed countries. This appears to be the case.[11] Model 3 reveals that in more developed countries younger entrepreneurs (18-24 years) have a higher contribution to economic growth as compared to mid-age and older entrepreneurs, while in less developed countries the older entrepreneurs (45-64 years) have a higher contribution to economic growth. It

*Table 1.2   Explaining growth from TEA and age composition of
              entrepreneurship (N = 36)*

	Model 1	Model 2	Model 3
Constant	25.0**	36.5**	37.8**
	(3.4)	(3.5)	(3.7)
TEA	0.006		
	(0.1)		
TEA rich		0.11*	0.14**
		(1.8)	(2.2)
TEA poor		−0.11	−0.072
		(1.1)	(0.8)
Share young	0.022	0.043	
	(0.5)	(0.9)	
Share old	0.009	0.015	
	(0.3)	(0.7)	
Share young, rich			0.098*
			(1.9)
Share old, rich			0.023
			(0.9)
Share young, poor			−0.039
			(0.6)
Share old, poor			0.10**
			(2.1)
log (GNIC)	−3.0**	−4.2**	−4.4**
	(3.0)	(3.2)	(3.5)
GCI	1.4	1.2	1.2
	(1.5)	(1.4)	(1.5)
R^2	0.522	0.598	0.662
Adjusted R^2	0.443	0.515	0.561
Log-likelihood	−59.2	−56.1	−53.0

Note: Absolute heteroskedasticity consistent *t*-values are between parentheses.
Dependent variable is average annual growth of GDP for the period 2002–05. TEA is
Total Entrepreneurial Activity rate (*Global Entrepreneurship Monitor*); GCI is Growth
Competitiveness Index 2001 (*Growth Competitiveness Report*); GNIC is per capita income
of 2001. * Significant at 0.10 level; ** significant at 0.05 level.

appears that in the more developed countries, with a well-developed infrastructure supporting entrepreneurship, it is beneficial to have many young
entrepreneurs challenging the established routines with new ideas, thereby
introducing more dynamics into the system.[12] In less developed countries,
on the other hand, entrepreneurship is a less well-known and stimulated
phenomenon and it may be expected that people have less experience with

Table 1.3   Explaining growth from TEA and education composition of entrepreneurship (N = 33)

	Model 1	Model 2	Model 3
Constant	26.7**	37.4**	37.2**
	(3.4)	(3.7)	(4.5)
TEA	0.014		
	(0.2)		
TEA rich		0.12*	0.17**
		(1.7)	(2.9)
TEA poor		−0.093	−0.23
		(1.1)	(1.4)
Share low educated	0.012	0.020	
	(0.6)	(0.9)	
Share high educated	0.020	0.026	
	(0.9)	(1.2)	
Share low educated, rich			0.033
			(1.2)
Share high educated, rich			0.019
			(1.1)
Share low educated, poor			0.040
			(0.9)
Share high educated, poor			0.092**
			(2.5)
log (GNIC)	−2.9 **	−4.0 **	−4.4 **
	(3.1)	(3.5)	(4.8)
GCI	0.81	0.60	1.4 **
	(1.0)	(0.8)	(2.1)
R^2	0.608	0.666	0.731
Adjusted R^2	0.535	0.589	0.641
Log-likelihood	−52.2	−49.6	−46.0

Note: Brazil, Mexico and New Zealand are missing. See also note in Table 1.2.

starting up and running a business. In many cases people start firms to escape a situation of low-pay wage jobs or unemployment, without the knowledge and skills required to successfully run a business. In such a setting it is important to have more experienced (successful) entrepreneurs around who not only have an important contribution themselves, but are also able and willing to engage in mentoring of new entrepreneurs.

Table 1.3 focuses on entrepreneurial diversity in terms of education. Here we have included the share of low-educated and that of high-educated entrepreneurs in the analysis. Coefficients for these two variables

Table 1.4   *Explaining growth from TEA and gender composition of*
              entrepreneurship (N = 36)

	Model 1	Model 2	Model 3
Constant	29.1**	38.7**	36.4**
	(3.7)	(3.6)	(3.5)
TEA	0.025		
	(0.4)		
TEA rich		0.12**	0.15**
		(2.0)	(2.2)
TEA poor		−0.071	−0.11
		(0.8)	(1.1)
Share female	−0.039	−0.026	
	(1.2)	(0.8)	
Share female, rich			−0.049
			(1.3)
Share female, poor			−0.012
			(0.3)
log (GNIC)	−3.3**	−4.2**	−4.1**
	(3.3)	(3.4)	(3.5)
GCI	1.4	1.2	1.5*
	(1.6)	(1.3)	(1.8)
R^2	0.532	0.590	0.603
Adjusted R^2	0.472	0.522	0.520
Log-likelihood	−58.8	−56.4	−55.9

Note: Note in Table 1.2 applies.

should be interpreted relative to the reference group (mid-level education). For Models 1 and 2 we see that the education variables do not have a significant impact. For Model 3 we find a relatively strong effect for the share of high-educated entrepreneurs in less developed countries (significant at 5 percent level). This is in line with van Stel et al. (2005) who argue that in developing countries it is the quality of entrepreneurial supply (measured by education levels of entrepreneurs) rather than the quantity of entrepreneurial supply (as measured by TEA) that contributes to economic growth. Indeed, developing countries tend to be characterized by a relatively high share of so-called necessity entrepreneurs (vis-à-vis opportunity entrepreneurs).[13] It has been argued that necessity entrepreneurs have a lower contribution to economic growth than opportunity entrepreneurs (Reynolds et al., 2002).[14]

Finally, Table 1.4 focuses on gender diversity. Although not statistically significant we find a negative sign for the share of female entrepreneurs across the three models. The negative impact seems to be more pronounced for developed countries. This raises questions about the relevance of policies designed to increase levels of female entrepreneurship. It is important for governments to clearly formulate and understand the targets to be pursued by policy. For example, do governments aim to stimulate the number of female entrepreneurs or the female share in entrepreneurship (that is, the gender diversity of entrepreneurship)? This distinction is relevant since Verheul et al. (2006) show that there may be different mechanisms involved in achieving these targets. The results in Table 1.4 suggest that, if the underlying goal of economic policy is to enhance economic growth, generic entrepreneurship policy (that is, stimulating entrepreneurial activity in general) may be preferred over policies specifically designed to stimulate female entrepreneurship. Although in more developed countries female entrepreneurs – like male entrepreneurs – contribute positively to economic growth (as can be seen by the positive impact of the TEA rate), there is no evidence that a higher share of women within the entrepreneurship population enhances growth beyond this 'general' impact of the number of female entrepreneurs. From this perspective it may be argued that policies specifically aimed at creating advantages for women (for example, 'positive discrimination') are not favorable for achieving economic growth.

Our regression results should be interpreted with some care as the analysis is based on a limited number of observations (36 countries). However, despite the small number of observations, the results appear to be robust. First, the coefficients for the control variables are intuitive in all model specifications. In particular, we find a negative sign for the catching-up variable (log(GNIC)) and a consistently positive effect for the Growth Competitiveness Index across all specifications. Second, although we measure our independent variables at a time preceding the period of the dependent variable – on the basis of which we decided not to include lagged GDP growth in our models – we did run model variants including lagged GDP growth (period 1998–2001) as a robustness test. The main results, as described above, remained unchanged although in some cases significance levels became somewhat lower.[15]

1.5   DISCUSSION AND CONCLUSION

Research suggests that there is substantial diversity among entrepreneurs and their ventures (Gartner, 1985). The aim of the present study is to investigate the extent to which entrepreneurial diversity has an effect on national economic growth over and above the sheer number of entrepreneurs. We distinguish between a competition effect of diversity (where economic growth results from a more fierce competition among a higher number of firms), measured by the size of the entrepreneurial population, and a 'pure' diversity effect (where entrepreneurial activity of different socio-demographic groups may have a different impact on macro-economic performance), measured in terms of the composition of the entrepreneurial population.

The empirical analysis shows that the contribution of entrepreneurship generally depends on the level of economic development. In conformity with van Stel et al. (2005) we find that the size of the entrepreneurship population has a positive impact on economic growth in more developed countries but has no impact in less developed countries. Hence, we find support for the existence of a competition effect in the developed economies: a higher number of entrepreneurs appears to serve as input for a selection process where the best performing firms survive, ultimately leading to higher levels of economic growth. In less developed countries an increase in the number of entrepreneurs is not associated with higher growth. It appears that, instead of intensifying the competition process through the wish to excel and challenge incumbent firms with new products or new techniques of production (that is, knowledge-intensive entrepreneurial activity), the many 'shopkeeper' and necessity type entrepreneurs in these countries may simply want to earn a living through starting up and running a business.

With respect to the 'pure' diversity effect of entrepreneurship there are several interesting results. First, we find that the age composition of the entrepreneurial population matters in explaining economic growth. More specifically, the effect of the share of younger or older entrepreneurs on economic growth depends upon the level of economic development. In more developed countries younger entrepreneurs appear to have a particularly important contribution to economic growth, whereas in less developed countries older entrepreneurs are more important. This suggests that more developed countries benefit from more dynamism and new ideas from young entrepreneurs, contributing to a process of creative destruction, whereas less developed countries benefit from more experienced entrepreneurs to create a knowledge infrastructure supporting successful new venture creation.

Second, we find that in less developed countries particularly high-educated entrepreneurs are important for achieving economic growth. However, these countries tend to be characterized by a relatively low share of high-educated entrepreneurs. In our sample the average share of high-educated entrepreneurs is significantly lower for the poor countries (24.6 percent) as compared to the more developed countries (43.9 percent). This may be due to the fact that higher educated people in developing countries often leave their country to find a job in more developed countries where they may receive a higher salary or facilities. From a policy perspective, it is important that less developed countries prevent the negative consequences of this 'brain drain' and the relatively low level of education characterizing its population by creating a more attractive work environment for higher educated people; investing in education of the labor force and in particular (potential) self-employed people; and attracting higher educated entrepreneurs to help stimulate the economy.

Finally, we did not find evidence for a differential impact on economic growth of female and male entrepreneurs. As discussed earlier, our results suggest that stimulating female entrepreneurs is important (in the developed countries entrepreneurship has a positive influence on growth), but not at the expense of male entrepreneurs by way of 'positive discrimination' measures.

The findings in our study have important policy implications. In particular, one may argue that a significant effect of the size of a country's entrepreneurial population calls for creating generic entrepreneurship policies that are applicable to all types of entrepreneurs, whereas the significant effects of the different entrepreneurial groups calls for programs targeting these specific groups. Our results suggest that in highly developed countries generic entrepreneurship policy is important (since the impact of the TEA rate is positive), with a special focus on stimulating entrepreneurship among young people (the impact of the share of young entrepreneurs is also positive). For less developed countries our results indicate that it is important to stimulate entrepreneurship among higher educated individuals and people within the age category of 45 to 64 years old. Governments in these countries should stimulate the accessibility of the know-how of these experienced entrepreneurs to the wider public. In general, generic entrepreneurship policies seem to be less efficient in less developed countries since they are likely to stimulate and attract necessity entrepreneurs.

There is a methodological issue that we did not discuss up until this point. It may be argued that, strictly speaking, it is not really diversity that we measure in this study. Diversity is often associated with measures of the spread or variance of a certain phenomenon. For instance, in this study one may argue that entrepreneurial diversity in terms of education is maximal if all three education levels represent one third of the total number of entrepreneurs. On the other hand, one may argue that diversity is low if this distribution would be skewed. These different situations could be measured with Herfindahl type measures. A disadvantage of such measures is that it is not possible to distinguish between the relative importance of the different entrepreneurial groups. For example, a positive impact of the variance over the different groups implies that economic growth can be enhanced by creating a skewed distribution over the different groups. However this does not indicate in which direction the distribution should be skewed, that is, which groups should be stimulated or discouraged (for example, entrepreneurs with low, middle or high education). By way of including the shares of all different groups in our model we are able to distinguish between the relative importance of different entrepreneurial groups.

In addition to gender, age and education, future research may focus on other types of entrepreneurs, such as ethnic, portfolio or habitual entrepreneurs. Our database prevented us from including other types of entrepreneurial diversity in the analysis. Moreover, as it can be expected that there is interaction between socio-demographic characteristics, it will be interesting to find out whether there are interaction effects, for example, whether young, high-educated people are more important for achieving growth than old, high-educated, self-employed individuals.

ACKNOWLEDGEMENTS

This chapter has been written in the framework of the research program SCALES carried out by EIM and financed by the Dutch Ministry of Economic Affairs. The authors are grateful to Jolanda Hessels for her support and valuable input.

NOTES

1. This reasoning is based on the population ecologist view that each new organization represents a unique formula (Hannan and Freeman, 1989).
2. See also Cohen and Klepper (1992).
3. This is true in particular for women entrepreneurs and entrepreneurs aged 50 years and older. In more developed countries higher educated entrepreneurs are now representing an important part of the entrepreneurial population.
4. This information is retrieved from wikipedia.org (accessed 28 November 2006).
5. The idea behind the relationship between these demographic characteristics and performance is that it is valuable for the business to have a workforce that resembles the population (in terms of race and gender composition) in order to be able to serve the diverse market demand.
6. Florida (2002, p.69) argues that at the core of this so-called creative class of people there are scientists and engineers, university professors, poets and novelists, artists, actors, designers and architects, writers and opinion makers.
7. Note that, when controlling for relevant factors (related to both gender and performance), performance differentials between firms run by female and male entrepreneurs diminish or disappear (Du Rietz and Henrekson, 2000; Kalleberg and Leicht, 1991; Watson and Robinson, 2003).
8. For the share of entrepreneurs with low education the percentages for the GEM

education variables 'none' and 'some secondary education' are summated. Furthermore, for the middle education category the GEM variable 'secondary education' is used, while the high education category is a summation of the GEM variables labeled 'post-secondary education' and 'graduate experience'.

9. The 36 countries in our sample are: Argentina[P], Australia, Belgium, Brazil[P], Canada, Chile[P], China[P], Taiwan, Denmark, Finland, France, Germany, Hong Kong, Hungary[P], Iceland, India[P], Ireland, Israel, Italy, Japan, Korea, Mexico[P], the Netherlands, New Zealand, Norway, Poland[P], Russia[P], Singapore, Slovenia, South Africa[P], Spain, Sweden, Switzerland, Thailand[P], UK and USA. Mark [P] indicates a poor country. The richest of the 11 relatively poor countries is Hungary with a 2001 per capita income of 12 570 US$. The poorest of the 25 relatively rich countries is Taiwan with a 2001 per capita income of 16 761 US$. Hence, there is a clear gap between the two groups of countries in terms of GNIC.

10. The minimum of 0 percent for low education corresponds to Russia. This does not imply that education levels among Russian entrepreneurs are extremely high. Instead the group of middle-educated entrepreneurs (secondary education) is relatively large (54 percent), according to our data. Also note that the number of observations is 33 here. Data on education were missing for Brazil and New Zealand while we judged the data for Mexico to be implausible (70 percent of entrepreneurs having high education according to the database). Therefore we removed Mexico as well for the education diversity analysis.

11. A likelihood ratio test comparing Models 2 and 3 reveals that the new variables in Model 3 add significantly to the model fit. The LR test statistic equals 6.2 while the critical value for two degrees of freedom at the 5 percent level equals 5.99.

12. From a Schumpeterian perspective it may be argued that in modern economies younger entrepreneurs particularly contribute to the process of creative destruction.

13. Opportunity-based entrepreneurship refers to people who start their own business by taking advantage of an entrepreneurial opportunity. Necessity-based entrepreneurship involves people who start a business because other employment options are either absent or unsatisfactory (Minniti et al., 2006).

14. Reynolds et al. (2002) find that about 20 percent of the entrepreneurs expect to provide no jobs, of which about 53 percent were necessity entrepreneurs. Also, more than 25 percent of the entrepreneurs expect to provide more than 20 jobs in five years, of whom 70 percent were motivated by opportunity. In addition, 9 percent of all opportunity entrepreneurs expect to create a new market, compared to 5 percent of necessity entrepreneurs.

15. These regression results are available upon request.

REFERENCES

Audretsch, D.B. and M. Keilbach (2004), 'Entrepreneurship capital and economic performance', *Regional Studies*, **38** (8), 949–59.

Blackburn, R., L. Mackintosh and J. North (1998), *Entrepreneurship in the Third Age*, Kingston upon Thames: Kingston University Entrepreneurship Centre.

Blanchflower, D.G., A. Oswald and A. Stutzer (2001), 'Latent entrepreneurship across nations', *European Economic Review*, **45**, 680–91.

Bosma, N., C.M. van Praag, A.R. Thurik and G. de Wit (2004), 'The value of human and social capital investments for the business performance of start-ups', *Small Business Economics*, **23**, 227–36.

Broda, C. and D.E. Weinstein (2006), 'Globalization and the gains from variety', *Quarterly Journal of Economics*, **121** (2), 541–85.

Burke, A.E., F.R. FitzRoy and M.A. Nolan (2000), 'When less is more: distinguishing between entrepreneurial choice and performance', *Oxford Bulletin of Economics and Statistics*, **62** (5), 565–87.

Carree, M.A., A.J. van Stel, A.R. Thurik and A.R.M. Wennekers (2002), 'Economic development and business ownership: an analysis using data of 23 OECD countries in the period 1976–1996', *Small Business Economics*, **19** (3), 271–90.

Chaganti, R. and S. Parasuraman (1996), 'A study of the impacts of gender on business performance and management patterns in small businesses', *Entrepreneurship Theory and Practice*, **21**, Winter, 73–5.

Cliff, J.E. (1998), 'Does one size fit all? Exploring the relationship between attitudes towards growth, gender, and business size', *Journal of Business Venturing*, **13**, 523–42.

Cohen, W.M. and S. Klepper (1992), 'The trade-off between firm size and diversity in the pursuit of technological progress', *Small Business Economics*, **4** (1), 1–14.

Cohen, W.M. and F. Malerba (2001), 'Is the tendency to variation a chief cause of progress?', *Industrial and Corporate Change*, **10** (3), 587–608.

Colombo, M.G. and M. Delmastro (2001), 'Technology-based entrepreneurs: does internet make a difference?', *Small Business Economics*, **16**, 177–90.

Colombo, M.G., M. Delmastro and L. Grilli (2004), 'Entrepreneurs' human capital and the start-up size of new technology-based firms', *International Journal of Industrial Organization*, **22** (8–9), 1183–211.

Congregado, E., A. Golpe and J.M. Millán (2005), 'Determinantes de la oferta de empresarios', in J. García and J. Pérez (eds), *Cuestiones Clave de la Economía Española*, Perspectivas actuales 2004, Seville: Centro de Estudios Andaluces, pp. 165–87.

Davidsson, P. and B. Honig (2003), 'The role of social and human capital among nascent entrepreneurs', *Journal of Business Venturing*, **18** (3), 301–31.

Delmar, F. and P. Davidsson (2000), 'Where do they come from? Prevalence and characteristics of nascent entrepreneurs', *Entrepreneurship and Regional Development*, **12** (1), 1–23.

Du Rietz, A. and M. Henrekson (2000), 'Testing the female underperformance hypothesis', *Small Business Economics*, **14** (1) 1–10.

Evans, D.S. and L.S. Leighton (1989), 'Some empirical aspects of entrepreneurship', *American Economic Review*, **79** (3), 519–35.

Florida, R. (2002), *The Rise of the Creative Class and How it is Transforming Work, Leisure, Community and Everyday Life*, New York: Basic Books.

Gartner, W.B. (1985), 'A conceptual framework for describing the phenomenon of new venture creation', *Academy of Management Review*, **10** (4), 696–706.

Gimeno, J., T.B. Folta, A.C. Cooper and C.Y. Woo (1997), 'Survival of the fittest? Entrepreneurial human capital and the persistence of underperforming firms', *Administrative Science Quarterly*, **42** (4), 750–83.

Grilo, I. and J.M. Irigoyen (2006), 'Entrepreneurship in the EU: to wish and not to be', *Small Business Economics*, **26** (4), 305–18.

Grilo, I. and A.R. Thurik (2005), 'Latent and actual entrepreneurship in Europe and the US: some recent developments', *International Entrepreneurship and Management Journal*, **1** (4), 441–59.

Hannan, M.T. and J. Freeman (1989), *Organizational Ecology*, Cambridge, MA: Harvard University Press.

Iyigun, M.F. and A.L Owen (1999), 'Entrepreneurs, professionals and growth', *Journal of Economic Growth*, **4** (2), 213–32.

Jackson, L.F. (1984), 'Hierarchic demand and the Engle curve for variety', *Review of Economics and Statistics*, **66**, 8–15.

Jacobs, J. (1984), *Cities and the Wealth of Nations; Principles of Economic Life*, New York: Random House.

Kalleberg, A.L and K.T. Leicht (1991), 'Gender and organizational performance: determinants of small business survival and success', *Academy of Management Journal*, **34** (1), 136–61.

Kilduff, M., R. Angelmar and A. Mehra (2000), 'Top management-team diversity and firm performance: examining the role of cognitions', *Organization Science*, **11** (1), 21–34.

Mata, J. (1996), 'Market, entrepreneurs and the size of new firms', *Economic Letters*, **52** (1), 89–94.

McArthur, J.W. and J.D. Sachs (2002), 'The growth competitiveness index: measuring technological advancement and the stages of development', in M.E. Porter, J.D. Sachs, P.K. Cornelius, J.W. McArthur and K. Schwab (eds), *The Global Competitiveness Report 2001–2002*, New York: Oxford University Press, pp. 28–51.

Minniti, M., P. Arenius and N. Langowitz (2005), *Global Entrepreneurship Monitor: 2004 Report on Women and Entrepreneurship*, Centre for Women's Leadership, London: Babson College and London Business School.

Minniti, M., W.D. Bygrave and E. Autio (2006), *Global Entrepreneurship Monitor, 2005 Executive Report*, London: Babson College and London Business School.

Nelson, R.R. and S.G. Winter (1982), *An Evolutionary Theory of Economic Change*, Cambridge, MA: Harvard University Press.

Parker, S.C. and C.M. van Praag (2006), 'Schooling, capital constraints, and entrepreneurial performance: the endogenous triangle', *Journal of Business and Economic Statistics*, **24** (4), 416–31.

Pelled, L.H. (1996), 'Demographic diversity, conflict, and work group outcomes: an intervening process theory', *Organization Science*, **7** (6), 615–31.

Peña, I. (2002), 'Intellectual capital and business start-up success', *Journal of Intellectual Capital*, **3** (2), 180–98.

Reynolds, P.D. (1997), 'Who starts new firms? Preliminary explorations of firms-in-generation', *Small Business Economics*, **9**, 449–62.

Reynolds, P.D., M. Hay and S.M. Camp (1999), *Global Entrepreneurship Monitor: 1999 Executive Report*, London: Babson College, Kauffman Center for Entrepreneurial Leadership and London Business School.

Reynolds, P.D., W.D. Bygrave, E. Autio, L.W. Cox and M. Hay (2002), *Global Entrepreneurship Monitor: Executive Report*, London: Babson College, London Business School and Kauffman Foundation.

Richard, O.C. (2000), 'Racial diversity, business strategy, and firm performance: a resource-based view', *Academy of Management Journal*, **43** (2), 164–77.

Robinson, G. and K. Dechant (1997), 'Building a business case for diversity', *The Academy of Management Executive*, **11** (3), 21–31.

Rosa, P., S. Carter and D. Hamilton (1996), 'Gender as a determinant of small business performance: insights from a British study', *Small Business Economics*, **8**, 463–78.

Salomon, M.F. and J.M. Schork (2003), 'Turn diversity to your advantage', *Technology Management*, July–August, 37–44.

Sapienza, H.J. and C.M. Grimm (1997), 'Founder characteristics, start-up process, and strategy/structure variables as predictors of shortline railroad performance', *Entrepreneurship Theory and Practice*, **22** (1), 5–24.

Saviotti, P.P. (1996), *Technological Evolution, Variety and the Economy*, Cheltenham, UK and Brookfield, VT, USA: Edward Elgar.

Schutjens, V. and E. Wever (2000), 'Determinants of new firm success', *Papers in Regional Science*, **79** (2), 135–53.

Simons, T., L.H. Pelled and K.A. Smith (1999), 'Making use of difference: diversity, debate, and decision comprehensiveness in top management teams', *Academy of Management Journal*, **42** (6), 662–73.

Singh, G. and A. DeNoble (2003), 'Early retirees as the next generation of entrepreneurs', *Entrepreneurship Theory and Practice*, **28** (3), 207–26.

Snel, D. and A. Bruins (2004), *Oudere versus jongere starters [Old Versus Young Start-up Entrepreneurs]*, EIM report A200410, Zoetermeer, Netherlands: EIM Business and Policy Research.

Storey, D.J. (1994), *Understanding the Small Business Sector*, London and New York: Routledge.

The Economist (1999), 'Face value: the pygmy problem', **353** (8144), 68–70.

Uhlaner, L.M. and A.R. Thurik (2007), 'Post-materialism influencing total entrepreneurial activity across nations', *Journal of Evolutionary Economics*, **17** (2), 161–85.

van Stel, A.J., M.A. Carree and A.R. Thurik (2005), 'The effect of entrepreneurial activity on national economic growth', *Small Business Economics*, **24**, 311–21.

Verheul, I. and A.R. Thurik (2001), 'Start-up capital: does gender matter?', *Small Business Economics*, **16** (4), 329–45.

Verheul, I., P.A. Risseeuw and G. Bartelse (2002), 'Gender differences in strategy and human resource management: the case of the Dutch real estate brokerage', *International Small Business Journal*, **20** (4), 443–76.

Verheul, I., A.J. van Stel and A.R. Thurik (2006), 'Explaining female and male entrepreneurship at the country level', *Entrepreneurship and Regional Development*, **18**, 151–83.

Watson, J. (2002), 'Comparing the performance of male- and female-controlled businesses: relating outputs to inputs', *Entrepreneurship Theory and Practice*, **26** (3), 91–100.

Watson, J. and S. Robinson (2003), 'Adjusting for risk in comparing the performances of male- and female-controlled SMEs', *Journal of Business Venturing*, **18**, 773–88.

Weber, P. and M. Schaper (2003), 'Understanding the grey entrepreneur: a review of the literature', paper presented at 16th Annual Conference of Small Enterprise Association of Australia and New Zealand, Ballarat, VIC 28 September–1 October.

2. High education, sunk costs and entrepreneurship

Jean Bonnet and Pascal Cussy

2.1 INTRODUCTION

Baumol (1990) observes that if the total number of entrepreneurs varies in different societies their contribution to growth varies even more according to their allocation in time and space between more or less productive activities depending on periods and cultures. The lack of entrepreneurship capital leads to the European paradox, a high level of knowledge investments for poor results in terms of growth and reduction of unemployment (Audretsch, 2007). Even though entrepreneurship has been acknowledged as a factor of growth by economists for a long time (Leibenstein, 1968), the difficulty in integrating all the idiosyncratic features of the entrepreneur[1] has prevented the entrepreneur being taken into account in a formalized theory. The microeconomic decision to get into entrepreneurship nevertheless enables an approach to entrepreneurship in terms of occupational choice. The decision to become an entrepreneur is mainly a decision of allocation of one's human capital considering the comparison between an entrepreneurship opportunity cost with a reward (financial, symbolic – social status – indeed psychological) prospect.

Part of the strong growth experienced over recent years in the USA comes from new knowledge economy companies. This contrasts with Europe where there is a need for developing entrepreneurial intensity, especially in innovative sectors. The setting up of innovative companies then constitutes the missing link to go from a knowledge economy to what can be named an innovation economy. There are numerous reasons for this deficit in entrepreneurship (culture, financial means, fiscal policy and so on). One of the main problems encountered in Europe is the insufficient involvement of elites in entrepreneurship. Especially in France graduate students from 'Grandes Ecoles'[2] are too few to choose the entrepreneurial career that contributes greatly to the inadequacy of entrepreneurial capital described by Audretsch.

This lack of entrepreneurial capital is partly due to the existence of a sunk cost for the graduates from 'Grandes Ecoles' which weighs up the loss of whole or part of the network and signal effects which create a rent and the stigma attached to entrepreneurial failure which turns into human capital depreciation when the entrepreneurial venture does not succeed. This stigma is strong in European countries.

It comes down to a standard problem of choice under uncertainty where the individual decides to get into entrepreneurship, the sunk cost reducing the incentive to get into entrepreneurship for the students coming from the more prestigious schools.

2.2   FRANCE, A REWARDING STRUCTURE DETERRING INNOVATIVE ENTREPRENEURSHIP

In most cases the decision to set up a firm is linked to the decision to create one's own job. Moskowitz and Vissing-Jorgensen (2002) have demonstrated that entrepreneurial investment does not bring about a profitability higher than investment on financial markets when risk (due to non-diversification) is important.

Two types of new entrepreneurs are then classically distinguished:

- The entrepreneurs pushed into entrepreneurship (push effect): entrepreneurs are more responsive to negative motivations, avoiding depreciation in their human capital, low opportunity cost to entrepreneurship.[3] Setting up a firm is an option for an individual facing unemployment or a mismatch with their salaried position.
- The entrepreneurs pulled into entrepreneurship (pull effect): entrepreneurs are responsive to the rather positive motivations to develop a new idea (innovative in the sense of Schumpeter, 1934) or to business opportunities (innovative in a more incremental way in the sense of Kirzner (1979, 1985) when the entrepreneur's alertness enables them to take part in the clearing of markets).

A simple representation of the valorization of the individual's human capital allows to account for these two types of motivations to entrepreneurship. When the labour market is functioning well, the observed human capital of the individual gets paid on average to its just value and the setting up of a company by a salaried employee is rather a good signal since it may be expected that there is a new idea to develop or a market niche to make the most of. Why go for a risky situation, unless there is a profit expectation higher than one's wage?

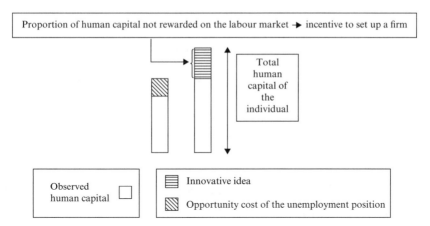

Figure 2.1   Human capital valorization and entrepreneurship

Conversely, a bad position on the labour market (for example, to be unemployed) results in one's human capital being paid less than what it should get on the labour market and simply because unemployment benefit is lower than wages. The setting up of a company by somebody who is unemployed is possible only because of a low opportunity cost to entrepreneurship and/or the will to avoid a depreciation of one's human capital. Therefore it tends to transmit less positively a priori than the setting up of a company by a salaried employee especially if the latter is experienced (Bhattacharjee et al., 2006, 2008). The previous graph in Figure 2.1 allows us to understand, starting from the valorization of the human capital of the individual, the various motivations to entrepreneurship in connection with the previous position of the entrepreneur.

For the same given level of the observed human capital there can be the same incentive to entrepreneurship (ratio of 45° hatched and horizontal hatched parts to white parts) with nevertheless on average a different informative content about the total level of the human capital of the individual and thus, all things being equal, about the capacity or the ability of the new firm to develop and even to survive. An illustration adapted from Stam (2008) fully illustrates the overlapping of these two effects at the level of the definition of entrepreneurship in society (Figure 2.2).

Entrepreneurship according to Stam corresponds to the notion of innovative companies' setting up (start-up, spinoff and also corporate venturing[4]). Non-innovative self-employment is excluded from the definition of entrepreneurial capital in the sense of Audretsch and innovation is not only due to new entrepreneurs. Nevertheless since rupture's innovations often go through entrepreneurship (Baumol, 2004), it is important

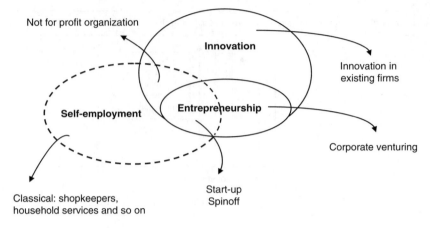

Note: Adapted from Stam (2008).

Figure 2.2   Innovative setting-up of firms

to encourage the second type of motivation to entrepreneurship which actually means encouraging or trying to understand why some categories of population (active salaried employees, young graduates and especially highly graduated ones) do not get into entrepreneurship enough. Mathias Fink (2008) observes that 'Entrusting innovation to big businesses is a mistake because they are afraid of breakthrough innovations. These latter are brought about by academics.'

The proportion of unemployed people in the population of new entrepreneurs (setting up/taking over) is around three to four times greater than the rate of unemployment. For example, in the Sine[5] 2006 survey the proportion of unemployed people in the population of new entrepreneurs is 40 per cent for an unemployment rate of 9.8 per cent. In the Sine 1998 survey the proportion of unemployed people in the population of new entrepreneurs is only 28 per cent for an unemployment rate of 11.7 per cent.[6]

Push motives are predominant in entrepreneurship in France. Among entrepreneurs people unemployed for less than a year are always slightly more numerous than people being unemployed for over a year, but the gap did reduce between 2002 and 2006. One reason might be the tougher stance regarding unemployment benefit which took place in early 2004. In the French case push effects are predominant in the population of new entrepreneurs partly because pull effects are deterred.[7]

Several explanations may be put forward as to the factors detering pull motives, that is, the setting up of innovative companies. A low involvement of French elites in innovative entrepreneurial activity may be pointed out among them (see Appendix 2.2 for the other explanations). This low involvement exists because their human capital gets better valorization within a smooth and unrisky career path (within which their graduate titles and alumni networks come into play). The network and signal effects of the fame of the 'Grandes Ecoles' create a privileged position through a lack of competition that Ribeill (1984, p. 84) describes as follows: 'The entrepreneurial propensity of engineers is inversely proportional to the fame of the schools they graduated from.' It seems to us that this latter argument is important in the French case. It may be indeed demonstrated that network effects deter the most highly graduated from getting into entrepreneurship, and this especially for the innovative sectors since the time required for the implementation of the project increases the sunk costs due to the loss of the networks in case of failure.

2.3 EDUCATION AND ENTREPRENEURSHIP: A COMPLEX LINK

The 'economy of innovation' means that the value of the firm is linked to the knowledge, skills, creativity and innovative capacity of its employees. The individual who runs their own business should be expected to be less risk averse than the individual who chooses to be hired as an in-house manager, in the line of Khilström and Laffont (1979). If we consider that risk aversion is equally distributed in the population, we will have different involvements in entrepreneurship at different levels of education. 'Education is generally insignificant in longitudinal studies of the transition to self-employment and studies which included controls for both human and financial capital generally find education to play an insignificant role in the transition' (Georgellis and Tsitsianis, 2005, p. 12). Nevertheless, when the firm is set up for good reasons, that is, not linked to weak opportunity costs or to depreciation motives but, for example, to the valuation of an innovative project, the rate of return of the new firm is linked to the knowledge, the skills and the creative and innovative capabilities of the owner/manager themself. Thus it seems logical to assume that elites' involvement in innovative entrepreneurship is critical for economic growth. Verheul and Van Stel (Chapter 1, this volume) identify in several works information indicating that 'entrepreneurs with a higher level of education are more successful in terms of performance or innovation than less educated entrepreneurs'. A recent study in the USA shows that over the 1983–2000 period 'There is a big increase in the earnings of college self-employed households over other groups and a much bigger concentration in wealth' (Terajima, 2006, p. 27).

In the French case the inadequate number of innovative companies being set up is critical. Fontagné (2008) deplores a shortage of new firms in computer engineering, in electronic games and so on. Lebret (2007, p.130) remarks that 'the greatest American success have tens of thousand of employees and that these firms are worth tens of billions of dollars [whereas] in Europe successes are rather creating thousands of employees and worth billions of dollars'. One of the explanations is linked to the insufficient involvment of French elites in entrepreneurship. Fayolle (2001) had already observed that few graduates from 'Grandes Ecoles' in France promote their human capital through setting up innovative companies.[8] The author also noticed following a 1994 survey that this specific group of entrepreneurs represents only about 2 per cent of all French entrepreneurs. Taking into account the fact that these entrepreneurial vocations mainly concern unemployed or old engineers in a jeopardized position, one sizes up how much the French educational system does not encourage a lot of young graduates to enhance their human capital getting into entrepreneurship. According to a recent study on student entrepreneurship,[9] 4 per cent of the new entrepreneurs (ex-nihilo startup) have declared a direct change of status from being a student to being an entrepreneur. Thus the total number of new ex-nihilo firms set up by students would be around 7000 to 9000 new firms per year. There is a great disparity behind these figures. Several courses of high education indeed appear to be correlated to various degrees of intensity in entrepreneurship. Students with two to four years spent at university represent 48 per cent of these new firms, students from management and engineering 'Grandes Ecoles', for their part represent only 3.3 per cent and 1.5 per cent, respectively (including university management education) (Bécard, 2007).

The application of the Shangaï school criterion throws some light on this shortage of entrepreneurial elites. Applying the criterion of scientific production, it downgraded French 'Grandes Ecoles'. The Mines school, by taking into account the position in the first 500 world firms of graduates from schools and universities, puts the emphasis back on French schools.[10] In this ranking an engineer is less prone to occupy an executive position than a Sciences P., HEC or ENA graduate, the Polytechnique school being an exception. Nevertheless, according to the detractors of this ranking, the main thing it highlights is cooptation and network effects taking place between 'Grandes Ecoles' alumni. Another explanation of the lack of engineers-entrepreneurs may be due to the fact that the best talents apply for comfortable positions of executives as civil servants or work in public firms with interesting wage trajectories. 'There are five main state bodies: l'inspection des Finances, le Conseil d'Etat, la Cour des comptes, les Mines et les Ponts et Chaussée.' The best ENA and Polytechnique school students are found there. The 'chef de corps' allocates the missions and looks after everyone's career. 'Better paid and more highly regarded than other civil servants, the members keep this advantage until the end of their career' (Lebègue and Walter, 2008). In other words, the existence of sunk costs attached to entrepreneurial failure diminishes the propensity to get into entrepreneurship for these populations. This career path thus increases the opportunity cost to get into entrepreneurship for this population and thus reduces its incentive to set up a firm.

2.4   ENTREPRENEURSHIP AND CAREER PATH

In economics the standard choice between entrepreneurship or wage earning is addressed in terms of occupational choice for which economic gains of each option are compared. In this case a necessary condition for an individual to set up a firm is that the discounted earnings the individual expects to get from it be higher than the discounted wage flows they get. The final decision is of course contingent upon the risk associated with the undertaking and the degree of aversion to risk of the individual. For the most risk averse people the profit expectation has to be significantly higher than the opportunity cost (the discounted wage flows). In this standard analysis the opportunity cost is not contingent upon the choice to get into entrepreneurship or not. One thus assumes that there is no depreciation of the human capital consequently to an entrepreneurial failure. This follows Evans and Leighton (1989, p. 520) who notice that: 'business experience has just about the same return in wage work as in self-employment'. It suggests that entrepreneurship is an effective means of preventing potential depreciation (in case of unemployment for example) even if the worker ends up returning to wage employment, whatever the level of education of the individual.

Yet two other effects come into play, a stigma effect and a network effect which are not taken into account in the standard analysis and which are particularly important in the French case:

The stigma effect of a potential failure leads to a decrease of the wage of an individual who returns to a salaried position after the failure of an undertaking. It arises from the negative perception of entrepreneurial failure which is especially strong in France,

The network effect derives from the fact that an individual graduating from a 'Grande Ecole' enjoys an advantageous and protected career path (privileged position) they will not get back easily should they come back after an entrepreneurial failure. Effectively there exists a wages' ranking according to the level of the diploma with some 'Grandes Ecoles' benefiting from a reputation effect (see Spence, 1973 for the signal effect of education).

The network effect creates a privileged position through lack of competition. One enjoys this effect only when one follows the standard career path (that is, without any rupture, straight following the mapped out path) and this effect continues for the whole active life of the individual. The signal effect is supposed to represent a higher productivity justifying the path's difference.

These two effects combine and result in a kind of depreciation of the human capital of the individual when the firm fails. They may also be seen as a sunk cost because the individual will never again find the position they would have been able to claim. The longer the time the individual is diverted from their standard career path, the more important is the depreciation effect (sunk cost). Furthermore, since the most innovative projects require more time, their opportunity cost then becomes higher which increases the disincentive to get into entrepreneurship for 'Grandes Ecoles' graduates.

A higher number of entrepreneurs will thus be found among the population of non-labelled graduates (that is, coming from less prestigious schools; assumption of Ribeill). This effect may nevertheless be alleviated by the fact that 'Grandes Ecoles' graduates may be holding better projects and a higher success probability.

To illustrate this let us consider a graduate individual who has the choice between occupying a salaried position, thus enjoying the support of a network, or undertaking a risky innovative project which requires time for preparation, research and commercial finalizing of a product or a process. This innovative project is contingent upon a random variable, a state of the world, the individual does not know at the time they have to make their decision. In order to simplify, this random variable is assumed to take only two possible values.

The career path of the individual, should they choose to get into entrepreneurship, proceeds in two stages. At the beginning of the first stage the agent decides to get into entrepreneurship or to occupy a salaried position and at the end of this stage they get to know about the random variable and thus about the future success or not of the undertaking.

When the favourable state of the world comes about, it is in their best interest to carry on their innovative project but when the unfavourable state of the world comes about, it is in their best interest to stop and take back a salaried activity. In this case they lose part of the advantage attached to belonging to a network, an advantage which is assumed to diminish in time.

Let us write:

W_1^s and W_1^e, the sum of the discounted income received during period 1 as a salaried employee or as an entrepreneur.

W_2^s and W_2^r, the sum of the discounted income received during period 2 as a salaried employee or after going back to work following the insufficient success of the undertaking.

$\overline{W_2^e}$ and $\underline{W_2^e}$, the sum of the discounted income received during period 2 following a firm being set up in the favourable or unfavourable state of the world.

q the probability of success (that it, the favourable state of the world which comes about).

Let us assume that $W_1^e + \overline{W_2^e} > W_1^s + W_2^s$ and that $\overline{W_2^e} > W_2^r$ (it is worthwhile to get into entrepreneurship and to carry on when it is a favourable state of the world). Let us also assume that $W_1^e + \underline{W_2^e} < W_1^s + W_2^s$ and that $\underline{W_2^e} < W_2^r$ (it is not worthwhile to get into entrepreneurship and to carry on the project when it is an unfavourable state of the world).

Altogether when the individual decides to get into entrepreneurship they receive a wealth $W^e = W_1^e + W_2$ with W_2 the random variable which is written:

$$
W_2 = \begin{cases} \overline{W_2^e} & W_2^r \\[2mm] q & 1 - q \end{cases}
$$

In other words, it comes down to a standard problem of choice under uncertainty where the individual decides to get into entrepreneurship if $U(W^e) \geq U(W^s)$ with $U(\cdot)$ a utility function.

However, in the absence of a network effect, the individual would receive in the second period the sum W_2^s and not W_2^r. The difference $W_2^s - W_2^r$ thus represents an additional and sunk opportunity cost. It is random since it is contingent upon the success probabilities of the firm. One also notices that a reduction in W_2^r diminishes the expected value of W_2 and increases its variance which reduces the incentive to get into entrepreneurship.

A graphic analysis which illustrates this problem is shown in Figure 2.3.

On the graph in Figure 2.3 w_t^s represents the discounted income at the t date when the individual is a salaried employee and $w_t^r(T)$ the discounted income when the individual goes back to a salaried activity from the T date onwards following an entrepreneurial lack of success. In this case, for example, W_2^r is the sum of $w_t^r(T)$ for all the periods from $t = T$ to $t = N$, the retirement period. The pay curve of the entrepreneurial project is added ($\overline{w_t^e}$ and $\underline{w_t^e}$, respectively, represent the discounted value of the income at the t date in the favourable or unfavourable state of the world).

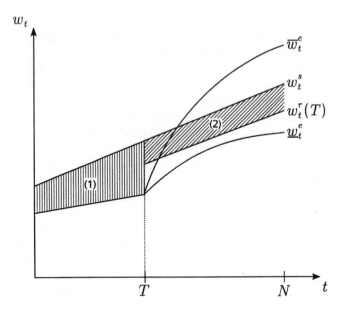

Figure 2.3   Sunk cost and entrepreneurial choice

An innovative firm undertaking a project leads to a period where the graduate will get paid less than if they had followed the standard path. So the vertical hatched zone represents the loss of income in the first period (this loss gets accentuated for a 'Grande Ecole' graduate due to the higher level of w_t^s). At the period T if the project is insufficiently beneficial the graduate comes back to a salaried position but on a lower career path. The 45° hatched zone represents the total loss of wages in case of return to a salaried position. The latter is specific to 'Grande Ecole' graduates. It is a sunk cost which reduces the incentive to get into entrepreneurship for this type of population. This zone diminishes when the first period prior to the revision date gets longer but the loss represented by the vertical hatched zone extends further, which adds up to the total surface increasing. Moreover it leads to a loss in the expected wage in case of coming back to a salary position (because $w_t^r(T') < w_t^r(T)$). Finally, an increase in the length of the period before the project review leads to an increase in the entrepreneurship opportunity cost (represented in 45° hatched zone in Figure 2.4) which leads to a reduction in the incentive to get into entrepreneurship.

As we assume that innovative projects require a long time for finalization, these innovative projects also imply the risk of a greater depreciation of the human capital when the project fails, and then the risk of a greater sunk cost for the graduate individual. Indeed, in every new innovative firm

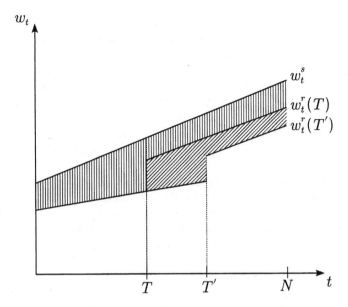

Figure 2.4   Innovative projects and sunk costs

there are phases of validation of the project (finalizing a new medicine for example) for which there is new information which means a revised project and thus a revised sunk cost. The sunk cost is random since it is contingent upon the success probabilities of the firm.

2.5   CONCLUSION

Numerous macroeconomic, institutional and cultural reasons account for differences in entrepreneurial intensity between countries. These reasons refer to what Baumol (1990) calls the rules of the game, that is, the structure of reward in the economy. He notices that some societies give priority to reward structures which are more or less favourable to firm development. Labour markets especially differ from country to country (more or less flexible with more or less network effects) and thus the qualified population is more or less prone to undertake innovative projects. Of course the effect of education on the appearance of rupture innovations is not obvious. Baumol (2004) observed that breakthrough innovations are very often achieved by independent and autonomous people very often endowed with a basic education. Education may then be considered as a help and a hindrance to innovation, as a help because it 'can stimulate creativity and imagination' and as a hindrance because 'the student who has mastered a large body of the received mathematical literature including theorems, proofs and methods of calculation, may be led to think in conventional ways that can be an obstacle to unorthodox approaches that favors creativity' (Baumol, 2004, p. 3). Too much of academic education harms creativity. In the USA, where specialization takes place at a later stage of the curriculum, it is well known that students fare less well than their European counterpart up to the PhD level and then demonstrate more imagination compared to European students taking the same diploma.

France is a country where the labour market is not as flexible as other countries. Collectively it leads to an insider/outsider tradeoff that is not favourable to risk taking and entrepreneurship, especially in the population of young students and qualified salaried people and among public researchers. For 1000 public researchers only 1.5 new innovative firms are set up each year (Emin, 2003), despite the 12 July 1999 law on innovation and the research which, among other things, aims at making it easier for researchers to get their research results into a stage of industrial development.[11] The USA, which has achieved a real innovation economy, finds entrepreneurial resources among young educated students that benefit from the stimulating environment of scientific parks and university campuses. Some young talented French go to the USA to set up their firms, especially in the Silicon Valley (Poncet, 2000). The entrepreneur finds funds there more easily but above all finds a more active labour market, more numerous and deeper relationships with the university, greater possibilities to change job and then to promote the experience previously acquired (Gilson, 1999). In other words, the functioning of the labour market is more favourable to entrepreneurship.

NOTES

1. Baumol (1968) remarks that people speak about clever tricks, ingenious schemes, brilliant innovations and charisma which differentiate entrepreneurs.
2. See Appendix 2.1.
3. Even though setting up one's own firm when being unemployed always remain a positive signal about the true level of the individual human capital (Bhattacharjee et al., 2008).
4. Corporate venturing provides an alternative to traditional methods of a growing company. A company invests in new products or technologies by funding businesses that have a reasonably autonomous management team and separate human resource policies. Four ways can be experienced: taking a passive, minority position in outside businesses (corporate venture capital), taking an active interest in an outside company, building a new business as a stand-alone unit or building a new business inside the existing firm with a structure allowing for management independence.

5. Système d'informations sur les nouveaux entrepreneurs, French database on new French firms.
6. These results also have to be qualified taking into account conjuncture and the evolution of public aid to unemployed people setting up or taking over a firm. For the 1994 Sine, one has to take into account the 1993 crisis (GDP–1 per cent); for 1998 the favourable conjuncture and thus the stronger job opportunities offered on the labour market. One actually notices that if the plans more or less favourable in time to entrepreneurship by unemployed people increase the number of firms receiving aid, they have a lesser effect on the number of unemployed people setting up their own firm who in many cases would have undertaken this anyway. Going through unemployment as a strategy may admittedly exist but it is not essential.
7. Wennekers (2006) has thus demonstrated that there is a negative relation between the unemployment rate and the setting up of firms' rate in the European case. This result corroborates the fact that the considerations of exiting unemployment on the labour market should be taken into account and bear an influence on entrepreneurial activity.
8. The ratio of entrepreneurs-engineers among the population of French active graduate engineers ranges between 5 and 7 per cent according to the socio-economical surveys conducted by the National Council of Engineers and Scientists of France (CNISF).
9. 'Créateurs-étudiants', *APCE*, August 2005.
10. The ranking attributes one mark to the education institute of the CEO of each of the 500 world firms of the 2007 Fortune ranking. If they graduated from several schools, the mark is shared.
11. Other accompanying measures are the innovative technology firm contests, setting up of public incubators and the April 2003 innovation plan for young innovative firms. The status of young innovative firms created by the 2004 finance law and implemented by the 21 June 2004 decree gives SMEs some advantages that have development-research expenses representing at least 15 per cent of their costs:

   - A tax exemption for profit and yearly fixed tax.
   - A tax exemption for the surplus values of securities transfer for the associates of the firm.
   - An employer's social security contribution on wages paid to the salaried employees taking part in research relief.

   Introducing the status of young university firm (JEU) from January 2008 onwards aims at favouring entrepreneurship by students or any other person taking part in research works of higher education institutions. It is about extending the status of young innovative firms, and their advantages, to young university firms.
12. Nevertheless, one has to be cautious when interpreting the results since projects which were not carried through owing to credit rationing are not taken into account.
13. *Le Figaro économie*, 18 May 2005.

REFERENCES

Aernoudt, R. (2004), 'Incubators: tool for entrepreneurship?', *Small Business Economics*, **23**, 127–35.

APCE (2005), 'Créateurs étudiants', August.

Audrestsch, D. (2007), 'Entrepreneurship capital and economic growth', *Oxford Review of Economic Policy*, **23** (1), 63–78.

Baumol, W.J. (1968), 'Entrepreneurship in economic theory', *American Economic Review*, **58**, March, 64–71.

Baumol, W.J. (1990), 'Entrepreneurship, productive, unproductive and destructive', *Journal of Political Economy*, **98**, October, 893–921.

Baumol, W.J. (2004), 'Education for innovation: breakthroughs vs. corporate incremental improvements', National Bureau for Economic Research paper, no. 5, April.

Bécard, F. (2007), 'Le renforcement des coopérations entre les structures d'appui à l'innovation et à la création d'entreprises, les écoles d'ingénieurs et les écoles de management', rapport Retis, à Mr le Ministre délégué à l'industrie, April.

Bhattacharjee, A., J. Bonnet, N. Le Pape and R. Renault (2006), 'Inferring the unobserved human capital of entrepreneurs', in M. Van Praag (ed.), *Entrepreneurship and Human Capital*, Amsterdam, Netherlands: Amsterdam Center for Entrepreneurship, Faculty of Economics and Business, University of Amsterdam, July, pp. 47–51.

Bhattacharjee, A., J. Bonnet, N. Le Pape and R. Renault (2008), 'Entrepreneurial motives and performance: why might better educated entrepreneurs be less successful?', ThEMA research laboratory working paper, University of Cergy-Pontoise, France.

Emin, S. (2003), 'L'intention de créer une entreprise des chercheurs publics: le cas français', Thèse de Doctorat de Sciences de Gestion de l'Université Pierre Mendès France de Grenoble.

Evans, D.S. and L. Leighton (1989), 'Some empirical aspects of entrepreneurship', *American Economic Review*, **79** (3), 519–35.

Fayolle, A. (2001), 'D'une approche typologique de l'entrepreneuriat chez les ingénieurs à la reconstruction d'itinéraires d'ingénieurs entrepreneurs', *Revue de l'Entrepreneuriat*, **1** (1), 77–97.

Fink, M. (2009), 'L'autonomie est la solution pour sauver les universités', *le Monde*, 17 February.

Fontagné, L. (2008), 'L'industrie va mal? Regardez plutôt les services', *Ouest France*, 23-24 February.

Fougères, D. (2000), 'La durée du chômage en France', in Jean-Paul Fitoussi, Olivier Passet and Jacques Freyssinet (eds), *Réduction du chômage: les réussites en Europe*, report for le Conseil d'Analyse Economique (CAE), La Documentation Française, pp. 239–59.

Georgellis, J.G. and N. Tsitsianis (2005), 'Self-employment longitudinal dynamics: a review of the literature', *Economic Issues*, **10** (2), 51–84.

Gilson, R. (1999), 'The legal infrastructure of high technology industrial district: Silicon Valley, Route 128, and covenants not to compete', *New York University Law Review*, **3**, 575–629.

Khilström, R. and J.J. Laffont (1979), 'A general equilibrium entrepreneurial theory of firm formation based on risk aversion', *Journal of Political Economy*, **87** (4), August, 719–48.

Kirzner, I.M. (1979), *Perception, Opportunity, and Profit*, Chicago, IL: University of Chicago Press.

Kirzner, I.M. (1985), *Discovery and the Capitalist Process*, Chicago, IL: University of Chicago Press.

Lebègue, T. and E. Walter (2008), *Grandes Ecoles: la fin d'une exception française*, Paris: Calmann-Lévy.

Lebret, H. (2007), *Start-up: ce que nous voulons encore apprendre de la Silicon Valley*, self-published book, 978 1 1434 817334.

Leibenstein, H. (1968), 'Entrepreneurship and development', *American Economic Review*, **2** (58), 72–83.

Moskowitz, T. and A. Vissing-Jorgensen (2002), 'The returns to entrepreneurial investment: a private equity premium puzzle?', *American Economic Review*, **4**, September, 745–78.

Poncet, J.-F. (2000), 'La fuite des cerveaux: mythe ou réalité?', report no. 388 de la commission des affaires économiques du Sénat.

Ribeill, G. (1984), 'Entreprendre hier et aujourd'hui: la contribution des ingénieurs', *Culture Technique*, **12**, 77–92.

Schumpeter, J. (1911 [1934]), *The Theory of Economic Development*, Cambridge, MA: Harvard University Press.

Spence, A.M. (1973), 'Job Market Signaling', *Quarterly Journal of Economics*, **87** (3), 355–74.

Stam, E. (2008), 'Entrepreneurship and innovation policy', Iena economic research papers, no. 2008-6.

Terajima, Y. (2006), 'Education and self-employment: changes in earnings and wealth inequalities', Bank of Canada, working paper, no. 40.

Wennekers, S. (2006), 'Entrepreneurship at country level: economic and non-economic determinants', Erasmus Research Institute of Management (ERIM), accessed 28 January 2010 at http://repub.eur.nl/publications/eco_man/erim/erim3/957613528/.

APPENDIX 2.1   FRENCH 'GRANDES ECOLES'

Extract from *Grandes Ecoles, la fin d'une exception française,* by Thomas Lebègue and Emmanuelle Walter published (2008) by Calmann-Lévy, Paris.

'A true "Grande Ecole" is independent from university, selects on entry via post-baccalauréat or post-preparatory school exams and delivers a diplôma (master) of a baccalauréat +5 acknowledged by the State. Engineering schools must be certified by the Commission of Engineers Titles. They are majority: there are some 224'.

'"Grandes Ecoles" train engineers, managers and executives, researchers-teachers, high civil servants. If the *Conference of Grandes Ecoles* numbers 236 members (among them 12 foreign schools), the higher education ministry estimates there are 431 "Grandes Ecoles" (engineering schools, business schools, les école normales supérieures, but also veterinary schools).'

'Among them are found the "très Grandes Ecoles", the ones which train the future senior executives of the State and the big firms. They come in particular from "Ecole nationale d'administration (Ena), Hautes études commerciales (HEC), Ecole normale supérieure de la rue d'Ulm (ENS Ulm), Ecole polytechnique (X)" . . . Courses preparatory to "Grandes Ecoles" are the corner stone of selective education in France. They are organized within secondary schools and had in 2007–2008, 77 600 pupils.'

APPENDIX 2.2   THE CHECKS TO THE SETTING UP OF INNOVATIVE FIRMS

Among other explanations put forward in the literature, one may observe:

- An inadequate education to creativity and entrepreneurship in public institutions.
- A slow development of incubators in France due to lack of entrepreneurship (technological start-up, spin off) and underdevelopment of seed money and private financing networks (venture capital, business angels) (Aernoudt, 2004). However, it must be noticed that in France entrepreneurs do not suffer from a very high bank rationing at the beginning of their activity even if quite an important self-constraint motive may be detected among them (Cieply and Dejardin, Chapter 5, this volume).[12] In addition there is no path of exclusion, a young firm rationed at the beginning of its activity may very well develop sustained banking relationships later.
- A lack of entrepreneurial spirit. In France according to an Ipsos survey conducted for the Confédération Générale des Petites et Moyennes Entreprises (CGPME, General Confederation of SME),[13] 36 per cent of young people wish to enter the civil service, in particular for job safety. The rate is higher than in the USA where admittedly the public sector is less represented.
- An inadequate flexibility of the labour market. The result is well established now that in the French case there is a time dependence in that a longer time in unemployment decreases the probability of exiting unemployment (Fougères, 2000). And yet one of the conditions for risk taking is to be able to get back a job quickly in case of failure, and even to give value to one's experience.

3. Entrepreneurship and its regional development: do self-employment ratios converge and does gender matter?

Dieter Bögenhold and Uwe Fachinger

3.1 INTRODUCTION

The idea of this chapter is to discuss the issue of self-employment not only within the conventional scope of entrepreneurship discussion but within an integrated framework which combines entrepreneurship studies with labour market research. The integration of entrepreneurship analysis with studies on social stratification and mobility provides some very relevant issues and further questions in the field of entrepreneurship. With growing solo self-employment a new social phenomenon in the structure of the labour market and the division of occupations has emerged in which different social developments are overlapping each other. The question for the landscape of self-employment in general and for solo self-employment in particular is of crucial research interest: what forces their emergence? Must they be regarded primarily as a result of 'pushes' by labour market deficiencies or are they a response to new lifestyles and working demands which act as 'pulling' factors into self-employment? In other words, does solo self-employment serve as a valve of a pressing labour market or must it be regarded more positively as a new option in the classic division of labour by which an increasing number of people find new self-reliant and also stable jobs?

If one wants to talk about structural changes, data are needed which cover a broader timeframe. Therefore, we use German microcensus data from the Statistical Office Germany which are available for the periods from 1989 until 2005 to obtain further indications and specifications of the changes within the field of self-employment. Our main interest is to ask for structural changes of self-employment by observing the period since 1991. The questions are:

1. Do we find significant differences in the development between West and East Germany and between administrative districts?
2. Which disparities can be located when asking for gender differences?

To make it simpler, we consider which factors matter when talking about changes in entrepreneurship and self-employment: regions, gender or occupations.

In the analysis we want to draw a more holistic picture of self-employment and related changes in economy and society and in the division of work and occupations, by taking numerous facets of self-employment into account. The chapter has two parts. The first part discusses the issues of entrepreneurship, innovation and self-employment as we find those items in current academic discussion and related policy recommendations. All related debate very often goes back to some basic assumptions which one finds in much broader scenarios within works provided by Schumpeter, Hayek and Kirzner, among others. They conceptualize a strong link between entrepreneurship, innovation and self-employment. What we want to convey is that entrepreneurship, innovation and self-employment only overlap in some parts. The category of self-employment is no guarantee for economic welfare success or innovation. It reflects structural changes within the economy and society which condition the division of labour and organizations and working opportunities and which come up with new breeding grounds for small grants of new forms of self-employment, sometimes only part-time self-employment. Many of these new organizational entities seem to be reactions to social and economic changes. Those self-employed cannot be regarded as innovators in a Schumpeterian sense.

The second part refers to empirical findings, which are exclusively based upon investigation on the German case. While many regional studies are carried out on an international scale, this section focuses on intranational differences as sources of regional disparities. Although a first inspection is carried out on a rather descriptive data inspection, the findings allow that variables such as population sizes, self-employment profiles and specifics of regions, economic sectors and gender matter.

3.2   ENTREPRENEURSHIP – THEORETICAL CONSIDERATIONS

3.2.1   Entrepreneurship, Innovation and Self-employment

Entrepreneurship cannot be translated directly into a category for labour market analysis for example, self-employment – because the term itself seems to be more or less an umbrella term for different or diverse economic phenomena of business life. The idiom 'entrepreneurship' covers diverse issues, such as those relating to small and medium-sized enterprises, innovative ventures, business start-ups, socioeconomic perspectives and market behaviour, among others. As this is the case, there is no precise and commonly shared statistical source from which an international comparisons of specific levels of entrepreneurship can be drawn. When discussing links between entrepreneurship and the division of occupations and changes in the labour market the analytical category of 'self-employment' seems more precise and adequate for operationalizing a quantifiable understanding of entrepreneurship. Self-employment as a labour market category can be numerically counted and individual fractions of the category can be compared. However, referring to self-employment raises the difficulty that it usually serves as a kind of proxy for entrepreneurship but self-employment and entrepreneurship are never the same. Entrepreneurship covers only parts of the category of self-employment and the population of self-employed people includes people who can rarely be identified as entrepreneurial agents (Stam, 2008).

Entrepreneurship is treated as a policy instrument to introduce innovation in order to initiate positive effects for the economy and the labour market. Regarding the question of what innovation really means it is necessary to operate with a wide understanding of the term innovation. Within the extremely extensive literature one can go back to classic thought provided by Joseph A. Schumpeter (1963) who provided a typology of different innovation segments in order to demonstrate that innovation processes may include very different items. He distinguished between five different matters of innovation (Schumpeter, 1963, p. 66):

1. The introduction of a new good.
2. The introduction of a new method of production, that is, one not yet tested by experience in the specific branch of manufacture, and which needs by no means to be scientifically new, even more, it can also be a new way of handling a commodity commercially.
3. The opening of a new market, that is, a market into which the particular branch of manufacture of the country in question has not previously entered, whether or not this market has existed before.
4. The conquest of a new source of supply of raw materials or half-manufactured goods, again irrespective of whether this source already exists or whether it has to be created first.
5. The carrying out of a new organization of any industry, such as the creation of a monopoly or the breaking up of a monopoly position.

Having in mind the broad scenario of interpretations and applications of innovation we should take into account that no single pattern of innovations exists but diverse ways of innovations as formerly not known 'new combinations'. Innovation research is an elementary part of the broader debate on stimulating economic growth. A long tradition exists in discussing how to implement further growth most appropriately. Competing approaches are still coexisting although recent debate is moving towards a so-called unified growth theory 'in which variations in the economic performance across countries and regions could be examined based on the effect of variations in educational, institutional, geographical, and cultural factors on the pace of the transition from stagnation to growth' (Galor, 2006, pp. 284–5).

Acknowledging that growth has become the strategically most crucial index of policy orientation, innovation is becoming of similar importance since innovation is always seen as initiating and keeping the driving force of growth in motion (Schumpeter, 1947, Part II, Ch. 2). One of the issues to foster innovation is fostering entrepreneurship. The link between innovation, entrepreneurship and growth (Audretsch and Thurik, 2001) has become centrally proclaimed and underlined. Many of the theoretical and empirical literature have been provided not only to each of the dimensions but also to their practical interplay. The multicomplex concert of entrepreneurial driven innovation as growth engine includes a wide and open understanding of the different elements of innovation and of competition as a discovery process (Hayek, 2002; Kirzner, 1973) which ultimately includes several soft dimensions (besides hard factors such as financing and given technology) as productive means, such as – among others – human resources, knowledge (including educational skill and education), system of industrial relations, social and organization networks, working behaviour and mentalities (Audretsch, 2002, 2007).

Creation and discovery are mysterious processes but whatever else may be required scientists are reasonably certain that incentives matter (Scotchmer, 2004, preface). Innovation is the key to competitiveness in a globalized economy, which opens the door to sustainable growth and to more employment. Innovation processes are highly embedded in societal trends towards increasing ratios of knowledge in diverse spheres (Warsh, 2006). Processes of industrial renewal in the global economy take place within a universal framework of permanent reconfigurations of the wider structure of economy and society. One of these tendencies is the internationally noticeable process of tertiarization which reduces employment and companies in the secondary sector – especially in the manufacturing industry – and which increases employment and ventures in services. Acknowledging this trend as a major source of change helps to demystify conventional debate in which especially rising numbers of entrepreneurs are glamorized and rhetorically sold as a positive outcome of policy activities. The general trend that in the production sector the relative number of white collar employees increases affects the division of labour within companies as well as between them (Bögenhold and Fachinger, 2008). Shifts in the sectoral division of national and international economies need to be acknowledged in order to see the potential for firm dynamics including niches for new small firms (Bögenhold and Fachinger, 2007).

3.2.2 Certainty and Uncertainty: Firm Strategies

The division of work and the division of private companies can be interpreted from the perspective of company strategies and from the perspective of global social changes. The first perspective rationalizes changes in the structure of corporations or the division of labour primarily as an effect of firm strategies. Firms can enlarge, move, downsize or close down and this will have certain effects on the system of the organization of the firms. The alternative view is based upon the idea that societies evolve globally as well as specifically and that those changes provide new and changing frameworks for the landscape of labour and business organizations.

Much of what we observe as firm strategies to increase flexibility is nothing else than an attempt to minimize uncertainties. A study, which addressed the phenomenon systematically and early, was the book by Frank H. Knight (1971). Knight discussed strategies of business organizations in relation to issues of planning certainties. While competition between enterprises is modulated under the premise of perfect competition where all participants share all the same relevant information, Knight argues that modern, dynamic, economic societies do not meet with this premise:

> With uncertainty absent, man's energies are devoted altogether to doing things; it is doubtful whether intelligence itself would exist in such a situation; in a world so built that perfect knowledge was theoretically possible, it seems likely that all organic readjustments would become mechanical, all organisms automata. With uncertainty present, doing things, the actual execution of activity, becomes in a real sense a secondary part of life; the primary problem or function is deciding what to do and how to do it. (Knight, 1971, p. 268)

Knight's premise is that we are in a world of dynamics and related uncertainties. If we want to understand the economic system adequately, we have to have a better understanding of uncertainties and corresponding zones of complexities. The issue of uncertainty separates expectations and certainties. In economic life nearly all future prospects and activities are based upon specific assumptions. These assumptions are adverted to data of competitors, the business cycle, labour markets, innovation and technology standards and institutional settings. The problem for business corporations is how to act despite uncertainties. 'The significance of change is that it gives rise to the problem of the control of action, and in this respect the difference between predictable and unpredictable change is conspicuous' (Knight, 1971, p. 315). Risks are distinguished as static or dynamic risks. Static risks are managed by routines while dynamic risks are related to challenges provoking new types of answers: 'Problems of action arise out of departures from routine in changes of all sorts' (Knight, 1971, p. 315).

The corporation does not only deal with uncertainties which are located outside the corporation but also within the organization. Organizational theory had started to discuss 'human factors' inside the organizational boarders, which were treated in different ways through theorems of 'bounded rationality' (Simon, 1955) or as 'moral hazards' (Alchian and Demsetz, 1972). Although the literature did not always discuss the issues systematically, one crucial point was often the question of how a corporation is changing over time. Does the administration change if companies are successfully growing? What about the emergence of organizational buffers and lack of controls?

According to Blau, two contradictory tendencies are emerging:

> The large homogeneous personnel components in large organizations simplify supervision and administration, which is reflected in a wider span of control of supervisors . . . and a lower administrative ratio . . . in large than in small organizations. Consequently, organizations exhibit an economy of scale in administrative manpower. . . . At the same time, however, the heterogeneity among organizational components produced by differentiation creates problems of coordination and pressures to expand the administrative personnel to meet these problems. (Blau, 1974, p. 320)

What Blau explained principally differs very much regarding to different economic sectors and to different organizational environments. Different transaction costs explain why companies come up with organizational answers this or that way but transaction costs are very difficult to estimate practically. Specific organizational structures are often the result of search strategies to minimize transaction costs. In wide part, these search routines reflect trial-and-error-strategies which gives an idea of what Chandler (1962) meant by his famous credo of 'structure follows strategy'.

Business historian Chandler discussed that:

1. Strategies are the result of routines of repetition.
2. The fact of uncertainties can sometimes imply contradictory strategies.
3. New moments of crisis are potentially new starting points of changing organizational conceptions and interpretations.

In *The Visible Hand* Chandler (1977) made clear that in order to reduce transaction costs strategies of vertical integration are favoured. In addition, in *Strategy and Structure* (1962) Chandler demonstrated just the opposite explanation, for example, how the emergence of organizational buffers may initiate company processes of reorganization. Here advantages of a multidivisional structure are related to a reduction of transaction costs.

> The basic reason for its success was simply that it clearly removed the executives responsible for the destiny of the entire enterprise from the more routine operational activities, and so gave them the time, information, and even psychological commitment for long-term planning and appraisal. . . . [The] new structure left the broad strategic decisions as to the allocation of existing resources and the acquisition of new ones in the hands of a top team of generalists. Relieved of operating duties and tactical decisions, a general executive was less likely to reflect the position of just one part of the whole. (Chandler 1962, p. 382)

3.2.3 Creative Destruction and Complexities

Empirically, company strategies, which deal with the issue of uncertainties, differ. In some cases strategic planning essentially leads to industrial dynamics. In case of certainty no scenario of planning is needed since all parameters are known but an economy which is interpreted as being in a permanent storm of 'creative destruction' (Schumpeter, 1947) is always in a flux of creating new things. Creative destruction is a contradictory expression, which seeks to highlight the fact that competition and inherent processes towards monopolistic and oligopolistic competition are only one part of the overall economic game. However, processes of creation of new firms, new ideas and even new business leaders, which are running simultaneously, are often neglected. Deaths and births are two sides of the same coin, and Schumpeter dubbed creative destruction as an essential fact about capitalism. Innovation is the steady, new 'fresh blood' through which new ideas and new people flow into the economy and which keeps the 'capitalist machine' going. However, creativity is almost combined with destruction elsewhere. When new products appear, consumer demands change, and existing production and related markets are rendered obsolete.

Innovation and technical progress are in the Schumpeterian framework due (not) to external factors but they belong to the economic system as internal factors. The crucial question is not what capitalism does with economic structures but how capitalism creates and destroys these structures. The basic assumption of its dynamics is the existence of competition for innovation: companies always compete for new ways of innovation.

Innovation is regarded as introducing a new combination of things which did not exist before or which were not done in that way before. Implementation of a new combination is the successful test on the market (Schumpeter, 1963).

Regarding this background, entrepreneurs are treated as agents to introduce new inputs into the economy. Schumpeter defined an entrepreneur as a person who comes up with the aforementioned 'new combinations' which are commonly called innovation. In this context the activity of entrepreneurs is fundamental for economic development.

Entrepreneurship is regarded as an institution that carries out the function of providing innovations. According to Schumpeter the economic function of entrepreneurship is to initiate and to continue the process of creative destruction as the 'permanent storm of capitalist development'. In this view entrepreneurs act as personifications of economically necessary functions of economic change. Schumpeter's definition is notable since he considers only those economic actors as entrepreneurs who create 'new combinations' and this almost with loaned capital. The last point is remarkable in that there are always risks taken. In this sense, entrepreneurial being is 'not a profession and as a rule not a lasting condition' (Schumpeter, 1963, p. 78).

Here Schumpeter introduces entrepreneurial activities ultimately linked to sources of uncertainties. Only those business people who deal with uncertainties are regarded as (innovative) entrepreneurs, since an entrepreneur is by definition only an entrepreneur when they are risk taking and innovative. The link between Knight, Schumpeter, Hayek and further ideas of evolutionary economics (Nelson and Winter, 1982) or evolutionary entrepreneurship (Kirzner, 1973, 1985) is given through the idea of management of uncertainties under conditions of asymmetric information. Management processes are always practised in and against dynamic environments under processes of uncertainties; they are realized under generalized hypotheses and normative assumptions in order to reduce complexities.

3.2.4   Institutional Context of Entrepreneurship

In economic models complexities are reduced to try to be as simple as possible in order to deduce core principles which can be applied to all situations. The institutional framing with particular socio-spatial-cultural characteristics, including social, legal and demographic specifics, is often neglected in such models. However, even if a social environment is recognized as a variable that has to be taken into account, it does not imply fully integrating the working mechanism of the inner principle adequately into the model. Engerman and Sokoloff (2003) express clearly that economic growth theories can be better formulated by a more sensitive understanding of institutions:

> Economists do not have a very good understanding of where institutions come from, or why societies have institutions that seem conducive to growth, while others are burdened by institutions less favourable for economic performance. Until they do, it will be quite difficult to specify the precise role of institutions in processes of growth. . . . [W]hat little we know about the evolution of institutions suggests caution about making strong claims about their relationship to growth. (Engerman and Sokoloff, 2003, p. 28)

The consequence for research on entrepreneurship is that not only the context of entrepreneurship has to be acknowledged (Baumol and Strom, 2007) but also its change in temporal sequences. Baumol (1990) exemplified that in his historical analysis of entrepreneurship and he expresses that entrepreneurship as such cannot always be equated with economic upswings and positive effects of innovations. He explains that 'entrepreneurs are always with us and always play *some* substantial role. But there are a variety of roles among which the entrepreneur's efforts can be reallocated, and some of those roles do not follow the constructive and innovative script that is conventionally attributed to that person' (Baumol, 1990, p. 894, emphasis in original). An analytic look on the development over centuries indicates that frameworks of economies can vary considerably and that mentalities and further cultural dispositions change (Munro, 2006), which is an argument that specifications of space and time should be considered when talking about entrepreneurship (Bögenhold, 1995).

Network research (Nohria and Eccles, 1995; Scott, 2007) increased the conceptual understanding that economic cycles are best interpreted as socially controlled and organized interaction processes of individual and corporate actors. Economic activities function along specific 'ties' of contacts which are organized according to specific social circles of communication. Organizational networks can be seen analogously to social networks. The difference is that organizational networks focus on interaction between organizations compared to ego-centred networks based on social action of human agents. Michael E. Porter (1990) argues that it is more reasonable to compare regions instead of referring to aggregate economies and their aggregate data. Regions are the core subject of socioeconomic analysis. When talking about 'microeconomics of prosperity' (Porter, 2000) the term serves as a research programme. Nowadays discussion on growth and regional policies often claims the need to foster clusters, a discussion which is based upon a perspective spread by Porter (see Stern et al., 2000).

A great part of the recent literature on innovation (Kaiserfeld, 2005) is led by questions for adequate socioeconomic contexts generating innovation. Social networks are explicitly treated as 'extra-market externality' (Westlund, 2006) and a direct link between 'networking' and 'entrepreneurial growth' is postulated (Johannisson, 2000). In the discussion clusters as sources of innovation through cooperation has increased significantly (Karlsson, 2007), and the growth of socioeconomic elements is simultaneously expressed within the entrepreneurship literature. Looking at specific models of economic success and growth we arrive at a matrix of particular combinations of information processing, product generation, opportunity and market finding and regional characteristics (Asheim and Coenen, 2005; Asheim et al., 2006), which are based upon issues of material and immaterial dimensions of production and organization (in the same direction, see the findings of Mugler et al., 2006). In particular, the rising importance of knowledge as a factor of production (Bell, 1973; Castells, 2004, 2005 as sociologists; and Warsh, 2006 as a historian of economic thought) underlines those dramatic changes in economic regimes of production (Dolfsma and Soete, 2006). Audretch (2007) makes clear that knowledge has evolved as the key factor within discussions on economic progress.

Acknowledging the institutional context of entrepreneurship implies the recognition of social factors being of strategic importance to arrive at an adequate understanding of growth patterns. These social factors include items such as language, mentalities, family structures, systems of basic and higher education, industrial relations, trust or knowledge. They constitute different societal regimes of production, which always have specific faces in divergent regional contexts. In that sense business historians explained it as 'cultural factors in economic growth' (Cochran, 1960) and Buchanan and Ellis stated that 'the really fundamental problems of economic growth are non-economic' (Buchanan and Ellis, 1955, p. 405).

If one agrees with Buchanan and Ellis, one also has to agree with far-reaching consequences since non-economic factors have to be analysed and understood in order to explain economic growth. According to these ideas, Audretsch (2002) listed in his discussion of major factors several social soft factors as key factors influencing entrepreneurship beside catchwords such as finance and taxes. The most important of these soft factors are culture, networks and social capital. Finally, the focus of analytical observation must be narrowed down to local entities that are regions rather than nations. Here Porter's ideas on the microeconomics of prosperity matches with thought on the core-periphery model as delivered by Krugman (1991). Looking at regions enables us to see specific paths and path dependencies of economic and social development, which allow the analysis of regional prosperities within their own logics of evolution (Audretsch et al., 2008).

Having discussed entrepreneurship in context with innovation and self-employment (Bjerke, 2007), the partial overlap of the three items was considered. Self-employment often serves as the practical translation of what is sometimes somewhat mysteriously coined entrepreneurship. While entrepreneurship has a close link with innovation and the dynamics of capitalism, self-employment as analytical category often stands apart. The question is whether all forms of self-employment are closely connected to the innovative and dynamic parts of the economy where new elements and ideas are set up keeping the capitalist engine in motion. The next section aims to shed light on the question by referring empirically to the German case.

3.3   FROM ENTREPRENEURSHIP TO THE STUDY OF SELF-EMPLOYMENT: OBSERVATIONS ON THE GERMAN CASE

The main interest of the empirical research is to ask for structural changes within the category of self-employment by observing a period of 15 years.

Since public discussion on entrepreneurship is often done in a very glamorizing way in which self-employed people are regarded as personalized agents of entrepreneurship, which operate as heroes of capitalist dynamics, our study is led by the attempt to develop the field more realistically. In the following we want to take some important facets of self-employment into account to draw a more holistic picture of self-employment within the division of work and occupations. The questions are do regions, does gender or do occupations matter when talking about changes in self-employment.

3.3.1   Trends of Self-employment

In Germany over the time span of 51 years, the percentages of self-employed to the labour force has decreased from 13.0 per cent to 8.1 per cent in 1991 and since then a small increase has taken place. The development of the portion of self-employed people and family workers to the labour force, which started from 24.1 per cent and decreased until 1991 to 9.5 per cent, with a small raise since then, is a reflection of the structural changes in the economy that is characterized by the term 'tertiarization': an increase of the service sector, for example, portrayed by the rising numbers of employed people and the growing share of GDP. Service sector increases are often mirrored by a decline of the agricultural sector. The decline is for a large part due to the shrinking number of farmers and therefore also a result of the ongoing concentration within the economy. Hence, over the period, not only a reduction of self-employed people took place but also the number of family workers decreased drastically, which further indicates the structural changes in the economy (for more information see, for example, Bögenhold and Fachinger, 2009).

The overall development of the two rates hides structural changes that took place within self-employment and no information about the underlying forces can be yielded. For a closer look, an analysis on an individual basis is necessary. The microcensus database enables a closer look at the development of self-employment. Unfortunately, we could only use data since 1989 and 1991, respectively, and not for the whole time period of 51 years. On the other hand, as we are especially interested in comparing the development in West and East Germany, the relevant time span is covered.

The data show the somewhat unexpected development of the number of self-employed people in West and East Germany as the profiles have nearly the same shape – only the number is much lower in East Germany (for a clear picture, see Bögenhold and Fachinger, 2009). As the labour market structure in East Germany was totally different from West Germany, the growth at the same pace is astounding. East Germany was a former communist country where the transition phase with its dramatic institutional and economic shocks might have lead to a different entrepreneurial engagement level, when compared to the longstanding market economy of West Germany which did not experience such an abrupt change (Grilo and Thurik, 2005a, p. 146). Therefore one would have expected a sharp increase over the first years after the unification due to the restructuring of the economy and the process of adaptation to the 'capitalistic' market structure in West Germany – but the development is as stable as in West Germany without any sharp alterations.

Another view is gained, when self-employed people as a percentage of the labour force is considered. The development of the rate of self-employment in West and East Germany is quite different between 1991 and the mid-1990s. During this time an adjustment of East to West German structures took place. Here the somehow expected steep increase until 1993 can be seen as an indication of the economic transition and the adjustment of the labour market structure in East Germany to the structures of West Germany. From 1993 to 2003 the development of the self-employment rate is more or less the same for West and East Germany. A new phase of increasing percentage of self-employment in East Germany began in 2003, so that in 2005 the percentage of self-employed people in West and East Germany is nearly the same. However, the increase is mainly caused by a reduction of the labour force and not by an increase of the number of self-employed people.

3.3.2 Solo Self-employment: A New Matter of Investigation

To get a better understanding of the underlying forces of the development of self-employment, the self-employed people are differentiated into those who work alone (possibly having officially or unofficially support from family members) and those who have at least one employee. Even this somewhat crude measure delivers a clear result: the development of self-employment is mainly due to an above-average increase in the numbers of solo self-employed people as can be seen in Figure 3.1. The analysis shows that the steady rise in the numbers of self-employed people in Germany led to the fact that more than 50 per cent of all self-employed people belong to the category of solo self-employment in the meantime – and this applies for West and East Germany.

Furthermore, it is noteworthy that the rise in solo self-employment took place especially in West Germany and that the process happened in two phases. The first started in 1995 and ended two years later and the second phase started in 2002.

The development during the first period is an indication of the effect of at least two changes in law. The first bundle of causes is the changes of labour market regulations and of the industrial law since 1995. Since then it is easier for firms to outsource jobs and to do business with the same people as freelancers. The second bundle consists of changes of welfare state regulations. A new scheme was introduced in 1995: the statutory long-term care insurance. With this scheme, the market concept was introduced. The expectation was that with more competition the quantity and quality of the services would improve, and – as a result – many new one-person firms emerged especially by women who formerly worked as nurses in hospitals or nursing homes.

The second phase of drastic increase in solo self-employment is due to another severe change of labour market regulations in connection with further reforms of the welfare state system which took place at the beginning of the third millennium: the so-called Agenda 2010. The effect of this reworking yielded essentially the other increase of solo self-employment beginning in 2002.

Overall, the analysis indicates that the increase of self-employment is due to special 'innovations' and the reorganization of labour. The two pushes of solo self-employment are for once a reflection of changing laws and administrative regulations, fostering explicitly or implicitly people to

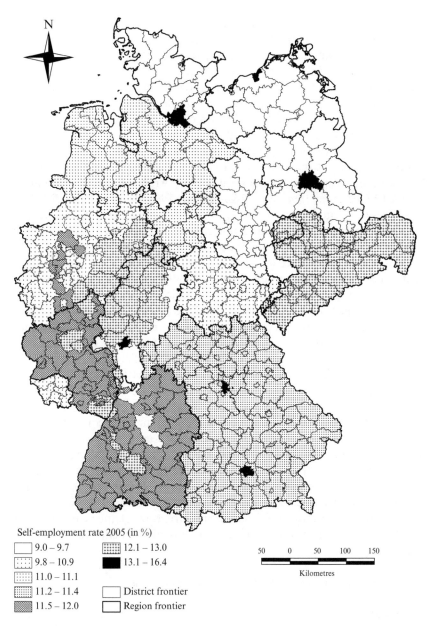

Self-employment rate 2005 (in %)

☐ 9.0 – 9.7	▦ 12.1 – 13.0		
☐ 9.8 – 10.9	■ 13.1 – 16.4		
▦ 11.0 – 11.1			
▦ 11.2 – 11.4	☐ District frontier		
▦ 11.5 – 12.0	☐ Region frontier		

50   0   50   100   150

Kilometres

Source: Authors' calculations based on the scientific use files of the microcensus of the Federal Statistical Office Germany; we are grateful to Helmut Bäurle, who drew the map.

Figure 3.1   Regional specific self-employment rate 2005

become self-employed. The introduction of the new body of law regarding long-term care as the '11. Book of the Social Security Statute Book' opened a new market in the sense of Schumpeter (Schumpeter, 1963, p. 66). This was accompanied by measures reducing the administrative complexities, which are regarded as an obstacle for becoming self-employed (see, for example, Grilo and Thurik, 2005b). On the other hand, the organization of labour was restructured by companies, which led to outsourcing of work to previous employees and led to a new legislation concerning the social security of those dependent self-employed people. The new legislation took place at the end of the 1990s ('Gesetz zur Korrekturen in der Sozialversicherung und Versicherung von Arbeitnehmerschutzrechten' from 19 December 1998, Bundesgesetzblatt 1998, Teil I, No. 85, S. 3843-3852, and its modification 'Gesetz zur Förderung der Selbständigkeit' from 20 December 1999, Bundesgesetzblatt 2000, Teil I, No. 1, S. 2-4. For an early discussion of the impacts, see Bögenhold et al., 2001).

Considering the combination of solo self-employment and gender indicates that the structural development is parallel to each other. The profiles of solo self-employed men and solo self-employed women follow the same time path – just the level is different and the profile for women is steeper. This result is somewhat contradictory to the results of Henrekson and Roine (2005 p. 33) where 'the fact still remains that an entrepreneurial culture and a welfare state seem very remotely related' with 'a vibrant entrepreneurial culture and the set of institutions that underpins such a culture seen very remotely related to the welfare state culture and its institutions'.

The effect of the increase in solo self-employment is compensated by a decline of self-employed with employees. Overall the relation of self-employed women to self-employed men is reasonably stable over the period. There is only a small increase in the percentage of self-employed women in West Germany from 26 per cent to 29 per cent and in East Germany from 28 per cent to 30 per cent. Concerning the division of gender, no indications of a fundamental structural change can be found as the relation between male and female self-employment proved to keep relatively stable.

3.3.3 Self-employment and Regional Diversification

The matter of regional differentiation is hardly acknowledged although the process of structural changes is very specific in respect to different regions. The consequences of structural changes become more transparent when looking at the regional division. In order to follow the arguments of Michael E. Porter (1990) and to give an impression about the heterogeneous situation within Germany, in Figure 3.1 self-employment rates are shown for the administrative districts of Germany for the year 2005.

A look at the regional distribution yields an inconsistent picture and backs up the argumentation of Porter (1990): there is a high self-employment rate in some metropolitan regions such as Munich, Berlin, Frankfurt and Hamburg, but not in Bremen or Hanover. In Saxony and in northern parts of Hesse the self-employment rate is above average as well. Very remarkable is also the fact that regions with high self-employment rates border on regions with very low rates. It may be deduced that there is no smooth transition from one region to another: regions with high and regions with low self-employment rates are coexisting within the nearest neighbourhood. This raises the question as to the reasons behind this pattern, which can only be answered by detailed comparative regional studies.

Considering the sectoral structure of the economy with respect to self-employment the situation turned out to be even more heterogeneous. Given a high rate of self-employment, for some regions the degree of tertiarization is inconsistent (Figure 3.2). There are regions with a low rate of self-employed people in the tertiary sector, where the rate of self-employment is also low – as, for example, in the Weser-Ems region – and there are other regions with a high rate of self-employment in the tertiary sector and a high self-employment rate.

In general, the findings show that differences between regional levels cannot be reasonably explained simply according to the East-West scheme which has been done very often. Sometimes the simple relationship of high self-employment rate and a high rate of self-employed people in the tertiary sector that has been supposed is not the case.

Regarding our findings and with respect to future developments, the question concerning the nature of self-employment is of particular interest. As Figure 3.2 indicates, in almost all regions the majority of self-employed people are working on their own in one-person firms. However, the share of solo self-employed people also varies from region to region: the ratio is between 69.0 per cent in the Munich region or 71.1 per cent in the Berlin region down to 50.1 per cent in regions in Lower Saxony.

Dealing with special subgroups of occupational independence is thoroughly complex. New facets of self-employment have to be discussed. Under the label of self-employment, losers in the labour market – whose place in the structure of dependent work is uncertain – are summed up, just like the emerging new and highly autonomous forms of entrepreneurial activities due to the ever-increasing importance of knowledge (see for a recent analysis about entrepreneurial decision Hessels et al., 2008).

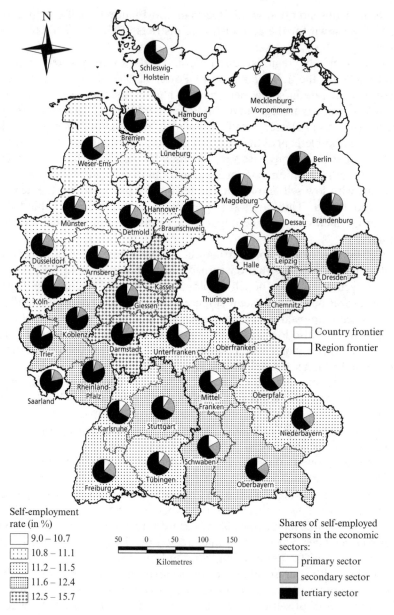

Self-employment
rate (in %)

☐ 9.0 – 10.7
⬚ 10.8 – 11.1
▦ 11.2 – 11.5
▦ 11.6 – 12.4
▦ 12.5 – 15.7

50   0   50   100   150

Kilometres

Shares of self-employed
persons in the economic
sectors:

☐ primary sector
▨ secondary sector
■ tertiary sector

Source: Authors' calculations based on the scientific use files of the microcensus of the
Federal Statistical Office Germany; we are grateful to Helmut Bäurle, who drew the map.

Figure 3.2   Regional and sector specific self-employment rate 2005

Over the last decades we have witnessed an advance of women in occupational independence. But this development also differs from region to region and no general effect for Germany can be formulated. The same is true for the increase of solo self-employment: We cannot say that a high rate of solo self-employment definitely goes hand in hand with a high rate of self-employed women. Sometimes the contrary is the case as the numbers for the administrative district of Frankfurt show with an above-average rate of 63 per cent for solo self-employment and a rate of 27.4 per cent for self-employed women, which is well below the average. Overall, there are regions where nearly every third self-employed person is female, while in other regions only every fourth person is female. However, there are regions with a low rate of female self-employment and a high rate of solo self-employment, whereas in the administrative district of Stuttgart both rates are high.

3.4 ENTREPRENEURSHIP, SELF-EMPLOYMENT, REGIONS: FROM GLAMORIZING VISION TO DIFFERENTIATED ANALYSIS

Our discussion has touched on many crucial aspects for a better understanding of entrepreneurship. While following ideas introduced primarily by Schumpeter that economies always need 'fresh blood' out of social and economic innovations in order to keep the capitalist engine in motion, we partly agreed that entrepreneurship might be an appropriate instrument to 'transport' diverse forms of innovation. However, the conventional equation that entrepreneurship has to be translated by the labour market category of self-employment was questioned theoretically and empirically. Self-employment is heterogeneous and has diverse elements, social logics and social path-dependencies, leading to the fact that fractions of self-employment can be very constitutive as sources and agents of innovation but other fractions are simultaneously very non-entrepreneurial in a Schumpeterian sense of running enterprises in routines without ever having ideas of innovation. The last group is very often driven by needs to keep the firms running to secure living and they are created out of diverse motives, very often also against a background of unemployment.

The idea of this chapter was to discuss the issue of self-employment in a framework which combines labour market research with a wider socio-economic context. Which forces push self-employment and how much do regions and gender matter? And how can we explain the explosion of solo self-employment compared to 'regular' self-employment?

What we have tried to explain is that the introduction of an institutional context to the debate on entrepreneurship, innovation and self-employment considerably helps to arrive at a better understanding of many phenomena under discussion. The turn to an economy within an institutional context helps to realize a turn from an economy *in abstracto* to an economy *in concreto*. When talking about entrepreneurship it must be related to real societies and economies with concrete time-space coordinates. Empirical results and economic history provide the genuine background which indicates how economies and societies are really evolving (Baumoll et al., 2007).

The shift towards markets creates new business opportunities opening up for other already established firms or for business start-ups through self-employment trying to cover these segments. The ups and downs of business activities in economies must always be taken as the balance between births and deaths, the idea of the metaphor of creative destruction. In that understanding an analysis of self-employment in a given year or in a short period of time is almost no more than a snapshot of capitalist dynamics.

Our findings illustrate that the social and economic process after the German reunification proves the adjustment of the ratio of self-employed people in East Germany to the West German level. In 2005 the gap between East and West Germany is nearly closed. Therefore persisting differences between regional levels cannot reasonably be explained anymore simply according to the East-West scheme, but must be better interpreted in a multicomplex framework of intranational relations and different growth and labour market patterns within Germany. Attempts to explain variation primarily with the German history of having post-communist parts in the East and 'purely' capitalist parts in the West will fall too short. What we can empirically observe is that all of Germany is fragmented.

At first sight, the heterogeneity has no clear and systematic logic of economic and social evolution. The unity of variation in regional levels of self-employment ratios concerning sectoral and further classification is contradictory when trying to relate different levels to different sizes of metropolitan or rural areas or to different levels of economic prosperity. All possible explanations according monocausal explanatory schemes can be confronted with counterfactual examples of regional development elsewhere. Regional differences within self-employment ratios which have no one-to-one fit with different levels of economic prosperity or different levels of unemployment are striking and make monocausal explanations difficult. Our findings suggest that self-employment has to be explained by inherent modes of regional working and dynamics.

What Porter labelled the 'microeconomics of prosperity' (Porter, 2000) seems to provide the analytic key for future analyses in order to decode different patterns of development. A first inspection and evaluation of the data suggests that we can conclude with a slogan that 'regions matter'. In this respect, we observe a unity of diversity and a diversity of unity. Following the conclusion that regions matter we can further suggest that 'culture matters' (Harrison and Huntington, 2000), since regional differences can be regarded as different levels of historically grounded specific socioeconomic differences. Regional differences are heterogeneous and contradictory as well as homogeneous from different perspectives of analysis and must be taken as elements and variables of a holistic entrepreneurship research (Bögenhold, 2007).

The non-identity of entrepreneurship and self-employment has been discussed at the beginning of the chapter: not everything labelled entrepreneurship can be translated with the category of self-employment and vice versa not all self-employed people can be regarded as proper entrepreneurs. Too heterogeneous are standards of living, labour, biographies, expectations and aspirations of people. In particular, the high and increasing portion of solo self-employment among the category of self-employment highlights the fact that not all self-employed people match with the idea of an 'entrepreneur as permanent opportunity seeker and finder' (Kirzner, 1973) but many of them are close to low incomes and their existence is to be explained against a background of experienced or feared unemployment.

Celebrating a revival of entrepreneurship by indicating the increasing numbers of self-employment is not serious since the explosion of solo self-employment does not have very much in common with a revival of entrepreneurship. These tendencies are better explained by global sectoral changes including labour market trends, secular processes towards tertiarization and the emergence of new professions which can be operated through freelanced activities or micro-firms.

BIBLIOGRAPHY

Alchian, A.A. and H. Demsetz (1972), 'Production, information costs, and economic organisation', *American Economic Review*, **62**, 777–95.
Asheim, B. and L. Coenen (2005), 'Knowledge bases and regional innovation systems: comparing Nordic clusters', *Research Policy*, **34**, 1173–90.
Asheim, B., L. Coenen and J. Vang (2006), 'Face-to-face, buzz and knowledge bases: socio-spatial implications for learning, innovation and innovation policy', working paper, Universities of Lund, Aalborg und Oslo.
Audretsch, D.B. (2002), *Entrepreneurship: A Survey of the Literature*, Brussels: Commission of the European Union, Enterprise Directorate General.

Audretsch, D.B. (2007), *The Entrepreneurial Society*, Oxford: Oxford University Press.

Audretsch, D.B. and R. Thurik (2001), 'Linking entrepreneurship to growth', OECD Science, Technology, and Industry working paper 2001/2, OECD Publishing, Paris.

Audretsch, D., O. Falck, M. Feldman and S. Heblich (2008), 'The lifecycle of regions', discussion paper no. 6757, CEPR, Munich.

Baumol, W.J. (1990), 'Entrepreneurship: productive, unproductive, and destructive', *Journal of Political Economy*, **98** (5), 893–921.

Baumol, W.J. and R.J. Strom (2007), 'Entrepreneurship and economic growth', *Strategic Entrepreneurship Journal*, **1**, 233–327.

Baumol, W.J., R.E. Litan and C.J. Schramm (2007), *Good Capitalism, Bad Capitalism and the Economics of Growth and Prosperity*, Yale: Yale University Press.

Bell, D. (1973), *The Coming of Post-industrial Society. A Venture in Social Forecasting*, New York: Basic Books.

Bjerke, B. (2007), *Understanding Entrepreneurship*, Cheltenham, UK and Northampton, MA, USA: Edward Elgar.

Blau, P.M. (1974), *On the Nature of Organizations,* New York: Wiley.

Bögenhold, D. (1995), 'Selbständige Erwerbsarbeit in sozial- und wirtschaftshistorischer Perspektive', in J. Schmude (ed.), *Neue Unternehmen: Interdisziplinäre Beiträge zur Gründungsforschung*, Wirtschaftswissenschaftliche Beiträge, 113, Heidelberg: Physica Verlag, pp. 11–23.

Bögenhold, D. (2004), 'Creative destruction and human resources: a labor market perspective on firms and human actors', *Small Business Economics,* **22** (3–4), 165–77.

Bögenhold, D. (2007), 'Entrepreneurship im Kontext: Zur Wichtigkeit sozialwissenschaftlicher Aspekte der Gründungsforschung', in M. Fink, D. Almer-Jarz and S. Kraus (eds), *Sozialwissenschaftliche Aspekte des Gründungsmanagements – Die Entstehung und Entwicklung junger Unternehmen im gesellschaftlichen Kontext*, Stuttgart: IBIDEM, pp. 28–51.

Bögenhold, D. and U. Fachinger (2007), 'Micro-firms and the margins of entrepreneurship: the restructuring of the labour market', *International Journal of Entrepreneurship and Innovation,* **8**, 281–93.

Bögenhold, D. and U. Fachinger (2008), 'Do service sector trends stimulate entrepreneurship? A socio-economic labour market perspective', *International Journal of Services, Economics and Management*, **1** (2), 117–34.

Bögenhold, D. and U. Fachinger (2009), 'Entrepreneurship, innovation and spatial disparities: divisions and changes of self-employment and firms', working paper 2009-2, University of Vechta, Centre for Research on Ageing and Society, Vechta.

Bögenhold, D., U. Fachinger and R. Leicht (2001), 'Self-employment and wealth creation. Observations on the German case', *International Journal of Entrepreneurship and Innovation*, **2** (2), 81–91.

Buchanan, N.S. and H.S. Ellis (1955), *Approaches to Economic Development*, New York: Twentieth Century Fund.

Castells, M. (ed.) (2004), *The Network Society: A Cross-cultural Perspective*, Cheltenham, UK and Northampton, MA, USA: Edward Elgar.

Castells, M. (2005), *The Rise of the Network Society*, Malden, MA: Blackwell.

Chandler, A.D. (1962), *Strategy and Structure. Chapters in the History of the American Industrial Enterprise,* Cambridge, MA: Harvard University Press.

Chandler, A.D. (1977), *The Visible Hand: The Managerial Revolution in American Business,* Cambridge, MA: Harvard University Press.

Cochran, Th.C. (1960), 'Cultural Factors in economic growth', *Journal of Business History*, **20** (4) 515–30.

Davidsson, P., F. Delmar and J. Wiklund (2006), 'Entrepreneurship as growth; growth as entrepreneurship', in P. Davidsson, F. Delmar and J. Wiklund (eds), *Entrepreneurship and the Growth of Firms*, Cheltenham, UK and Northampton, MA, USA: Edward Elgar, pp. 21–37.

Dalfsma, W. and L. Soete (2006), *Understanding the Dynamics of a Knowledge Economy*, Cheltenham, UK and Northampton, MA, USA: Edward Elgar.

Engerman, S.L. and K.L. Sokoloff (2003), 'Institutional and non-institutional explanations of economic differences', working paper 9989, National Bureau of Economic Research (NBER).

Galor, O. (2006), 'From stagnation to growth: unified growth theory', in P. Aghion and S. Durlauf (eds), *Handbook of Economic Growth*, Amsterdam: Elsevier, pp. 171–293.

Grilo, I. and R. Thurik (2005a), 'Entrepreneurial engagement levels in the European Union', *International Journal of Entrepreneurship Education*, **3** (2), 143–68.

Grilo, I. and R. Thurik (2005b), 'Latent and actual entrepreneurship in Europe and the US: some recent developments', *International Entrepreneurship and Management Journal*, **1** (1), 441–59.

Harrison, L.E. and S.P. Huntington (eds) (2000), *Culture Matters. How Values Shape Human Progress*, New York: Basic Books.

Hayek, F.A. (2002), 'Competition as a discovery procedure', *Quarterly Journal of Austrian Economics*, **5** (3), 9–23.

Henrekson, M. and J. Roine (2005), 'Promoting entrepreneurship in the welfare state', working paper, IUI, Research Institute of Industrial Economics, Stockholm.

Hessels, J., M. van Gelderen and R. Thurik (2008), 'Entrepreneurial aspirations, motivations, and their drivers', *Small Business Economics*, **33**, 323–39.

Johannisson, B. (2000), 'Networking and entrepreneurial growth', in D.L. Sexton and H. Landström (eds), *Blackwell Handbook of Entrepreneurship*, Oxford: Blackwell, pp. 368–86.

Kaiserfeld, T. (2005), 'A review of theories of invention and innovation', working paper, Royal Institute of Technology, Stockholm, Sweden.

Karlsson, C. (2007), 'Clusters, functional regions and cluster policies', CESIS, working paper no. 84, Jönköping.

Kirzner, I. (1973), *Competition and Entrepreneurship*, Chicago, IL: University of Chicago Press.

Kirzner, I. (1985), *Discovery and the Capitalist Process*, Chicago, IL: University of Chicago Press.

Knight, F.H. (1971), *Risk, Uncertainty and Profit*, Chicago, IL: University of Chicago Press.

Krugman, P. (1991), *Geography and Trade*, Cambridge, MA: MIT Press.

Mugler, J, M. Fink and S. Loidl (2006), *Erhaltung und Schaffung von Arbeitsplätzen im ländlichen Raum*, Wien: Manz.

Munro, J. (2006), 'Entrepreneurship in early-modern Europe (1450–1750): an exploration of some unfashionable themes in economic history', working paper no. 30, Institute for Policy Analysis, University of Toronto.

Nelson, R.R. and S.G. Winter (1982), *An Evolutionary Theory of Economic Change*, Cambridge, MA: Harvard University Press.

Nohria, N. and R.G. Eccles (eds) (1995), *Networks and Organizations. Structure, Form, and Action*, Boston, MA: Harvard Business School Press.

Porter, M.E. (1990), *The Competitive Advantage of Nations*, New York: Free Press.

Porter, M.E. (2000), 'Attitudes, values, beliefs, and the microeconomics of prosperity', in L.E. Harrison and S.P. Huntington (eds), *Culture Matters. How Values Shape Human Progress*, New York: Basic Books, pp. 14–27.

Schumpeter, J.A. (1947), *Capitalism, Socialism and Democracy*, London: Allen & Unwin.

Schumpeter, J.A. (1963), *The Theory of Economic Development*, New York and Oxford: Oxford University Press.

Scotchmer, S. (2004), *Innovation and Incentives*, Cambridge, MA: MIT Press.

Scott, J. (2007), *Social Network Analysis*, London: Sage.

Simon, H.A. (1955), 'A behavioral model of rational choice', *Quarterly Journal of Economics*, **69**, 99–118.

Stam, E. (2008), 'Entrepreneurship and innovation policy', Jena Economic Research Paper, no. 006-2008.

Stern, S., M.E. Porter and J.L. Furman (2000), 'The determinants of national innovative capacity', working paper no. 7876, National Bureau of Economic Research (NBER), Cambridge.

Warsh, D. (2006), *Knowledge and the Wealth of Nations. A Story of Economic Discovery*, Norton: New York.

Westlund, H. (2006), 'The social capital of regional dynamics: a policy perspective', working paper no. F423, University of Tokyo, Center for International Research on the Japanese Economy.

PART II

Understanding the importance of access to finance and to available support systems

Entrepreneurial activity is often said to be hampered by limited access to banking loans because of informational asymmetries. The literature describes two types of situations. Firms are able to display formalized information such as financial accounts, legal status, formal agreements and all other reporting devices. This 'hard' information can be opposed to the 'soft' information which is 'in the air' and is mainly based on the reputation of firms and owners–managers themselves (Stein, 2002). Generally it is considered that the lack of information is more important for new innovative firms. Thus among new firms credit rationing should be higher for innovative firms. Because banks are not fully geared towards financing the specific investments of innovative firms, other devices such as venture capital, business angels and facilities to access capital from private investors are crucial for enhancing this kind of firm and also constitute factors of differentiation among regions and countries.

In the first contribution Ginés Hernández-Cánovas, Antonia Madrid-Guijarro and Howard Van Auken (Chapter 4) show that qualitative factors related to the personality and experience of the entrepreneur, characteristics of the product and services offered by the firm, and strategy and organization of the firm are as important as quantitative information to assess the creditworthiness of technological-based firms in Spain.

Sylvie Cieply and Marcus Dejardin (Chapter 5) study financial constraints that new French firms experienced during the mid-1990s. Strong rationing and self-constraint rationing are higher for innovative firms, which supports the idea that the proportion of discouraged borrowers is higher in innovative sectors than in non-innovative ones.

Antonio Aragón, Alicia Rubio Bañón and Paula Sastre Vivaracho

(Chapter 6) explore the context of entrepreneurship in Spain, focusing on regional environment factors assessed by a pool of experts disseminated in all the 17 Spanish regions (plus Ceuta and Melilla). Access to finance but also according to the experts, education and training are key factors to promote entrepreneurship that needs quite urgent action.

Rafik Abdesselam, Sylvie Cieply and Anne-Laure Le Nadant (Chapter 7) show that the role of private equity firms is deeply influenced by the nature of financial systems which remains different among European countries.

REFERENCE

Stein, J. (2002), 'Information production and capital allocation: decentralized vs. hierarchical firms', *Journal of Finance*, **57**, 1891–1921.

4. Role of information in the debt financing of technology-based firms in Spain

**Ginés Hernández-Cánovas,
Antonia Madrid-Guijarro and
Howard Van Auken**

4.1 INTRODUCTION

Capital structure theory states that owners should select a financing mix that minimizes the firm's overall cost of capital by identifying the optimal levels of equity and debt capital. While appropriate for firms having great access to the capital markets, the capital acquisition by technology-based firms may not be consistent with wealth maximization due to numerous market-related constraints (Ang, 1992; Petty and Bygrave, 1993). Issues such as high risk, unproven markets, motivation of owners, lead-time on product development, limited asset base, intellectual property rights and limited experience with raising capital by the owners often present important constraints on the ability of technology-based firms to raise capital. As a consequence, these firms are often faced with a limited set of choices that may limit their ability to achieve a minimum cost of capital.

The above problems would be mitigated assuming a free flow of information between users and providers of capital (Brigham and Ehrhardt, 2007). However, obstacles confronting technology-based firms in their search for capital have been attributed to high agency costs that result from asymmetric information between the firm and investors (Carter and Van Auken, 1992; Landstrom, 1992). In this environment banks have an informational advantage over other providers of capital because they make higher investments in screening and monitoring technologies to reduce informational asymmetries. Since technological-based firms lack reliable quantitative information, much of banks' competitive advantage comes from their ability to gather soft or qualitative information and combine it with financial data to assess the creditworthiness of the firm. Although this aspect is recognized by most bankers, we lack empirical studies of qualitative factors used by banks when analysing technological-based firms.

In an attempt to fill in this gap, this chapter uses a new survey data set to identify the main qualitative and quantitative factors used by Spanish banks to assess the creditworthiness of technological-based firms. In addition, our data set allows us to compare the importance of different factors between and within each subset of information and consider if the financial entity is a bank or a savings bank. Our results show that financial entities evaluate qualitative information when assessing the creditworthiness of the firm. Qualitative factors evaluated are the entrepreneur's honesty and integrity, knowledge about the sector and experience. Other qualitative information evaluated included product, market, customers, employee qualifications, technology and product quality. This information was found to be as important as the accounting information. The results also suggest that Spanish banks more highly value quantitative information relative to Spanish savings banks.

The chapter is organized as follows. Section 4.2 provides background on the financing of technology-based firms. Section 4.3 discusses the questionnaire development, data collection and methods of analysis. Section 4.4 presents the results, and Section 4.5 concludes the chapter.

4.2   BACKGROUND

The assumptions underlying capital acquisition theory assume conditions that facilitate the flow of capital between providers and users. In friction-less capital markets, internal and external finance would be perfect substi-tutes (Manigard et al., 2002). However, capital acquisition is commonly the result of managerial preferences and constrained by the financial context in which the firm operates (Jordan et al., 1998). Market conditions in which technology-based firms operate may not be consistent with some of these assumptions due to numerous constraints (Petty and Bygrave, 1993). Previous studies have suggested that the lack of information may be a significant obstacle to good financial decisions among technology-based firms (Berger and Udell, 1998; Van Auken, 2001). Busenitz and Barney (1997) recognized that financing decisions are often made before all the necessary information is available. Timely and accurate information are foundations for good capital financial decisions (Gibson, 1992; Lang et al., 1997).

The costs associated with innovation, especially technology innovation, will commonly require external funding because the costs of development occur prior to revenue. Financial institutions are reluctant to fund innovation because of the high risk originated by the existence of information asymmetries between the firm and providers of capital. Informational asymmetries reduce the accuracy with which banks can assess the creditworthiness of technology-based firms (adverse selection problem) as well as the efficiency of monitoring mechanisms during the life of a loan (moral hazard problem). Stiglitz and Weiss (1981) believed that the main consequence of these problems is credit rationing. Credit rationing cannot be eliminated by raising interest rates because of the negative effect on the bank's return. As the interest rate is raised, the risk borne by the banks increases because more qualified borrowers will not apply for a loan (adverse selection effect) and the remaining will choose riskier investment projects (moral hazard effect). These problems, which are particularly an obstacle to debt financing when the innovation is intended rather than developed (Freel, 2007), are difficult to mitigate due to lack of assets for collateral, and lack of near-term revenues to repay loans.

Cross-country research shows that firms can overcome asymmetric information problems and obtain enhanced access to bank debt, establishing a close banking relationship (Petersen and Rajan, 1994, Berger and Udell, 1995, in the USA; Angelini et al., 1998, in Italy; Harhoff and Körting, 1998, and Lehmann and Neuberger, 2001, in Germany; De Bodt et al., 2005, in Belgium; Hernández-Cánovas and Mártinez-Solano, 2010, in Spain). Grünert et al. (2005) stated that financial intermediaries such as banks reduced information asymmetry through monitoring. This enables the bank to get private information about the firm over time through multiple interactions and/or the provision of several financial services (Boot, 2000). Based on this property information, Grünert et al. (2005) indicate that banks assign internal credit rating to appraise the creditworthiness of their borrowers and use it for loan approval, pricing, monitoring and loan loss provisioning.

Berger et al. (2001) distinguished between two kinds of private information flows inside a firm–bank relationship. On the one hand, firms provide the bank with hard information, which is easily observable quantitative data. This information is backward looking and may include, for example, financial statements, asset returns and other quantitative data about the projects of the firm. On the other hand, banks can also obtain soft (for example, qualitative) information through interaction between the loan officer and the firm over time. This information is forward looking and primarily concerns opinions, ideas and comments related to management quality, position within the industry, organization of the firm and accounting behaviour.

The above characteristics imply several advantages for the use of hard information relative to soft information. According to Godbillon-Camus and Godlewski (2005), hard information requires less expensive technology, is easier to collect and transmit, allows better comparability and reduces the likelihood of manipulation. Despite the advantages of hard information, which have been confirmed by several empirical studies (Berger et al., 2002; Feldman, 1997a, 1997b; Frame et al., 2001), soft information appears to be the most important in bank relationships for technology-based firms since they usually lack reliable hard information. This is supported by the requirement of the Basel Committee on Banking Supervision (2001) that banks not only have to consider quantitative but also qualitative factors. However, there is a lack of empirical research on qualitative factors in internal credit ratings for high technological-based firms.

Günther and Grüning (2000) found that almost 50 per cent of German banks combine quantitative and qualitative factors to obtain credit risk assessments. About 77.6 per cent recognize that the inclusion of soft factors raises the accuracy of the default prediction. Hesselmann (1995), Blochwitz and Eigermann (2000), Lehmann (2003) and Grünert et al. (2005) showed that the use of soft information increased the ability to discriminate between defaulting and non-defaulting firms. Weber et al. (1999) and Brunner et al. (2000) reported that ratings using qualitative factors were more stable than quantitative ratings.

4.3 DATA AND METHODOLOGY

4.3.1 Questionnaire and Data

A questionnaire was developed and pre-tested in spring 2008. Data were collected in March and April 2008 through a questionnaire addressed to the person in charge of the risk assessment department. The contacts were made by telephone calls, and then the questionnaire was sent by e-mail, fax or internet.

The purpose of this questionnaire was to collect data associated with lending decisions for high tech industrial companies. Questionnaire development was based on previous research and input from a panel of experts. The questionnaire was divided into five sections. The first section asked information about the respondent age, gender, years of experience as a risk analyst, total assets and job description. The next four sections asked the respondent to rank the importance (1–5 Likert scale, where 1 = not important and 5 = very important) of various aspects regarding (1) the entrepreneur's personality and experience; (2) characteristics of products/services; (3) strategy/organization of the firm; and (4) financial information (see tables 4.1, 4.2, 4.3 and 4.4, respectively, for the variables list).

The questionnaire was sent to 97 financial entities whose operations are national in scope. A total of 30 useable questionnaires were returned (17 savings banks and 13 banks), providing a response rate of 30.9 per cent. The mean total assets of respondents is 62 463 325.50 million euros. The mean age of respondents is 40.17 years, and mean experience as a risk analyst is 12.30 years.

4.3.2 Analysis

Initially the data were summarized using univariate statistics (means and frequencies) to provide a better understanding of the respondents and characteristics of the data. The analysis was carried out in several steps. First, correlations between variables in each of the four sections (entrepreneur's personality and experience, product/services, strategy and organization, and financial information) of the questionnaire were calculated to better understand interaction between variables.[1]

In order to identify the most valued items within each part of the questionnaire, in Tables 4.1–4.4 we used Friedman's non-parametric tests for related sample determining if the rankings in each part of the questionnaire were different. Once Friedman's test verified differences in the respondents' ranking, we analysed the five highest ranked items in each section of the questionnaire and their relationship with other items. To do this, we completed a Wilcoxon non-parametric test for a related sample, comparing the rankings in pairs of items.

With the purpose of comparing the information among the four different parts of the questionnaire, Table 4.5 shows four factor analyses used to reduce the number of items without losing important information. The factor analyses were completed using the five most valued variables from each of the four sections of the questionnaire. The principle components analysis resulted in one useable factor for each of the four sections of the questionnaire; these useable factors have mean 0, taking negative and positive values as they are estimations of rotated factors. Second, we ran non-parametric tests to identify differences among factors behaviour.

These four factors were used in Table 4.6 to assess differences in lending requirements by characteristics of the financial entities: (1) banks versus savings banks in panel A and (2) small versus large financial institutions in panel B.

4.4   RESULTS

4.4.1   Correlations

Most correlations between the variables are relatively low. The variables related to entrepreneur's personality and experience that are most highly correlated with other variables are entrepreneur's capacity to react/evaluate risks, analytical ability and continuity of the business if the entrepreneur is suddenly lost. The variables associated with product and service characteristics that are most highly correlated with other variables are proven successful product in the market, product developed to the point of a functioning prototype, product's cycle of life and suppliers have higher negotiation power than the firms of the sector. The variables included in the strategy and organization of the firm dimension that are most highly correlated with other variables are firm controls quality of the products and technology of the productive facilities. The variables considered in the accounting information section that are most highly correlated with other variables are clear valuation procedures and accounting principles, economic and financial situation of firm analysed frequently, growth ratios, contribution of own resources in the firm and working capital.

4.4.2   Entrepreneur's Personality and Experience Variables

Friedman's non-parametric tests denote the existence of differences among the variable rankings. Table 4.1 (entrepreneur's personality and experience) shows that 'honesty and integrity of the manager' (4.2) is ranked as being the most important factor when lending to high tech firms, followed by 'knowledge of the sector' (4.167), 'management ability' (4.133), 'work experience' (4.100) and 'team organization' (3.867). The Wilcoxon non-parametric range tests indicate no significant differences between the majority of the five most valued factors, whereas they show significant differences with the lowest ranked items 'articulate in discussing venture' (2.667), 'search for independence' (2.733) and 'attention to detail' (3.067).

4.4.3   Product/Services Characteristics Variables

Table 4.2 (product/service characteristics) shows that 'firm's customers' was ranked as the most important factor (4.267) when lending to high tech firms, followed by 'proven successful product in the market' (4.2) and 'market with a significant growth rate' (4.067). The Wilcoxon non-parametric range tests indicate no significant differences between the

Table 4.1 Means and significance of the difference among the items associated with entrepreneur's personality and experience

Entrepreneur's personality and experience (n = 30)	Mean value	Ranking	Significance p value Wilcoxon non-parametric range test for related samples												
			P0	P1	P2	P3	P4	P5	P6	P7	P8	P9	P10	P11	P12	P13
P0 Capacity to react/evaluate risks	3.600	9														
P1 Honesty and integrity	**4.200**	**1**	**0.005**													
P2 Capable of sustained intense effort	3.621	8	0.854	0.002												
P3 Analytical ability	3.400	11	0.193	0.001	0.334											
P4 His wish to make money	3.167	12	0.105	0.001	0.028	0.234										
P5 Articulate in discussing venture	2.667	15	0.001	0.000	0.001	0.001	0.000									
P6 His team organization	**3.867**	**5**	0.059	0.122	0.102	**0.002**	**0.009**	**0.000**								
P7 Attends to detail	3.067	13	0.001	0.000	0.017	0.056	0.695	0.038	0.000							
P8 His search for independence	2.733	14	0.000	0.000	0.000	0.007	0.016	0.655	0.000	0.025						
P9 Management ability	**4.133**	**3**	**0.001**	0.712	**0.003**	**0.000**	**0.003**	**0.000**	**0.046**	**0.000**	**0.000**					
P10 Work experience	**4.100**	**4**	**0.002**	0.581	**0.003**	**0.000**	**0.001**	**0.000**	0.127	**0.000**	**0.000**	0.782				

85

Table 4.1 (continued)

Entrepreneur's personality and experience (n = 30)	Mean value	Ranking	Significance p value Wilcoxon non-parametric range test for related samples													
			P0	P1	P2	P3	P4	P5	P6	P7	P8	P9	P10	P11	P12	P13
P11 Knowledge of the sector	**4.167**	**2**	**0.002**	**0.976**	**0.004**	**0.000**	**0.000**	**0.000**	0.088	**0.000**	**0.000**	**0.675**	**0.414**			
P12 Proven leadership skill	3.733	6	0.419	0.013	0.581	0.057	0.009	0.000	0.405	0.000	0.000	0.042	0.032	0.012		
P13 Linking degree with the sector	3.600	10	1.000	0.007	0.978	0.157	0.061	0.000	0.087	0.005	0.000	0.009	0.002	0.001	0.317	
P14 Continuity of the business if the leader's loss takes places suddenly	3.667	7	0.670	0.009	0.671	0.074	0.049	0.001	0.257	0.005	0.000	0.018	0.027	0.013	0.653	0.672

Note: Friedman non-parametric test for related samples: χ^2: 147.419 sig.: 0.000.

Table 4.2 Means and significance of the difference among the items associated with product or service characteristics

Product or service characteristics (n = 30)	Mean value	Ranking	Significance p value Wilcoxon non-parametric range test for related samples													
			P15	P16	P17	P18	P19	P20	P21	P22	P23	P24	P25	P26	P27	P28
P15 Proven successful product in the market	**4.200**	**2**														
P16 High-tech product	3.400	12	0.000													
P17 Foreigner potential market	3.300	14	0.000	0.581												
P18 Product developed to the point of a functioning prototype	3.200	15	0.000	0.157	0.499											
P19 Product's cycle of life	3.567	9	0.001	0.388	0.101	0.005										
P20 Marketing strategy	3.533	11	0.000	0.559	0.142	0.032	0.827									
P21 Distribution net	**3.900**	**4**	**0.039**	**0.012**	**0.005**	**0.000**	**0.046**	**0.016**								
P22 The firm's customer	**4.267**	**1**	**0.637**	**0.000**	**0.000**	**0.000**	**0.000**	**0.000**	**0.035**							
P23 The firm's suppliers	**3.800**	**5**	**0.023**	**0.054**	**0.007**	**0.002**	**0.159**	**0.142**	**0.536**	**0.002**						
P24 Market with a significant growth rate	**4.067**	**3**	**0.396**	**0.003**	**0.000**	**0.000**	**0.003**	**0.015**	**0.393**	**0.196**	**0.135**					
P25 Barriers of entry in the sector are low	3.310	13	0.000	0.664	0.825	0.499	0.078	0.310	0.004	0.000	0.001	0.000				

Table 4.2 (continued)

Product or service characteristics (n = 30)	Mean value	Ranking	Significance p value Wilcoxon non-parametric range test for related samples													
			P15	P16	P17	P18	P19	P20	P21	P22	P23	P24	P25	P26	P27	P28
P26 Inter-firm competition in the sector is high	3.600	8	0.005	0.418	0.128	0.072	0.906	0.937	0.086	0.002	0.221	0.022	0.052			
P27 The customers have higher negotiation power than the firms of the sector	3.533	10	0.001	0.373	0.088	0.019	0.782	1.000	0.031	0.000	0.124	0.004	0.166	1.000		
P28 The suppliers have higher negotiation power than the firms of the sector	3.700	6	0.009	0.106	0.014	0.005	0.378	0.314	0.227	0.003	0.491	0.033	0.012	0.552	0.096	
P29 It is easy to create substitutive products to those manufactured in the sector	3.700	7	0.012	0.116	0.067	0.013	0.333	0.319	0.398	0.002	0.564	0.077	0.008	0.513	0.377	0.978

Note: Friedman non-parametric test for related samples: χ^2: 92.163 sig.: 0.000.

majority of the five most valued factors, whereas they show significant differences with the lowest ranked items 'product developed to the point of a prototype' (3.200), 'foreigner potential market' (3.3) and 'entry barriers in the sector are low' (3.310).

4.4.4   Strategy and Organization Variables

Table 4.3 (strategy and organization) shows that 'qualified employees' (4.138) was ranked as the most important factor when lending to high tech firms, followed by 'firm controls the product quality' (3.966) and 'technology of the productive facilities' (3.897). The Wilcoxon non-parametric range tests indicate no significant differences between the majority of the five most valued factors, whereas they show significant differences with the lowest ranked items 'firm has a quality certificate' (3.379) and 'work atmosphere is good' (3.414).

According to the strategic and management literature, the most valued qualitative factors in the above analyses are related to the key factors explaining the success or failure of SMEs. Ooghe and De Prijcker (2008) and Sudarsanam and Lai (2001) believe that human resource issues are important determining factors of success. Education and prior experience in business are crucial to explain the success of small firms (Van Gils, 2005), whereas poor management is often associated with firm failure (Gaskill et al., 1993). In addition, many failure factors are related to products and services, customers and markets, and cooperation with other stakeholders. For example, the likelihood of a firm success increases with the range of products (Reid, 1999) and decreases with dependency on few customers (Reid, 1999). Shin (2006) and Rickne (2006) highlight that the adoption of new technologies enhances the performance of the firm.

4.4.5   Financial Information

Table 4.4 (financial information) shows that 'indebtedness ratios' (4.40) is the most important variable when lending to high tech firms, followed by 'audited firm' (4.267), 'contribution with own resources to the investment' (4.267), 'growth ratios' (4.233) and 'firm doesn't appear in register of unpaid acceptances' (4.233). The Wilcoxon non-parametric range tests indicate no significant differences between the majority of the five most valued factors, whereas they show significant differences with the lowest ranked items 'firm carries out inventory of the existences at least once a year' (3.567), 'firm does reliable cost accounting' (3.667) and 'repayment capacity according to the business plan' (3.700).

Table 4.3 Means and significance of the difference among the items associated with strategy and organization of the firm

Strategy and organization of the firm (n = 30)	Mean value	Ranking	Significance p value Wilcoxon non-parametric range test for related samples								
			P30	P31	P32	P33	P34	P35	P36	P37	P38
P30 The firm has a quality certificate	3.379	10									
P31 The firm owns the facilities where the activity is developed	3.690	7	0.134								
P32 Qualified employees	**4.138**	**1**	**0.003**	**0.022**							
P33 There is a coherent price policy	**3.793**	**5**	**0.044**	**0.681**	**0.025**						
P34 The firm controls the quality of the products	**3.966**	**2**	**0.014**	**0.257**	**0.166**	**0.166**					
P35 The work atmosphere is good. The employees are happy	3.414	9	0.914	0.172	0.000	0.038	0.002				
P36 Technology of the productive facilities	**3.897**	**3**	**0.003**	**0.235**	**0.520**	**0.491**	**0.617**	**0.005**			
P37 The firm uses computers and information technologies	3.690	6	0.060	0.860	0.009	0.499	0.046	0.101	0.083		
P38 Position of the business	3.621	8	0.159	0.864	0.014	0.417	0.101	0.319	0.046	0.685	
P39 Impression caused by the business during the visit	**3.897**	**4**	**0.007**	**0.260**	**0.287**	**0.514**	**0.968**	**0.027**	**0.796**	**0.253**	**0.039**

Note: Friedman non-parametric test for related samples: χ^2: 34.163 sig.: 0.000.

Table 4.4 *Means and significance of the difference among the items associated with accounting information*

Accounting information (n = 30)	Mean value	Ranking	Significance p value Wilcoxon non-parametric range test for related samples															
			P40	P41	P42	P43	P44	P45	P46	P47	P48	P49	P50	P51	P52	P53	P54
P40 Audited firm	**4.267**	**2**															
P41 The volume of existences in the stores coincides with those in the balance sheet	3.833	13	0.012															
P42 The firm carries out an inventory at least once a year	3.567	16	0.002	0.087														
P43 The firm does some reliable cost accounting	3.667	15	0.005	0.265	0.695													
P44 There is a systematic control of customers that are behind in their payments	4.100	8	0.388	0.124	0.030	0.003												
P45 The valuation procedures and accounting principles used by the firm are clear, defined and constant in time	4.033	10	0.118	0.153	0.044	0.044	0.564											
P46 The economic and financial situation of the firm is analysed frequently	4.100	9	0.353	0.128	0.014	0.011	1.000	0.557										

Table 4.4   (continued)

Accounting information (n = 30)	Mean value	Ranking	Significance p value Wilcoxon non-parametric range test for related samples															
			P40	P41	P42	P43	P44	P45	P46	P47	P48	P49	P50	P51	P52	P53	P54
P47 The firm doesn't appear in the RAI (Registro de Aceptaciones Impagadas)	4.233	5	0.842	0.067	0.016	0.039	0.479	0.311	0.415								
P48 Personal indebtedness of the firm's manager	3.900	12	0.110	0.711	0.173	0.367	0.353	0.388	0.235	0.063							
P49 Growth ratios (net turnover, investment, added value)	4.233	4	0.675	0.044	0.008	0.018	0.400	0.130	0.356	1.000	0.084						
P50 Liquidity ratios	4.133	7	0.552	0.145	0.049	0.048	0.843	0.509	0.740	0.548	0.253	0.453					
P51 Indebtedness ratios	4.400	1	0.544	0.004	0.002	0.003	0.087	0.033	0.039	0.268	0.015	0.160	0.058				
P52 Profitability ratios	3.967	11	0.140	0.498	0.122	0.157	0.437	0.729	0.559	0.137	0.678	0.109	0.166	0.008			
P53 Repayment capacity according to the business plan	3.700	14	0.009	0.438	0.516	0.860	0.047	0.080	0.014	0.013	0.184	0.007	0.040	0.001	0.293		
P54 Contribution with own resources to the investment	4.267	3	0.780	0.047	0.012	0.010	0.282	0.108	0.198	0.796	0.029	0.796	0.467	0.614	0.068	0.012	
P55 Working capital	4.133	6	0.378	0.059	0.011	0.016	0.827	0.439	0.808	0.592	0.220	0.317	0.951	0.059	0.337	0.010	0.438

Note: Friedman non-parametric test for related samples: χ^2: 53.672 sig.: 0.000.

4.4.6 Factor Analysis

Table 4.5 shows scale reliabilities and component loadings of the factors for each of the four sections. These factor analyses have been carried out considering only the five most valued items in each section of the questionnaire. The factor analysis for the entrepreneur's personality and experience variables indicated that work experience, management ability and knowledge of the sector were the three highest loading variables. Regarding market and product characteristics, the firm's customer, the proven successful product and the distribution net were the items with the highest loading components. Additionally, the variables with the highest loading for the strategy and resources section were technology of the productive facilities, qualified employees and firm controls quality of products. Finally, concerning the financial information items, growth ratios, contribution of resources to investment and firm doesn't appear in the RAI, were the variables with the highest loading component in the factor.

The Friedman non-parametric test among these four factors shows no significant differences in their importance ($\chi 2$: 1.103 sig.: 0.894), implying that Spanish financial entities give the same importance to soft and hard information when assessing the creditworthiness of firms. Consistent with existing evidence, these results suggest that soft information increases the predictive capacity of hard information, making it highly valuable. Until now financial institutions owned soft information through proprietary knowledge that the loan officers obtain over the years. However, current rotation of loan officers increases the incentives of financial institutions to save this qualitative knowledge and prevent the cost associated with its loss.

4.4.7 Further Analyses

Following the standard classification of financial institutions in Spain, Table 4.6, panel A, shows the differences in the use of information between banks and savings banks. The parametric and non-parametric tests do not indicate differences for the soft information (entrepreneur's abilities; market and product; strategy and resources), but they do for the hard information (accounting information). To go further in this issue we build Table 4.7 where we present mean differences between banks and savings banks in relation to each single item used in the questionnaire. At first glance, the five most valued items by banks are related to accounting information (indebtedness ratios, contribution with own resources to the investment, liquidity ratios, audited firm and growth ratios), while

Table 4.5   Scale reliability for the new variables built with the five most valued items in each section

Variable items (n = 30)	Component Loadings		Scale Reliability
Entrepreneur's abilities	P1 Honesty and integrity	0.747	Cronbach = 0.880
	P11 Knowledge of the sector	0.818	Factorial: 1 factor
	P9 Management ability	0.885	Explained variance:
	P10 Work experience	0.902	68.86%
	P6 His team organization	0.788	Sig. Bartlett: 0.000
			KMO: 0.701
Market and product	P22 The firm's customers	0.835	Cronbach = 0.809
	P15 Proven successful product in the market	0.814	Factorial: 1 factor
	P24 Market with a significant growth rate	0.619	Explained variance: 58%
	P21 Distribution net	0.769	Sig. Bartlett: 0.000
	P23 The firm's suppliers	0.730	KMO: 0.736
Strategy and resources	P32 Qualified employees	0.866	Cronbach = 0.823
	P34 The firm controls the quality of the products	0.888	Factorial: 1 factor Explained variance:
	P36 Technology of the productive facilities	0.905	82%
	P39 Impression caused by the business during the visit	0.835	Sig. Bartlett: 0.000 KMO: 0.700
	P33 There is a coherent price policy	0.846	
Accounting information	P51 Indebtedness ratios	0.780	Cronbach = 0.875
	P40 Audited firm	0.675	Factorial: 1 factor
	P54 Contribution with own resources to the investment	0.895	Explained variance: 68%
	P49 Growth ratios (net turnover, investment, added value)	0.902	Sig. Bartlett: 0.000 KMO: 0.758
	P47 The firm doesn't appear in the RAI (Registro de Aceptaciones Impagadas)	0.848	

Note: Friedman non-parametric test for related samples: χ^2: 1.103 sig.: 0.894.

four out of the five most valued items by savings banks are related to soft information (proven successful product in the market, the firm's customer, indebtedness ratio, qualified employees, entrepreneur's work experience). Furthermore, we find significant differences in the assessment made by

Table 4.6   Panel A: Banks versus savings banks: t-test of mean differences in ranking of importance of the four types of information

Variable	Type of financial entity	Mean	t-statistic
Entrepreneur's abilities	Savings banks (n = 17)	−0.033	−0.212
	Banks (n = 13)	0.044	
Market and product	Savings banks (n = 17)	−0.1584	−0.992
	Banks (n = 13)	0.207	
Strategy and resources	Savings banks (n = 17)	−0.1099	−0.373
	Banks (n = 13)	0.1353	
Accounting information	Savings banks (n = 17)	−.373	−2.743**
	Banks (n = 13)	0.488	

Panel B: Small versus large financial entities

Variable	Type of financial entity	Mean	t-statistic
Entrepreneur's abilities	Small (n = 15)	0.091	0.492
	Large (n = 15)	−0.091	
Market and product	Small (n = 15)	0.284	0.153
	Large (n = 15)	−0.2847	
Strategy and resources	Small (n = 15)	0.0195	0.108
	Large (n = 15)	−0.02099	
Accounting information	Small (n = 15)	−0.1365	−0.742
	Large (n = 15)	0.165	

Note: **$p < 0.05$; these analysie have been carried out running the non-parametric Wilcoxon test and the results are extremely similar.

banks and savings banks. In this sense, banks assign more importance to the following items in comparison with the savings banks: indebtedness ratios (4.769 versus 4.118), audited firm (4.615 versus 4), contribution with own resources (4.769 versus 3.882), growth ratios (4.615 versus 3.914), working capital (4.462 versus 3.882), liquidity ratios (4.692 versus 3.706), the economic and financial situation of the firm is analysed frequently (4.462 versus 3.824), profitability ratios (4.462 versus 3.588), the firm owns facilities where the activity is developed (4.154 versus 3.313) and the firm carries out an inventory at least once a year (4.077 versus 3.176). Banks take into account the hard information to a higher extent than savings banks. In recent years a significant reduction in the number of bank offices has increased the distances between firms and their bank lenders, whereas savings banks' offices have proliferated throughout the country, getting close together with their borrowers. Existing literature (DeYoung et al., 2008) suggests that most bank lenders might have implemented

Table 4.7   Banks versus savings banks: t-test of mean differences in ranking of importance of all the items

All the Items	All sample		Saving banks		Banks		p-value
	Ranking	Mean	Ranking	Mean	Ranking	Mean	
P51 Indebtedness ratios	1	4.400	3	4.118	1	4.769	0.027
P22 The firm's customer	2	4.267	2	4.176	13	4.385	0.463
P40 Audited firm	3	4.267	6	4.000	4	4.615	0.065
P54 Contribution with own resources to the investment	4	4.267	18	3.882	2	4.769	0.02
P49 Growth ratios (net turnover, investment, added value)	5	4.233	13	3.941	5	4.615	0.019
P47 The firm doesn't appear in the RAI (Registro de Aceptaciones Impagadas)	6	4.233	7	4.000	8	4.538	0.12
P1 Honesty and integrity	7	4.200	10	3.941	7	4.538	0.13
P15 Proven successful product in the market	8	4.200	1	4.235	18	4.154	0.799
P11 Knowledge of the sector	9	4.167	8	4.000	14	4.385	0.239
P32 Qualified employees	10	4.138	4	4.063	17	4.231	0.598
P55 Working capital	11	4.133	14	3.882	9	4.462	0.046
P50 Liquidity ratios	12	4.133	26	3.706	3	4.692	0.007
P9 Management ability	13	4.133	11	3.941	15	4.385	0.222
P10 Work experience	14	4.100	5	4.059	19	4.154	0.754
P44 There is a systematic control of customers that are behind in their payments	15	4.100	15	3.882	16	4.385	0.155
P46 The economic and financial situation of the firm is analysed frequently	16	4.100	21	3.824	10	4.462	0.051
P24 Market with a significant growth rate	17	4.067	9	4.000	20	4.154	0.608
P45 The valuation procedures and accounting principles used by the firm are clear, defined and constant in time	18	4.033	29	3.647	6	4.538	0.01
P52 Profitability ratios	19	3.967	34	3.588	11	4.462	0.016
P34 The firm controls the quality of the products	20	3.966	19	3.875	22	4.077	0.591
P21 Distribution net	21	3.900	20	3.824	24	4.000	0.593
P48 Personal indebtedness of the firm's manager	22	3.900	12	3.941	31	3.846	0.809

Table 4.7   (continued)

All the Items	All sample		Saving banks		Banks		p-value
	Ranking	Mean	Ranking	Mean	Ranking	Mean	
P36 Technology of the productive facilities	23	3.897	22	3.813	25	4.000	0.454
P39 Impression caused by the business during the visit	24	3.897	23	3.813	26	4.000	0.564
P6 His team organization	25	3.867	16	3.882	30	3.846	0.919
P41 The volume of existences in the stores coincides with those in the balance sheet	26	3.833	41	3.412	12	4.385	0.006
P23 The firm's suppliers	27	3.800	17	3.882	39	3.692	0.508
P33 There is a coherent price policy	28	3.793	24	3.750	32	3.846	0.79
P12 Proven leadership skill	29	3.733	30	3.647	33	3.846	0.523
P28 The suppliers have higher negotiation power than the firms of the sector	30	3.700	37	3.529	29	3.923	0.229
P29 It is easy to create substitutive products to those manufactured in the sector	31	3.700	32	3.647	35	3.769	0.734
P53 Repayment capacity according to the business plan	32	3.700	31	3.647	34	3.769	0.776
P37 The firm uses computers and information technologies	33	3.690	27	3.688	40	3.692	0.987
P30 The firm owns the facilities where the activity is developed	34	3.690	45	3.313	21	4.154	0.015
P14 Continuity of the business if the leader's loss takes place suddenly	35	3.667	39	3.412	27	4.000	0.159
P43 The firm does some reliable cost accounting	36	3.667	38	3.471	28	3.923	0.223
P38 Location of the business	37	3.621	36	3.563	41	3.692	0.695
P2 Capable of sustained intense effort	38	3.621	28	3.688	47	3.538	0.68
P0 Capacity to react/evaluate risks	39	3.600	35	3.588	44	3.615	0.941
P13 Linking degree with the sector	40	3.600	33	3.588	43	3.615	0.93
P26 Inter-firm competition in the sector is high	41	3.600	25	3.706	50	3.462	0.503
P19 Product's cycle of life	42	3.567	40	3.412	36	3.769	0.28

Table 4.7　(continued)

All the Items	All sample		Saving banks		Banks		p-value
	Ranking	Mean	Ranking	Mean	Ranking	Mean	
P42 The firm carries out an inventory at least once a year	43	3.567	50	3.176	23	4.077	0.007
P27 The customers have higher negotiation power than the firms of the sector	44	3.533	44	3.353	37	3.769	0.234
P20 Marketing strategy	45	3.533	42	3.412	42	3.692	0.344
P35 The work atmosphere is good. The employees are happy	46	3.414	52	3.125	38	3.769	0.078
P3 Analytical ability	47	3.400	47	3.294	46	3.538	0.532
P16 High-tech product	48	3.400	48	3.294	48	3.538	0.468
P30 The firm has a quality certificate	49	3.379	43	3.375	52	3.385	0.98
P25 Barriers of entry in the sector are low	51	3.310	46	3.313	53	3.308	0.989
P17 Foreigner potential market	52	3.300	53	3.118	45	3.538	0.103
P18 Product developed to the point of a functioning prototype	53	3.200	54	3.000	51	3.462	0.109
P4 His wish to make money	54	3.167	51	3.176	55	3.154	0.953
P7 Attends to detail	55	3.067	55	2.941	54	3.231	0.375
P8 His search for independence	56	2.733	56	2.824	57	2.615	0.525
P5 Articulate in discussing venture	57	2.667	57	2.588	56	2.769	0.55

Note:　This analysis has been carried out running the non-parametric Wilcoxon test and the results are extremely similar.

credit-scoring models, which are based on hard information, to evaluate the creditworthiness of corporate borrowers because this technology outperforms soft information, relationship-based lending approaches in long-distance situations.[2] This would explain why financial data are more important for banks than for savings banks.

During recent years financial intermediation literature has focused on the association between the organizational structure of financial institutions and the information they use in their lending decisions (Berger and Udell, 2002; Berger et al., 2005). According to Stein (2002), the use of soft information is mainly associated with small and decentralized organizations where loan officers have more authority and incentives to make efficient use of the information. This is in contrast with large and centralized organizations, where the use of hard information facilitates the transmission to hierarchical levels where the lending decisions are made. In Table 4.6, panel B, is an analysis of the use of information in large and small financial institutions, but we find no differences.

4.5   DISCUSSION AND CONCLUSIONS

During their early years in operations, technology-based firms are highly dependent on high amounts of external financing. New technology-based firms are faced with long product development lead-times, high R&D and limited/non-existent revenues during the early years of operations. Capital acquisition is even more challenging because of the high risk associated with developing new technology and the lack of understanding of technology commercialization among many traditional providers of capital.

High risk, deficiency of assets for collateral and weak cash flow result in a situation where lenders rely on a comprehensive assessment of information, including both quantitative (for example, hard data) and qualitative (for example, soft data) information to make lending decisions. Reliance on hard and soft information can enable lenders to overcome risk considerations and develop more insight into the quality of the firm as a borrower.

Lenders understand that they can better assess a firm's creditworthiness by combining financial data with qualitative factors. However previous studies have not examined this issue to determine which qualitative variables are evaluated or if a difference exists between banks and savings banks. The results in this study provide insight into the process followed by a sample of Spanish financial institutions when screening technological-based firms and identifies the main qualitative factors used in their credit assessments.

The results of this study demonstrate that qualitative factors are as important as quantitative information to assess the creditworthiness of technological-based firms. Qualitative factors related to the personality and experience of the entrepreneur, the characteristics of the product and services offered by the firm, and the strategy and organization of the firm are evaluated in addition to the traditional quantitative factors. The value of soft information together with high rotation of loan officers would explain why financial institutions incentivize the use of more complete credit files where this information can be stored.

Additionally, the results provide insight into differences relative to the type of financial institution (banks versus savings bank) and size of the financial institution. The evidence shows no statistical difference relative to the size of the financial institution. The results show that financial information is more important for banks than for savings banks when screening technological-based firms. Greater geographic separation between lender and borrower has likely resulted in greater reliance on financial information among banks.

The evidence presented in this chapter has clear implications for firms, financial institutions and policy makers. Financial institutions have a responsibility and financial interest in facilitating the flow of capital to borrowers (including technology-based firms). Financial institutions can use the findings in this study to help owners of technology-based firms to understand what factors (qualitative and quantitative) owners need to present when seeking loans. Owners of technology-based firms who seek loans can use the results of this study to better understand the process through which lenders evaluate applications. Owners can use the results to develop better loan applications that incorporate both quantitative and qualitative factors. The flow of capital from providers to users of capital is required for a healthy and dynamic economy. Policy makers can use the results from this study to develop better policies, training programmes and support information to help all stakeholders more fully understand each other.

NOTES

1. The correlations tables are provided on request to the authors.
2. See Petersen and Rajan (2002), Degryse and Ongena (2005) and Carling and Lundberg (2005) for further discussions on the association between distance and business lending.

BIBLIOGRAPHY

Ang, J. (1992), 'On the theory of finance for privately held firms', *Journal of Small Business Finance*, **1**, 185–203.
Angelini, P., R. Di Salvo and G. Ferri (1998), 'Availability and cost of credit for small businesses: customer relationships and credit cooperatives', *Journal of Banking and Finance*, **22**, 925–54.
Basel Committee on Banking Supervision (2001), 'The new Basel capital accord', consultative document, January.
Berger, A. and G. Udell (1995), 'Relationship lending and lines of credit in small firm finance', *Journal of Business*, **68**, 351–81.
Berger, A. and G. Udell (1998), 'The economics of small business finance: the roles

of private equity and debt markets in the financial growth cycle', *Journal of Business*, **22**, 613–73.

Berger, A. and G. Udell (2002), 'Small business credit availability and relationship lending: the importance of bank organizational structure', *Economic Journal*, **112**, 32–53.

Berger, A., S. Frame and N.H. Miller (2002), 'Credit scoring and the price and availability of small business credit', Board of Governors of the Federal Reserve System finance and economics discussion papers series 2002–26.

Berger, A., L. Klapper and G. Udell (2001), 'The ability of banks to lend to informationally opaque small businesses', *Journal of Banking and Finance*, **25**, 2127–67.

Berger, A., N. Miller, M. Petersen, R. Rajan and J. Stein (2005), 'Does function follow organizational form? Evidence from the lending practices of large and small banks', *Journal of Financial Economics*, **76**, 237–69.

Blochwitz, S. and J. Eigermann (2000), 'Unternehmensbeurtejlung durch diskriminanzanalyse mit qualitativen merkmalen', *Zeitschrift für betriebswirtschaftliche Forschung*, **52**, 58–73.

Boot, A. (2000), 'Relationship banking: what do we know?', *Journal of Financial Intermediation*, **9**, 7–25.

Brigham, E. and M. Ehrhardt (2007), *Financial Management: Theory and Practice*, 12th edn, Cincinnati, OH: South-Western College Publishers.

Brunner, A., J.P. Krahnen and M. Weber (2000), 'Information production in credit relationships, on the role of internal ratings in commercial banking', Center for Financial Studies working paper no. 2000/10, Frankfurt am Main.

Busenitz, L. and J. Barney (1997), 'Differences between entrepreneurs and managers in large organizations: biases and heuristics in strategic decision-making', *Journal of Business Venturing*, **12** (1), January, 9–30.

Carling, K. and S. Lundberg (2005), 'Asymmetric information and distance: an empirical assessment of geographical credit rationing', *Journal of Economics and Business*, **57**, 39–59.

Carter, R. and H. Van Auken (1992), 'Effect of professional background on venture capital proposal evaluation', *Journal of Small Business Strategy*, **3** (1), Spring, 45–55.

De Bodt, E., F. Lobez and J.C. Statnik (2005), 'Credit rationing, customer relationship and the number of banks: an empirical analysis', *European Financial Management*, **11**, 195–228.

Degryse, H. and S. Ongena (2005), 'Distance, lending relationships, and competition', *Journal of Finance*, **60**, 231–66.

DeYoung, R., D. Glennon and P. Nigro (2008), 'Borrower-lender distance, credit scoring, and loan performance: evidence from informational-opaque small business borrowers', *Journal of Financial Intermediation*, **17**, 113–43.

Feldman, R. (1997a), 'Credit scoring and small business loans', *Community Dividend*, April, Federal Reserve Bank of Minneapolis, accessed at www.minneapolisfed.org/publications_papers/pub_display.cfm?id=3206.

Feldman, R. (1997b), 'Small business loans, small banks and a big change in technology called credit scoring', *The Region*, September, Federal Reserve Bank of Minneapolis, accessed at www.minneapolisfed.org/publications_papers/pub_display.cfm?id=3631.

Frame, W., A. Srinivasan and L. Woosley (2001), 'The effect of credit scoring on small-business lending', *Journal of Money, Credit and Banking*, **33**, 813–25.

Freel, M. (2007), 'Are small innovators credit rationed?', *Small Business Economics*, **28**, 23–35.

Gaskill, L., H. Van Auken and R. Manning (1993), 'A factor analytic study of the perceived causes of small business failure', *Journal of Small Business Management*, **31**, October, 18–31.

Gibson, B. (1992), 'Financial information for decision making: an alternative small firm perspective', *Journal of Small Business Finance*, **1**, 221–32.

Godbillon-Camus, B. and C.J. Godlewski (2005), 'Gestion du risqué de crédit dans la banque: Information hard, information soft et manipulation', LaRGE working paper.

Grünert, J., L. Norden and M. Weber (2005), 'The role of non-financial factors in internal credit ratings', *Journal of Banking and Finance*, **29**, 509–31.

Günther, T. and M. Grüning (2000), 'Einsatz von insolvenzprognoseverfahren bei der kreditwürdigkeitsprüfung im firmenkundenbereich', *Die Betriebswirtschaft*, **60**, 39–59.

Harhoff, D. and T. Körting (1998), 'Lending relationships in Germany – empirical evidence from survey data', *Journal of Banking and Finance*, **22**, 1317–53.

Hernández-Cánovas, G. and P. Martínez-Solano (2010), 'Relationship lending and SME financing in the continental European bank-based system: empirical evidence from a unique survey data set, *Small Business Economics*, **34** (4), 465–82.

Hesselmann, S. (1995), *Insolvenzprognose mit Hilfe qualitativer faktoren*, Aachen, Germany: Shaker Verlag.

Jordan, J., J. Lowe and P. Taylor (1998), 'Strategy and financial policy in UK small firms', *Journal of Business Finance and Accounting*, **25**, 1 January–March, 1–27.

Landstrom, H. (1992), 'The relationship between private investors and small firms: an agency perspective', *Entrepreneurship and Regional Development*, 9 September, **4** (3) 199–223.

Lang, J., R. Calantone and D. Gudmundson (1997), 'Small firm information seeking as a response to environmental threats and opportunities', *Journal of Small Business Management*, **35**, 11–23.

Lehmann, B. (2003), 'Is it worth the while? The relevance of qualitative information in credit rating', University of Konstanz working paper.

Lehmann, E. and D. Neuberger (2001), 'Do lending relationships matter? Evidence from bank survey data in Germany', *Journal of Economic Behavior and Organization*, **45**, 339–59.

Manigard, S., K. Baeyens and I. Verschueren (2002), 'Financing and investment interdependencies in unquoted Belgain companies: the role of venture capital', Vlerick Leuven Gent Management School working paper.

Ooghe, H. and S. De Prijcker (2008), 'Failure processes and causes of company bankruptcy: a typology', *Management Decision*, **46** (2), 223–42.

Petersen, M. and R. Rajan (1994), 'The benefits of lending relationships: evidence from small business data', *Journal of Finance*, **49**, 3–37.

Petersen, M. and R. Rajan (2002), 'Does distance still matter? The information revolution in small business lending', *Journal of Finance*, **57**, 2533–70.

Petty, J. and W. Bygrave (1993), 'What does finance have to say to the entrepreneur', *Journal of Small Business Finance*, **2**, 125–37.

Reid, G.C. (1999), 'Complex actions and simple outcomes: how new entrepreneurs stay in business', *Small Business Economics*, **13**, 303–15.

Rickne, A. (2006), 'Connectivity and performance of science-based firms', *Small Business Economics*, **26**, 393–407.

Shin, I. (2006), 'Adoption of enterprise application software and firm performance', *Small Business Economics*, **26**, 241–56.

Stein, J. (2002), 'Information production and capital allocation: decentralized versus hierarchical firms', *Journal of Finance*, **57**, 1891–921.

Stiglitz, J. and A. Weiss (1981), 'Credit rationing in markets with imperfect information', *American Economic Review*, **71** (3), 393–410.

Sudarsanam, S. and J. Lai (2001), 'Corporate financial distress and turnaround strategies: an empirical analysis', *British Journal of Management*, **12**, 183–99.

Van Auken, H. (2001), 'Financing small technology-based companies: the relationship between familiarity with capital and ability to price and negotiate investment', *Journal of Small Business Management*, **30** (3), July, 240–58.

Van Gils, A. (2005), 'Management and governance in Dutch SMEs', *European Management Journal*, **23** (5), 583–9.

Weber, M., J.P. Krahnen and F. Vossmann (1999), 'Risikomessung im kreditgeswchäft: eine empirische analyse bankinterner ratingverfahren', *Zeitschrift für betriebswirtschaftliche Forschung, Sonderheft*, **41**, 117–42.

5. Entrepreneurial finance in France: the persistent role of banks

Sylvie Cieply and Marcus Dejardin

5.1 INTRODUCTION

Since the early 1980s scientific observers and policy practitioners have drawn attention to the role of new firms for their positive contribution to employment and to local development (Acs and Audretsch, 1993; Loveman and Sengenberger, 1991; Piore and Sabel, 1984). Small has become beautiful but small is often perceived as difficult to finance. Financial constraints are indeed among the most cited impeding factors for entrepreneurial dynamics to flourish (for a review, see Parker, 2004). New firms are not profitable enough to be self-financed. Because of both informational standards and costs associated with initial public offerings, they cannot raise equity on financial markets. Those whose growth rate is not exponential are not the targets of venture capital funds or business angels. Finally, their external financing is mainly based on loans, especially banking loans.

In comparison with other creditors, banks indeed benefit from advantages in financing opaque firms, and in particular new firms. Banks are specialized in gathering private information and treating it (Freixas and Rochet, 1997) and, as they manage money and deposit accounts, they own highly strategic information on firms' receipts and expenditures and on the way firms develop themselves or not (Diamond and Rajan, 2001; Ruhle, 1997). However, the credit market is not perfect and, since Turgot (1766 [1970]), Smith (1776) and Keynes (1930 [1971]), the idea that some firms may suffer from a lack of access to credit is widespread.

The credit gap finds strong theoretical support in the model of Stiglitz and Weiss (1981). Due to informational asymmetries, banks do not know about the risk of projects although they can observe the expected returns of projects. In this situation prices cannot clear the market; credit is allocated with rationing and equilibrium arises with a fringe of unsatisfied borrowers. This conclusion is not accepted by all the scientific community. In particular, in the framework of De Meza and Webb (1987), banks know about the return of any project if successful but not the probability of success and this situation leads to overlending. More recently, research tends to consider the cases described by Stiglitz and Weiss (1981) and De Meza and Webb (1987) as the two polar cases of a more general model of financing new investment under asymmetric information (Boadway and Keen, 2004).

Despite the fact that any consensus does not exist from a theoretical point of view and because credit rationing could hamper small firms' growth, an extensive empirical literature deals with credit rationing and small firms. In this chapter, we deal with this question in the French context of the mid-1990s. We focus on new firms which can be supposed to suffer more than others from credit rationing if credit rationing may exist. These firms indeed suffer from a lot of problems. Their risk of default is high. They are short of collaterals, particularly when they are innovative. They cannot produce any track record to bankers. Their informational system is not formalized enough and can generate informational asymmetries between managers and external investors.

This chapter is organized as follows. In Section 5.2 we introduce all kinds of credit rationing that new firms can suffer from. We define classical weak and strong credit rationing and introduce the concept of self-rationing based on the theory of discouraged borrowers (Kon and Storey, 2003; Levenson and Willard, 2000). In Section 5.3 we introduce the Sine surveys on new French firms by the French National Institute of Statistics (INSEE). These surveys gather individual data on entrepreneurs and new firms and allow us to build direct measures of financial constraints. In Section 5.4 we assess empirically the importance of credit rationing in entrepreneurship. We show that credit rationing 'à la Stiglitz-Weiss' is not very widespread among new firms. However, we highlight other financial constraints that illustrate either the old theory of weak credit rationing or the new theory of discouraged borrowers. We stress the specific case of innovative start-ups and the determinant role of banking finance for new firms. Section 5.5 concludes the chapter.

5.2 THEORETICAL FRAMEWORK: THE DIVERSITY OF CREDIT RATIONING

In this chapter we want to estimate the probability that a firm's access to credit is denied for reasons other than creditworthiness. In the academic literature we can distinguish three different kinds of credit rationing. The first two types, 'weak credit rationing' and 'strong credit rationing', have been analysed for a very long time. This typology was indeed introduced by Freimer and Gordon in 1965 and popularized by Keeton in 1979.[1] The last type, which we name 'auto-constraint' or 'self-rationing', is directly linked to the recent theory of discouraged borrowers (Kon and Storey, 2003).

'Weak credit rationing' (or type I) corresponds to the situation where a borrower i does not succeed in getting credit enough, at the moment t (Keeton, 1979). This borrower accesses credit but for a level of debt which is inferior to the desired level. This rationing occurs when some applicants receive, at the ruling interest rate, smaller loans than the amount they desire. Many reasons can justify this situation. The first reason, mentioned by the tenants of disequilibrium credit theory, is the rigidity of prices on the credit market which hampers the clearing of this market. Prices can be rigid because of laws on ceiling rates. The potential negative influence of these laws was mentioned very early by Turgot (1766 [1970]). We must note that in France laws on ceiling rates have been abolished for firms, except for overdrafts, since 2005. Prices can be rigid as well because of some commercial practices. Jaffee and Modigliani (1969) and Cukierman (1978) stressed the commercial habit of charging a single interest rate to a class of heterogeneous borrowers. With the increasing use of internal models of credit risk, this commercial practice is surely now obsolete; the determination of prices and non-prices conditions are based on the individual analysis of risk. However, the high level of competition among banks in nearly all developed countries can limit the flexibility of interest rates below the equilibrium interest rate and can give a new reality to this argument of price rigidity on the credit market. The second reason why firms cannot get the quantity of credit they want is the existence of bankruptcy costs which increase with the size of credit (Jaffee and Russel, 1976). Because bigger loans involve higher repayments, they are associated with more defaults and it can be rational for bankers to cap loan size in order to limit risks of defaults. In this chapter we consider that creditworthy firms suffer from a weak credit rationing if they ask for a banking loan, get acceptance for it but do not get enough credit.

'Strong credit rationing' (or type II) occurs when some borrowers' demands are turned down by banks although these borrowers are ready to pay all prices and non-price elements of the loan contract and where apparently identical demands are accepted by banks. In this situation a customer i does not receive credit at all at moment t although a customer j, which does not differ apparently from i, gets it. This situation was first described by Stiglitz and Weiss (1981). It is due to informational asymmetries which can cause adverse selection and moral hazard. In these situations changes in interest rates cannot restore market equilibrium and lenders, being unable to influence price levels effectively, may prefer to influence quantity and limit, rationally and independently of the regulatory context, the amount of credit. Williamson (1986) confirms the existence of credit rationing, though uses rather different arguments. In Williamson's view, on a market where information is imperfect, lenders must cope with opportunistic behaviors of borrowers though costly monitoring devices. When costs of monitoring exceed expected benefits, lenders prefer not to lend. In this chapter we consider that creditworthy firms suffer from a strong credit rationing if they ask for a banking loan and are denied it.

The two precedent approaches are static. They consider the case of firms which are unable to get access to credit, partially or completely, at time *t*. Levenson and Willard (2000) and Kon and Storey (2003) question the duration of this situation and introduce a new kind of credit rationing called 'discouraged borrowers'. Kon and Storey (2003) define discouraged borrowers as good firms requiring finance, which choose not to apply to the bank because they feel their application will be rejected. Levenson and Willard (2000) explain why this kind of rationing may exist: if the firm receives the credit after waiting a period of length α and if α is very small, then the firm is rationed for only a short period of time and the effects of credit rationing may be negligible. If α is large, then the delay to get access to credit can affect the firm's ability to expand or even survive and finally some firms that anticipate a large α may be discouraged from applying for credit. In this case firms do not ask for credit at all as they anticipate the refusals of banks for a rather long period: they are self-rationed. In this chapter we consider that firms are self-constrained (type III) if they do not ask for a banking loan although they should have asked for it as their financial needs illustrate it.

5.3   THE DATA

We exploit information contained in the Sine dataset. This dataset allows the description of the financing policy of young firms when they are created and for the two years following the beginning of their activities. The Sine dataset does not refer to the general entrepreneurial intention within the French population but to entrepreneurial projects that are concretized in new firms. As a consequence, entrepreneurial intentions that are aborted due to financial constraints are not reported. The point is of importance as the firm financing conditions are considered.

The survey (Sine 94-1) was conducted by the French National Institute of Statistical and Economic Studies[2] in 1994 and takes into account 30778 firms which had been set up or taken over during the first half of 1994 and which had survived at least for one month. The sample[3] is originally representative of the total population of entrepreneurs comprising 96407 new firms (it is a compulsory survey which obtained a 98.8 percent rate of reply). In this survey new firms are identified on the basis of their registration in the 'Système d'Informations et de Répertoire des Entreprises et des Etablissements' (SIRENE repertory[4]). The units, under review, belong to the private productive sector in the fields of industry, building, trade and services. The survey contains variables related to the entrepreneur and to the context of entrepreneurship.

Some questions concern the access of new firms to banking loans. In particular, we know first if firms ask for credit at the beginning of their life or not and second if credit is granted or denied. Thanks to the answers to these two questions, we can identify strong credit rationing which occurs when creditworthy firms asking for credit are denied. However, when credit is granted, we do not know if the quantity offered corresponds exactly to the quantity firms desire or not. Quite symmetrically, when firms do not ask for credit, we do not know if they are self-constrained or if they really have no financial need. To come near this information, we consider the second survey carried out in 1997 (Sine 94-2). This survey gives information about the status of the same firms (closed down or still running). For the firms that are still running, this survey also explores the financial behavior of the firm during the last two years and the financial problems they faced. On the basis of this second survey, we construct classes of credit rationing. For a more appropriate homogeneity of our data basis we consider only new firms without legal change (firms which are transformed from sole proprietorship into limited partnership), set up by a man or a woman (without subsidiaries) in the metropole area (overseas department excluded). At this stage we obtain 12681 units which represent 36509 firms.

With this second survey, we know if firms have to cope with financial problems during 1996–7. Financial problems in the post start-up stage reveal either a lack of access to funding at the beginning of their life or unanticipated financial needs. Whatever may be the reasons for the problem, this situation translates to a financial constraint for firms. If firms asked at the beginning of their life for credit and got it but still faced financial difficulties in the post start-up stage, we identify a weak credit constraint which is an (imperfect) proxy of the weak credit rationing. If firms did not ask for credit at the beginning and faced financial difficulties in the post start-up stage, we identify a self-credit constraint which is a proxy for the self-credit rationing.

Finally, the variable 'financial constraints' that is proposed includes four modalities:

1. The modality 'no rationing' is composed of two kinds of firms. The first ones asked for a banking loan and got acceptance for it. The second ones did not ask for a banking loan and did not face financial problems during 1996–7.
2. The modality 'weak constraint' groups together firms that did ask for a banking loan and got acceptance for it but they faced financial problems during 1996–7.
3. The modality 'strong rationing' gathers firms that did ask for a banking loan and were refused it in 1994.
4. The modality 'self-constraint' concerns firms that did not ask for a banking loan but should have asked for it as they faced financial constraints during 1996–7.

Because of the lack of information about the building of the credit rationing variable, the data basis is now restrained to 12 231 units which represent 35 115 firms. At the end we consider only firms which have invested during the last two years. The sample is now restricted to 26 622 firms.

To go further in analysing self-constraint, we study the nature of the relationships between banks and new firms during the post start-up stage. In Kon and Storey (2003) borrowers do not ask for credit at moment t as they anticipate a large delay before being able to access the banking loan. To study the duration of credit rationing, we analyse access of new firms to a banking loan during the post start-up stage when they do not ask for credit at the beginning and when they ask for it but were denied. We compare relationships with banks with relationships with other investors, in particular, proximity investors ('family, friends and fools' – the 3F – according to Ang (1991), outsiders and other firms. The variables that are representative for financial relationships are constructed using the combination of several questions from the 1997 survey regarding the financial management policy of the cash requirement and the financial management policy of the investments and the inter-firm financial cooperation links in 1994.

Concerning financial relationships, four dummy variables are constructed:

1. The first one is 'high intensive relationships' with banks. Firms in this class manage cash requirement by overdrafts or banking loans and/or finance investments by banking loans.
2. The second one is 'high intensive relationships' with '3F' or proximity finance. Firms in this class manage their cash requirements and finance their investments by private resources (from managers, relatives and/ or existing associates).

3. The third dummy variable is 'high intensive relationships' with external finance providers. Firms manage their requirements and/or finance their investments by raising new equities.
4. The last dummy variable is about financial links between enterprises (high intensive relationships with other firms). Strong financial links of cooperation with other firms are identified in 1994 and firms manage financial difficulties during 1996–7 by increasing terms of payments.

In order to identify financial constraints, we need to work only with creditworthy firms. This aim is achieved by considering the situation of firms which were established in 1994 and which were still alive in 1997. This methodological approach allows us not to consider as rationed firms that were 'lame ducks' and that were identified as bad firms by bankers. A good discrimination process, which consists not to lend to bad firms (firms that will quickly die), must not be considered as a rationing process. That is, some selection bias may occur as we consider only firms that were effectively created and still alive after two years of activities. Note, however, that, although rationed firms represent 5.20 percent of the firms that ceased their activities before 1997, they represent 3.26 percent of the firms that are still alive in 1997.

Moreover, we consider not only the global sample of firms but the sub-sample of innovative firms too. Innovative firms are the ones which belong to the classification of innovative branches given by the OECD and used in the French system of statistics (see Appendix 5.1). Their financial situation is specifically analysed as all informational problems and risk exposure for lenders are more acute when borrowers are innovative; so we expect credit rationing to be more sensitive on this sub-sample.

5.4   RESULTS

To study the importance of financial constraints and the nature of financial relationships new firms develop with banks, we refer to descriptive and contingent analysis of the results we obtain for the modalities of the variable 'financial constraint' and for the four variables that describe the nature of financial relationships.

In Table 5.1 we observe that 58.04 percent of our sample does not suffer from any financial constraint; less than half of the sample (41.96 percent) feel financially rationed. When firms suffer from financial constraints, we show the diversity of credit rationing. Strong credit rationing only concerns 3.64 percent of the sample whereas 16.02 percent of firms suffer from a weak credit rationing and 22.30 percent are self-constrained. Finally,

Table 5.1   Cross table of credit rationing in the population of firms still alive in 1997

		Not innovative	Innovative	Total
Frequency	**No credit rationing**	14909	543	15452
Cell chi-square		*0.0301*	*0.7944*	
Percent		56.00	2.04	58.04
Row percent		96.49	3.51	
Col. percent		58.12	55.86	
	Self-constraint	5649	287	5936
		0.8634	*22.783*	
		21.22	1.08	22.30
		95.17	4.83	
		22.02	29.53	
	Weak constraint	4181	84	4265
		1.251	*33.032*	
		15.71	0.32	16.02
		98.03	1.97	
		16.30	8.64	
	Strong rationing	911	58	969
		0.5481	*14.463*	
		3.42	0.22	3.64
		94.01	5.99	
		3.55	5.97	
	Total	25650	972	26622
		96.35	3.65	100.00
	3 degrees of freedom			
	Pb(Chi² >73.76 = 0.00)			

we must note that strong credit rationing is not highly widespread among firms still alive in 1997. The most important constraint that surviving new firms suffer from is self-constraint.

These results apply when only innovative sectors are taken into account, represented by 972 firms in our sample. In the sample 44.14 percent are concerned with credit rationing. At this global level the situation of innovative firms appears to be very similar to the situation of all new firms. When we distinguish between banking constraints, we observe that, with significance, strong rationing is higher for innovative firms (5.97 percent) whereas the weak rationing is less developed (8.64 percent). Self-constraint is more important for innovative firms (29.53 percent) than for non-innovative ones. According to this result, the proportion of discouraged borrowers is higher in innovative sectors than in non-innovative ones.

The entrepreneurial society

Table 5.2　*Financial relationships in the population of firms still alive in 1997*

		Not innovative	Innovative	Total
Observed frequency Theoretical	**High intensive relationships with banks**	14 385 14 188	341 538	14 726
	1 degree of freedom **Pb(0.05)(Chi² >167.02 = 0.00)**			
Observed frequency Theoretical	**High intensive relationships with 3F**	3619 3650	168 137	3787
	1 degree of freedom **Pb(0.05)(Chi²>7.74 = 0.00)**			
Observed frequency Theoretical	**High intensive relationships with external finance providers**	291 328	50 13	341
	1 degree of freedom **Pb(0.05)(Chi² >119.06 = 0.00)**			
Observed frequency Theoretical	**High intensive relationships with other firms**	264 311	58 11	322
	1 degree of freedom **Pb(0.05)(Chi² >201.33 = 0.00)**			

Table 5.2 underlines the importance of banking relationships in financing the growth of new firms. Of new firms 76.79 percent manage their financial problems with banks in their post start-up stage. The role of other providers of finance, proximity investors (owners, their family, friends and associates), outsiders and other firms is less important. For external finance providers and other firms, this role is quite insignificant; 3.46 percent of our sample develops high intensive relationship with these taken together. According to Kremp (1998), Kremp and Sevestre (2000) and Cayssals et al. (2007), we should have expected a more important role of other firms in financing new firms. The cited literature shows the increasing role of groups in France and the role of non-financial firms in capital structure. In a sample of very young firms (less than three years), we do not observe this situation which may concern well-established small and medium-sized firms or subsidiaries.

In contrast, when we only consider innovative sectors, the frequency of

Table 5.3   Cross table of high intensive relationships with banks with
               credit rationing in the population of firms still alive in 1997

		High intensive relationships with banks		
		No	Yes	Total
Frequency	**No credit rationing**	7885	7567	15452
Cell chi-square		*139.18*	*112.43*	
Percent		29.62	28.42	58.04
Row percent		51.03	48.97	
Col. percent		66.28	51.39	
	Self-constraint	2329	3607	5936
		39.45	*31.871*	
		8.75	13.55	22.3
		39.24	60.76	
		19.58	24.49	
	Weak constraint	1213	3052	4265
		251.85	*203.45*	
		4.56	11.46	16.02
		28.44	71.56	
		10.20	20.73	
	Strong rationing	469	500	969
		2.99	*2.42*	
		1.76	1.88	3.64
		48.40	51.60	
		3.94	3.40	
	Total	11896	14726	26622
		44.68	55.32	100.00
	3 degrees of freedom			
	Pb(Chi² >783.65 = 0.00)			

high intensive banking relationships decreases whereas the frequency of high intensive relationships with proximity investors, outsiders and other firms tends to increase, especially for the last two external suppliers of finance.

The correlation between the hypothesis of financial constraints and each indicator of the financial relationship is highlighted by the Chi-square test between the different level of financial constraints and banking relationships (complete sample). It can be observed (Table 5.3) that firms that are financed by banks in the third and the fourth years after their creation are less often classified as not being rationed. They become intensive in banking relationships, whereas, at the beginning of their life, they suffer from a credit gap. The same trend can be observed concerning the weak financial constraint and the self-constraint. Firms that suffer from a weak financial constraint often appear as being high intensive in banking relationships. Firms that constrain themselves on the credit market appear more than the average classified as developing high intensive relations with banks in the two years after their establishment.

On the one hand, banking relationships in the years that follow the start of firms cannot be associated with the absence of credit rationing at the beginning of their life. This observation underlines the fact that no path of exclusion can be identified on the credit market. On the other hand, banking relationships can be associated with weak financial constraints and auto constraints. This observation can be the expression of the rent expropriation described by Sharpe (1990) and Rajan (1992). Banks can profit from their informational advantage by financing firms with relatively bad conditions, albeit better conditions than the conditions that another bank could propose to its new customers.

5.5 CONCLUSION

In this chapter we studied financial constraints that new firms suffered from in France during the mid-1990s. We distinguished three types of credit rationing: the well-known weak and strong credit rationing and a self-constraint bound to the discouragement of entrepreneurs on the credit market. We obtained two major results.

We first show that a large part of new firms are not credit constrained. In particular, the strong credit rationing hypothesis only concern 3.64 percent of our sample and 5.97 percent of the sub-sample of the most innovative firms. Credit rationing à la Stiglitz-Weiss (1981) is the reality of a very small proportion of new firms in France during the mid-1990s. Weak rationing concerns 16.02 percent of the sample and only 8.64 percent of the sub-sample of the most innovative firms. Finally, auto constraint is the most important financial impediment that new firms have to suffer from as it concerns 22.30 percent of the total sample and 29.53 percent of the sub-sample of innovative firms. These results lead us to put the contribution of Stiglitz and Weiss into perspectives when new firms are concerned. These results support all academic backgrounds based on entrepreneurs' expectations of investors' future decisions. The new theory of credit rationing based on discouragement of entrepreneurs seems to be very realistic and promising.

Second, despite the existence of financial constraints when new firms want to access banking loans, banks still remain the main provider of external finance for new firms. Inter-firm finance and external finance are quite unimportant. When only innovative sectors are concerned, the frequency of high intensive relationships between new firms and these two kinds of investors tend to increase but remains at a very low level.

To conclude, all our results confirm the persistent role of banks in the financing of new firms in France during the mid-1990s. Other means of financing, such as venture capital, business angels and trade credit, played a minor role in the financing of French new firms in this period. These findings minimize the hypothesis of a new firm credit gap but may support as well the general direction of public aid in France which favors guaranteeing funding granted by banks to finance the riskiest firms and in particular new firms.

ACKNOWLEDGEMENT

The authors thank Jean Bonnet for comments on this chapter based on previous joint works.

NOTES

1. For a review of the literature on credit rationing, see Baltensperger and Devinney (1985), Jaffee and Stiglitz (1990) and Swank (1996).
2. INSEE (Institut National des Statistiques et des Etudes Economiques).
3. The sample was built by randomly drawing out samples from the 416 ($2 \times 8 \times 26$) elementary strata. These strata are classified according to the origin (start-up or takeover: two modalities), the branch (eight modalities) and the localization (22 French regions plus four overseas departments). The dataset must then be used with the correction of a weight variable (the reverse of the draw rate per branch, per region and per origin).
4. Economic 'activations' and 'reactivations' are excluded from the surveyed sample. Economic 'activations' correspond to units which do not have any activity and which decide afterwards to exercise one. Economic 'reactivations' corresponding to units which had stopped their activity and which start up again. They only deal with individual entrepreneurs. Financial and agricultural activities and the French units established abroad are set aside as well.

REFERENCES

Acs, Z.J. and D.B. Audretsch (1993), *Small Firms and Entrepreneurship: A Comparison Between West and East Countries*, Cambridge: Cambridge University Press.

Ang, J.S. (1991), 'Small business uniqueness and the theory of financial management', *Journal of Small Business Finance*, **1** (2), 1–13.

Baltensperger, E. and T. Devinney (1985), 'Credit rationing theory: a survey and synthesis', *Journal of Institutional and Theoretical Economics*, **141** (4), 475–502.

Boadway, R. and M. Keen (2004), 'Financing new investments under asymmetric information: a general approach', Queen's University Department of Economics working paper no. 1017.

Cayssials, J.-L., E. Kremp and C. Peter (2007), 'Dix années de dynamique financière des PME en France', *Bulletin de la Banque de France*, **165**, 31–48.

Cukierman, A. (1978), 'The horizontal integration of the banking firm, credit rationing and monetary policy', *Review of Economic Studies*, **45** (1), 165–78.

De Meza, D.E. and D.C. Webb (1987), 'Too much investment: a problem of asymmetric information', *Quarterly Journal of Economics*, **102**, 281–92.

Diamond, D. and R. Rajan (2001), 'Liquidity risk, creation and financial fragility: a theory of banking', *Journal of Political Economy*, **2**, 287–327.

Frelmer, M. and M.-J. Gordon (1965), 'Why bankers ration credit', *Quarterly Journal of Economics*, **3**, 397–416.

Freixas, X. and J.-C. Rochet (1997), *Microeconomics of Banking*, Cambridge, MA: MIT Press.

Jaffee, D. and F. Modigliani (1969), 'A theory and test for credit rationing: reply', *American Economic Review*, **5**, 918–20.

Jaffee, D. and T. Russel (1976), 'Imperfect information, uncertainty, and credit rationing', *Quarterly Journal of Economics*, **90** (4), 651–66.

Jaffee, D. and J. Stiglitz (1990), 'Credit rationing', in B. Friedman and F. Hahn (eds), *Handbook of Monetary Economics*, vol. 2, Amsterdam: North Holland, pp. 838–88.

Keeton, W. (1979), *Equilibrium Credit Rationing*, New York: Garland Press.

Keynes, J.M. (1930 [1971]), *A Treatise on Money*, reprinted, in D. Moggridge (ed.), *The Collected Writings of John Maynard Keynes*, vol. 6, The Applied Theory of Money, New York: Cambridge University Press.

Kon, Y. and D.J. Storey (2003), 'A theory of discouraged borrowers', *Small Business Economics*, **21** (1), 37–49.

Kremp, E. (1998), 'Structure du capital des entreprises françaises en 1996', *Bulletin de la Banque de France*, no. 55, 81–91.

Kremp, E. and P. Sevestre (2000), 'L'appartenance à un groupe facilite le financement des enterprises', *Economie et Statistique*, no. 336, 79–92.

Levenson, A. and K. Willard (2000) 'Do firms get the financing they want? Measuring credit rationing experienced by small businesses in the U.S.', *Small Business Economics*, **14** (2), 83–94.

Loveman, G. and W. Sengenberger (1991), 'The re-emergence of small-scale production: an international comparison', *Small Business Economics*, **1** (3), 1–37.

Parker, S.C. (2004), *The Economics of Self-employment and Entrepreneurship*, Cambridge: Cambridge University Press.

Piore, M.J. and C.F. Sabel (1984), *The Second Industrial Divide. Possibilities for Prosperity*, New York: Basic Books.

Rajan, R. (1992), 'Insiders and outsiders: the choice between relationship and arm's length debt', *Journal of Finance*, **47** (4), 1367–400.

Ruhle, I. (1997), 'Why banks? Microeconomic foundation of financial intermediaries', *Development and Finance*, **3**, 10–99.

Sharpe, S. (1990), 'Asymmetric information, bank lending and implicit contracts: a stylized model of customer relationship', *Journal of Finance*, **45** (4), 1069–87.

Smith, A. (1776 [1881]), *Recherche sur la nature et les causes de la richesse des nations*, French translation of *the Wealth of Nations* by Germain Garnier.

Stiglitz, J.E. and A. Weiss (1981), 'Credit rationing in markets with imperfect information', *American Economic Review*, **71** (3), 349–410.

Swank, J. (1996), 'Theories of the banking firms: a review of literature', *Bulletin of Economic Research*, **48** (3), 173–207.

Turgot, A.R.J. (1766 [1970]), 'Réflexions sur la formation et la distribution des richesses', reprinted in A.R.J. Turgot, *Écrits économiques*, preface by B. Cazes, Paris: Calmann-Lévy.

Williamson, S.D. (1986), 'Costly monitoring, financial intermediation and equilibrium credit rationing', *Journal of Monetary Economics*, **18** (4), 158–79.

APPENDIX 5.1   DEFINITION OF INNOVATIVE SECTORS BY DIGITIP-INSEE

Innovative sectors gather branches from information and communications technologies (ICT), and from the fields of pharmaceutical products, biotechnology and new materials.

The definition of branches relative to the ICT, given by the OECD, encompasses the following.

- The branches producing information technologies: computers and other computer equipment manufacturing (NAF 300C); equipment receiving, recording or reproducing sound and image manufacturing (323Z), hertz emitting and transmitting equipment and phoning equipment manufacturing (322A and B); navigational equipment manufacturing; apparatus of scientific and technical instrumentation manufacturing (332A and B and 333Z); connector industry (313Z), passive components' and condensators' manufacturing; and electronic components (321A, C and D).
- The branches distributing information technologies: wholesale computers and computers' equipment; and wholesale office equipment (NAF 518G and H).
- The services of information technologies: telecommunications services (NAF 642); data processing services, consulting in computer systems, software production, computer and office equipment hiring, data banks activities, computer and office equipment maintenance and fixing, and other activities related to computers (NAF 72 and 713E).
- The audio-visual services: TV film production, institutional and advertising film production, movie production, technical services for TV and cinema, movie distribution, videotape production and distribution, movie broadcasting, radio activities, TV programs production, and TV program broadcasting (921 and 922A, B, D, E and F).

The other branches encompass several sub-branches in chemistry (industrial gases production, other basic inorganic chemical products, other basic organic chemical products, basic plastic materials production and basic pharmaceutical products) (NAF 241A, E, G, L and 244A). They gather branches with a significant level of innovation technology measured by the number of patents registered by technological fields according to the study 'Key technologies for the French industry at the 2000 horizon'. This study published by the DiGITIP – Direction Générale de l'Industrie, des Technologies de l'Information et des Postes – has been realized on the basis of works of well-known experts in their field of competencies and the results of several surveys related to the innovation theme realized by INSEE – Institut national des statistiques et des etudes économiques – and the DiGITIP.

6. Contextual factors favouring entrepreneurship initiative in Spain

Antonio Aragón Sánchez, Alicia Rubio Bañón and Paula Sastre Vivaracho

6.1 OVERVIEW

The emergence and consolidation of business initiatives is a question that arouses growing interest among politicians, professionals and researchers, since it is the cornerstone for a nation to create employment and wealth in the medium and long term. Business initiatives are a vital issue in increasing employment and sustaining economic growth.

The importance of the creation of businesses can be observed in the day-to-day life of the economy. Indeed, as is shown in the Global Entrepreneurship Monitor (GEM) study in 2007, in Spain alone some 2 000 000[1] businesses were formed, between nascent initiatives (less than three months) and new ones (up to 42 months).

As a result, there is an increasing number of academic works that study the entrepreneurial phenomenon. An analysis of the literature places the research lines in four major groups. First, there are the studies which from an economic point of view explain the entrepreneur's function and the process of creation of businesses on a rational economic basis[2] (Ajzen, 1991; Krueger and Brazeal, 1994; Shapero and Sokol, 1982; Veciana, 2005). Second, there is the psychological perspective,[3] which analyses the personal characteristics that an entrepreneur should have to successfully create and manage a business (Brockaus, 1981; Contin et al., 2007; Delmar and Davidsson, 2000; Gartner et al., 2004; Johnson et al., 2006). A third research group, based on the fact that knowledge and capabilities are key factors to create a business, examines the entrepreneurship phenomenon from a management perspective[4] (McClellan, 1961; Collins et al., 1964). Lastly we find the works which from an institutional viewpoint analyse the factors conditioning the country's economic, political, social and cultural environment[5] for the creation of businesses (Audrestch et al., 2002; Gómez et al., 2007; Levie and Autio, 2008; Mira, 2007; Shane, 2003;

Sternberg and Wennekers, 2005; Veciana, 1999, 2005; Verheul et al., 2001, 2002).

A review of these works shows that there are very few studies that examine the importance of the factors of the business context in depth when it comes to consolidating the businesses created (Gao, 2008; Levie and Autio, 2008).

Based on this premise, the purpose of this chapter is to study in depth the knowledge of the entrepreneurship phenomenon and to try to find the main context factors that condition the creation of businesses.

To do this, all the literature on the subject will be reviewed to provide a definition and to determine the suitable theoretical framework, and to analyse the evolution of the main theoretic models. We will then analyse the different factors of the environment affecting the creation of new businesses. The study uses the results of a survey answered by 570 experts from all the Spanish regions. The differences in their replies are analysed according to the extent of entrepreneurial activity registered. The chapter concludes with a presentation and discussion of results and an analysis of their implications for future research in this area, as well as the applications that businesses may make at a practical level.

6.2   ENTREPRENEURSHIP

Entrepreneurship concerns the study of creating and initiating new corporate activities (Gartner, 1985; Veciana, 1988). The absence of a univocal definition of the term is one of the prime difficulties when it comes to developing research in this area (Audrestsch, 2003; Shane and Venkataraman, 2000).

One group of researchers considers that entrepreneurship is synonymous with creating a new business and that the entrepreneur will therefore be the person who fosters the birth of the new corporate initiative (Audrestsch, 2003; Brännback et al., 2006; Gartner, 1988; Gartner and Carter, 2003; Herbert and Link, 1989; Katz, 1990, 1992; Koppl and Minniti, 2003; Low and MacMillan, 1988; Shapero and Sokol, 1982).

Another group of researchers, headed by Schumpeter (1934), relates the entrepreneur concept with the innovator concept (Kirzner, 1973; Morris, 1998; Shane and Venkataraman, 2000; Sharma and Chrisman, 1999). Entrepreneurship will therefore be initiating activities that imply creativity, innovation, R&D and so on – activities that imply launching new products, implementing new production methods, opening new markets, incorporating new sources of supply or new forms of organization.

The definition used by Kirzner (1973) could be enshrined in these same lines, closely linked to innovation and the search for opportunities, considering entrepreneurship to be the ability to perceive new opportunities and how these influence the market equilibrium. Druker (1985) likewise defines the term as an innovation act that implies endowing the existing resources with new capabilities for the creation of businesses. On these lines, Rumelt's concept (1987), which considers entrepreneurship to be the creation of business that introduces some element of novelty, should be highlighted (Batjargal, 2005; Burns and Nielsen, 2006; Parto, 2005).

There is a third group of works that are characterized for combining both perspectives in their concepts, creating new businesses and taking advantage of opportunities and innovations to offer new goods and services (Cuervo, 2007; De Carolis and Saparito, 2006; Johnson et al., 2006; Li et al., 2006; Low and MacMillan, 1988; Venkataraman, 1997).

From the above concepts we may conclude that entrepreneurship is synonymous with starting business activity, and an entrepreneur is an individual who finds opportunities to perform an economic activity with the necessary resources (Audrestsch, 2003; Gao, 2007; Gartner, 1988; Gartner and Carter, 2003; Herbert and Link, 1989; Johnson et al., 2006; Katz, 1990, 1992; Koppl and Minniti, 2003; Low and MacMillan, 1988; Mira, 2006).

Our study will follow the definition provided by the GEM project researchers who consider that, together with the above characteristics, entrepreneurship seeks to capture any entrepreneur initiative without distinguishing its importance in terms of business volume, years of activity or dimension of the workforce. The definition used for entrepreneurship is specifically as follows: 'any attempt to start up a new business or enterprise by an individual, team or an already established company'. GEM furthermore understands that an entrepreneur will be any active person, aged between 18 and 64, who is engaged in the process of starting up a business initiative. Coverage is thus given to all kinds of entrepreneurial activities from self-employment to the development of any corporate activity (Bastida et al., 2007; Contín et al. 2007; Levie and Autio, 2008).

6.3   EVOLUTION AND ANALYSIS OF THE MODELS ON CREATION OF BUSINESSES

There is a very broad field of studies on the creation of businesses that covers different theories akin to the corporate function. The first research in the area of creation of businesses focused on determining the individual characteristics of the entrepreneurs. These studies started by highlighting certain traits and personal backgrounds that characterize the entrepreneur's behaviour (Collins et al., 1964; McClelland, 1961).

Although this orientation is important in order to know the individual characteristics an entrepreneur should have, it provides little or no information about the process of creation and consolidation of the future business. This calls for a change in direction in the research that, without overlooking the individual perspective, would introduce some other kind of variable in the models that would relate more to the process of the creation of businesses and to the external variables that condition the creation as well as to the future consolidation of the business (De Castro et al., 2008).

The work that reroutes the research in this new direction is that by Gartner (1985). It shows that to extend the process of the creation of businesses, the context of the problem must be analysed, taking the entrepreneur into account but as just one more element of the process. It specifically defines a theoretical framework composed of the interaction of a number of variables. It integrates four perspectives in the process of the creation of businesses: the individuals involved in the creation of businesses; the internal organization; the actual process; and the context surrounding the business that is created (Gartner et al., 1989).

When analysing the person, it integrates the individual perspective with a consideration of the factors related to the entrepreneur's background, capabilities, skills and motivations. As regards the variables related to the organization, it takes into account the competitive strategy and organizational structure of the new business. Third, the process variables include the activities to be performed by the entrepreneurs to create their business. Lastly, within the environment dimension the external characteristics are enshrined that condition the entrepreneur's decision and which the author terms the attraction of the environment.

Another key work that follows this perspective is that of Gnyawali and Folgel (1994). In this model the different dimensions of the environment are related to the opportunity, the predisposition and ability to create one's own business. The authors specifically affirm that the probability of initiating an entrepreneurial activity increases when three situations converge: (1) there are opportunities, alternatives with expectations of success for the creation of new businesses; (2) the entrepreneur is motivated and has the required attitude to create a business; and (3) the entrepreneur is capable – they have the necessary technical abilities to initiate and maintain their own business. The environmental factors are also defined. The laws and government policies, the social-cultural features, the support measures and training and qualification of the potential entrepreneur may affect some of the key components (opportunity, predisposition-motivation and ability) when taking the decision of creating one's own business. Thus, each environmental factor would be related to a specific feature of the process of the creation of businesses that could affect the final decision to create one's own business (Urbano, 2006).

Shane and Venkataraman (2000), corroborate the above, on these same lines, developing a model that, based on business opportunities, examines the need to introduce the economic and institutional features of the markets in any conceptual framework that analyses the entrepreneurship phenomenon. This makes variables such as technology, social standards, the law or government policies, among others, to be essential for the development of entrepreneurial initiatives.

Another model to be considered is the one proposed by Krueger and Brazeal (1994). In this model the factors that favour the intention to create a business are devised under a psycho-sociological approach. It proposes that to create a business the entrepreneur should identify that their business idea is credible. The credibility at the same time depends on two factors: the desire and interest to set up a new business, and the perceived feasibility of the entrepreneur.

Variables are in turn introduced in the model relating to the ability and preparation needed and the prior predisposition or propensity of the individual to act. Both variables will speed up the process, so increasing the intention to create the business.

Lastly, the authors consider that it is usual for some event to precipitate the creation process, and when an entrepreneurial opportunity is identified in the form of a real need to satisfy the market, this will decisively influence the final intention to create one's own business (Urbano, 2006).

The final model that should be highlighted is the one proposed by Reynolds et al. (2005) (Figure 6.1). This model, which is the basis of the GEM research programme, adopts a theoretical work framework, integrating different blocks of variables relating to the influence of the creation of businesses in a territory.

It considers that the level of entrepreneurship activity of a nation or territory is the outcome of the evaluations of corporate initiatives arising from ideas of new entrepreneurs as well as of companies created as consequences of alliances, agreements or ideas of already consolidated businesses.

Second, the model sustains that the environment decisively conditions the level of creation of businesses and consequently the level of economic growth in a given place. It differentiates between two types of factors, those that affect and modify the framework in which already established businesses compete, which it calls general environment of factors, and those that affect the level of opportunities and the capabilities of the new entrepreneurs, known as specific environmental factors of the entrepreneur.

Within the variables of the general environment we find those that

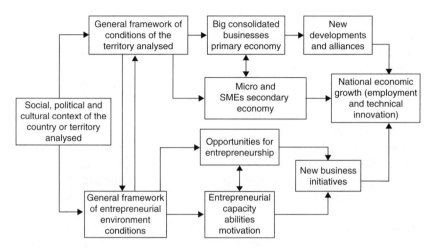

Source: Prepared by authors according to Reynolds et al. (2005).

Figure 6.1   Reynolds' model

affect a nation's general economy, such as the opening of markets, government, efficiency of the financial markets, technology, infrastructures,
entrepreneurial management skills, the labour market and institutions.
The general conditions of the national environment influence the characteristics of the economy and society where the entrepreneurial activity is
developed (specific environment).

Variables of the entrepreneur's specific environment include elements
such as financial support, government programmes and policies, education and training, R&D transfer, commercial and professional infrastructure, opening to the domestic market, access to physical infrastructure and
social and cultural standards.

Reynolds and colleagues argue that these variables in the entrepreneur's
specific environment have a direct influence on the opportunities open
to entrepreneurship and upon the level of knowledge, abilities and attitudes of the entrepreneurs. The model also assumes that a new business is
created each time an opportunity encounters an individual with the necessary motivation and ability to convert it into an entrepreneurial reality
(Reynolds et al., 1999).

We thus observe that the model shows the presence of a positive relationship between the factors of the entrepreneur's specific environment
and the entrepreneurial activity level (Levie and Autio, 2008). At an
empirical level, although some works have revealed a negative relationship between the general conditions of the environment and the rate of

entrepreneurial activity (Reynolds et al., 2002), very few works have until now corroborated that there is a positive relationship between the specific environmental factors and the rate of creation of businesses (Levie and Autio, 2008). This will be the main objective of our study: to ascertain that there is a positive relationship between the factors of the entrepreneur's specific environment and the rate of entrepreneurial activity.

Outside the conceptual framework of the GEM project research has focused on studying the influence of context factors in the creation of businesses, with the analysis centred on the effect of certain public policies and a suitable management of venture capital funds, tax incentives, programmes and services supporting new entrepreneurs, among other questions, such as financial support, governmental policies and access to R&D, because these are considered decisive factors in the creation of businesses (Levie and Autio, 2008). To advance in the analysis on how the specific environment affects the greater or smaller number of entrepreneur initiatives, this study will follow the model proposed by Reynolds et al. (2005) as mentioned in the previous paragraph.

6.4 THE ENTREPRENEUR'S SPECIFIC ENVIRONMENT

The entrepreneur's specific environmental factors are all those variables external to the entrepreneur that affect the creation of new businesses by influencing existing opportunities and the level of capabilities and abilities of the new entrepreneur directly and the rate of entrepreneurial activity indirectly.

The specific environment defines the rules of the game of the entrepreneurial activity in a given context, where the level and nature of the creation of new businesses depend on the environmental factors (Levie and Autio, 2008).

According to Reynolds et al. (2005) the variables that define the entrepreneur's specific environment are: (1) financial support; (2) government policies; (3) government programmes; (4) education and training; (5) R&D transfer; (6) commercial and professional infrastructures; (7) the openness of the domestic market; and (8) social and cultural standards. Each of these facets is described below.

6.4.1 Financial Support

When it comes to entrepreneurship we need to highlight the importance of financing.

Even though access to financing is one of the most important factors in creating a business, access to financial sources continues to be one of the main obstacles for the creation of businesses.

To obtain the necessary capital, the future entrepreneur must resort to financial institutions, other formal or informal investors, or obtain funds through their own means. Entrepreneurs usually resort first to banks, savings banks or credit cooperatives, although such financing is more expensive and difficult, and they do not usually cover the total demand for the required capital. In their initial stages the entrepreneur must complete the capital they need by going to private investors (business angels) that apart from providing financing may also participate in the management of the future business, and also be supported by family and friends.

To conclude, it is worth emphasizing the positive relationship between financing and the creation of businesses, because of the lack of initial capital, the little support through subsidies and aid and the high cost as well as the difficulty in finding outside resources may lead to the final decision not to undertake the planned activity (Urbano, 2006). In addition, to obtain the required outside financing the future entrepreneur must have a sound, innovating project with feasible guarantees (De Castro et al., 2008).

6.4.2 Government Policies

The decisions the administration may take regarding entrepreneur initiatives directly affect businesses and their creation, since they establish the rules and regulations to be fulfilled by the organizations and fix the public support for creating new businesses (Levie and Autio, 2008).

This item envisages how the policies of the different state and regional governments influence the creation of businesses; the priority these give to creating and developing new businesses; the level of administrative procedures to be completed to create a new business and the different taxes and charges that have to be paid. In Spain, depending on the type of initiative that is started, the formalities and procedures that the entrepreneur has to face are now becoming more flexible and less time consuming (De Castro et al., 2008).

6.4.3 Government Programmes

Government programmes are the actions that a government implements to facilitate the creation of businesses by making administrative formalities easier, providing professional support to the entrepreneurs to help them define and put their entrepreneurial initiatives into practice, support for innovation, starting up of business incubators and so on.

Today there is still a shortage of government programmes and rather than favouring entrepreneurial initiatives, they often make it difficult to create businesses (Coduras and Justo, 2002). To improve the support for entrepreneurial activity and increase the creation of businesses, the availability of public aid should be improved (Gómez et al., 2007). Government programmes that are in tune with the needs of entrepreneurs must, therefore, be fostered to increase the creation of businesses.

6.4.4 Education and Training

Education and training is a process that transmits knowledge, values, habits and forms of action.

The result of the process could also be called education, by which the individuals acquire abilities, knowledge, attitudes and values that potentially have the possibility of producing changes of a social, intellectual, emotional nature and so on in the person.

The purpose of training is to adapt human resources better to the job, and the training contents consequently seek to obtain a constant interaction between the demands of the actual job itself and the training contents taught (Levie and Autio, 2008).

The training will not only try to increase the competencies of the individuals but will also adapt them to their specific project, in which the training will accompany the implementation, should the individual decide to implement an entrepreneurial initiative (Contín et al., 2007; Levie and Autio, 2008).

There are different levels and relations in the creation of businesses with respect to education and training. The basic education levels do not specifically pay very much attention to training in questions relating to business management, which is a core factor for a suitable development and increase of the corporate activity (Gómez et al., 2007). In Europe there are a number of experiences aimed at fostering education for entrepreneurship, such as specifically qualifying teachers to transmit an attitude in which the figure of the entrepreneur is valued.

6.4.5 R&D Transfer

Innovation considers change in products and processes, their improvement, new marketing outlooks and new forms of distribution (North, 1993). These new ideas can improve the way in which things have been done until now, or else change them radically. Innovation may occur as a consequence of the internal development by the company itself or through acquiring licences to implement new technologies.

Authors such as Coduras and Justo (2002) and Bastida et al. (2007)

maintain that when the labour force dedicated to R&D and to innovation is increased, the technological base is strengthened and, consequently, the possibility of implementing new entrepreneurial initiatives.

To summarize, a good knowledge of the factors that favour creativity, together with an understanding of the elements conditioning innovation may be the starting point to create an entrepreneurial mentality in many sectors of the economy. Normally the entrepreneur is in themself already an innovator, a creator of new methods to respond to the market needs.

6.4.6 Commercial and Professional Infrastructures

Commercial infrastructures are the necessary means and services for the basic functioning of a business (sales, customer attention and so on) as well as the necessary public amenities that facilitate the exchange processes.

An entrepreneur needs to be able to count on sufficient suppliers, consultants and subcontractors that give support to the new businesses for their consolidation and subsequent commercial expansion.

In Spain there is ample access to good services and to good commercial infrastructures, although their cost is usually quite high (De Castro et al., 2008).

6.4.7 Internal Market Openness

The openness of the market is a dynamic process of modernization that assesses the entry barriers confronting an entrepreneur when creating a business (pre-established corporate benefits, effectiveness of the anti-monopoly regulations and so on) (Coduras and Justo, 2002).

Opening the market represents one of the solutions to a country's economic problems. It allows individuals to participate as a service provider and does not limit them to a given population. It also gives open market opportunities for entrepreneurship.

Opening the market solves the economic problem created by state monopolies because it encourages growth in terms of quantity and quality of the service and provokes cuts in prices. The opening generates wealth for everyone and facilitates the creation of new businesses (Levie and Autio, 2008; Pistrui, 2004).

6.4.8 Social and Cultural Standards

Social and cultural standards are disciplines that deal with features relating to the behaviour and activities of individuals. They examine both the material and the immaterial expressions of societies.

The most outstanding characteristic of social and cultural standards is that individuals possess specific cognitive abilities that create awareness and abstract mental representations that, generally speaking, influence their behaviour and create complex rules of interaction between individuals (Gómez et al., 2007).

It should be observed that social and cultural standards support and assess the individual success achieved by the entrepreneur through their personal efforts, as well as emphasizing self-sufficiency, autonomy and personal initiative. Another significant feature of social and cultural standards is that they stimulate taking entrepreneurial risk as well as the creativity and the innovation of the entrepreneur (Bastida et al., 2007; Levie and Autio, 2008).

The positive value of social and cultural standards must specifically be highlighted akin to the figure of the businessman and entrepreneur. A positive valuation of the businessman and of the actual entrepreneur and the risk that is taken on will without question be an incentive for an increasingly larger number of business initiatives to emerge in time. Individual aspects such as self-sufficiency, autonomy or personal initiative will also play a determining role.

In this section we support the idea provided by Reynolds et al. (2005) – the greater the weight in a specific context of: financial support, government programmes and policies oriented at supporting the business initiative, a suitable outlook on education and training, greater innovation and transfer of R&D, making commercial infrastructures available to businesses, opening the domestic market, counting on physical infrastructures and the social and cultural standards – explains a higher entrepreneurship activity index in a region or country.

6.5   METHODOLOGY

The data used in this work has been taken from the GEM 2007 project for Spain. To analyse how the environmental factors affect the propensity for the creation of businesses to a greater or lesser extent, this study has been produced using the opinions of 570 experts, from the 17 Spanish autonomous regions in addition to the opinions of experts from the autonomous cities of Ceuta and Melilla.

In the interviews and surveys the experts were asked to give their opinion on the state of the above-mentioned factors in each of their territories.

The consultation was based on a structured questionnaire containing a wide spectrum of statements relating to each of the environmental factors mentioned, in which the experts expressed their opinion on a score that ranged from 1 (absolutely untrue or I don't agree) to 5 (absolutely true or I agree).

6.5.1 Regions and Entrepreneurial Activity Index

The GEM report takes the levels of creation of businesses based on the synthetic index Total Entrepreneurial Activity Index (TEA), which measures the percentage of the adult population (aged 18 to 64 years) involved in setting up a business, in which they are going to own at least part of the capital. The TEA Index is at the same time made up of two kinds of initiatives, depending on the phase in which the business project is found: the nascent initiatives or Start-Up (SU), businesses with less than three months of activity; and the new initiatives or Baby-Business (BB), businesses with more than three and less than 42 months of activity.

To undertake the research the autonomous regions with a higher than the national average TEA and those with a TEA below that index have been categorized in two groups.

In the first group of regions we find Galicia, Madrid, Extremadura, Navarre, Catalonia, Valencia, Castile la Mancha, Balearic Islands and Canary Islands with TEA values equal to or higher than the average for Spain – 7.5 per cent in 2007 – and below that average we find Murcia, Aragon, Andalusia., Asturias, Ceuta, the Basque Region, Cantabria, Castile and Leon and Melilla.

An analysis on variance has been performed for each item to ascertain how each of the specific factors of the environment influence the entrepreneurship orientation to a greater or lesser extent. It defines the specific factors of the environment synthesized in Table 6.1. The analysis of the differences for the two groups into which the experts have been divided up will allow us to know to what extent more or less importance given to the specific environmental factors explains significant differences in the TEA Index.

6.6 RESULTS

As regards the first factor of the environment, financial support (Table 6.1, Figure 6.2), the results of the analysis performed show that for sources of self-financing, outside financing and public subsidies the values are around 3 and no statistically significant differences are observed, from which it can be deduced that these factors of the specific context of the businesses have no significant effect on the entrepreneurship orientation.

In contrast, the greater presence of private investors, the presence of

Table 6.1   Factors of the entrepreneur's specific environment

	Below TEA	Above TEA
Financial support		
Own financing sources	2.9	3
Outside financing	3.2	3.4
Public subsidies	3.2	3.1
Private investors	2.2***	2.6***
Venture capital	2.4**	2.6**
Equity offerings	1.6**	1.8**
Government policies		
Government policies	2.4	2.6
Support is a state priority	2.8	2.9
Support is a priority in the autonomous regions	3.4*	3.2*
Administrative procedures in one week	2.1	2.1
Taxes and fees do not represent a barrier	3.2	3
Predicted and coherent taxes and fees	3.2	3.2
Simple bureaucratic procedures	2.7	2.7
Governmental programmes		
Single window	3.4**	3.2**
Support of scientific parks and incubators	3.1*	3.3*
Suitable number of programmes	3.2	3.1
Competent and efficient professionals	3.2	3.3
Adjustment to the needs of the government programmes	3.3	3.2
Effectiveness of the government programmes	3.1	3.2
Education and training		
Education stimulates	2.3***	2***
Education provides knowledge	2.2**	2**
Education devotes attention to creating businesses	1.9***	1.7***
Higher education prepares for the creation of businesses	2.6*	2.5*
Training for management prepares for the creation of businesses	3	3
Professional training prepares for the creation of businesses	3***	2.8***
R&D transfer		
Efficiency of universities for creation of businesses	2.3	2.3
Same access to research	2.7	2.7
Businesses can finance the new technologies	2.2	2.1
Subsidies and aid are sufficient and adequate	2.7**	2.5**
Science and technology permits the creation of businesses	2.8*	3*
Economic support for engineers and scientists	2.3***	2.6***

Table 6.1   (continued)

	Below TEA	Above TEA
Commercial and professional infrastructure		
There are sufficient suppliers, consultants and subcontractors	3.3	3.4
The new businesses can assume the costs	2.6	2.6
The new businesses have easy access to third parties	2.9*	3.1*
The new businesses have good access to advisory services	3.5	3.5
The new businesses have good access to services	3.7	3.6

Note: X^2: *$p \leq 0.1$, **$p \leq 0.05$, ***$p \leq 0.01$.

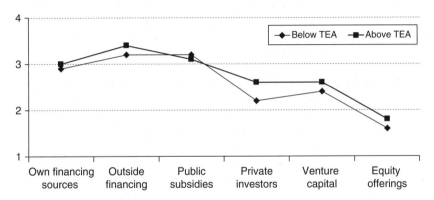

Figure 6.2   Financial support

venture capital companies and the possibility of resorting to the stock market, even though this is rather exceptional for an entrepreneur, are context factors that are significantly related to a greater entrepreneurship orientation by businesses in the different autonomous regions.

Regarding government policies as a factor of the specific environment for entrepreneurship (Table 6.1), the results of the analysis show that they have no significant effect on the greater or lesser entrepreneurship orientation of the businesses. In other words, the policies of the government that support entrepreneurship, the ease of administrative proceedings, the weight of taxes and charges, the fact that these are coherent or of greater simplicity in bureaucratic procedures do not explain greater entrepreneurship orientation by the businesses, in the experts' opinion. On the contrary, the fact that the support to develop entrepreneurship activities is a priority on the part of the autonomous regions is significantly related to better entrepreneurship orientation. This result may seem paradoxical, but it may be significant to have greater support by the autonomous regions when the businesses have a smaller entrepreneurship orientation.

Third, the results obtained for the items that form the variable government programmes are shown (Table 6.1). Again, as occurs with the variables of government policies, in this case counting on a suitable number of support programmes to entrepreneurs, the greater or lesser presence in the different territories of competent and efficient professionals, the adjustment to the needs of the government programmes or the effectiveness of the government programmes bear no significant relationship with the higher entrepreneurial activity index.

Support to the scientific parks and development of business incubators is related with a higher rate of entrepreneurial activity and by having a single window it is related with a smaller entrepreneurial activity index, but it seems that, in this case, it is significant that if we want to support the development of new entrepreneurial business initiatives, the information given to the potential persons interested should be simplified with the support of this action programme.

The results referring to education and training merit some consideration at a different level from those reviewed until now. The data shown in Figure 6.3 and in Table 6.1 reveal the importance of this variable.

If each item is analysed, it will be observed that the experts expressing disagreement that training simulates the entrepreneurial spirit, and that training provides knowledge for entrepreneurship, that it devotes attention to the creation of businesses or that higher education (university) or professional training prepares for the creation of businesses is clearly related with a lower entrepreneurial activity index. In other words, the training and education factor clearly penalizes the entrepreneurial initiative in Spain.

It should be considered in this respect that important efforts are called for in the medium and long term if we really want this situation to change, because it seems that the educational and training system is 'penalizing' the entrepreneurial initiatives of our students today.

The fifth factor of the environment that is analysed as explaining greater or lesser entrepreneurial orientation is R&D transfer. The experts agree in observing that science and technology favour the creation of businesses (this assertion corresponds to a greater entrepreneurial orientation), and also that the economic support for engineers and scientists is related to greater entrepreneurial orientation (Table 6.1 and Figure 6.4). In general, the experts do not agree that the subsidies and aid are sufficient and suitable, in particular in the case of smaller entrepreneurial activity in Spain.

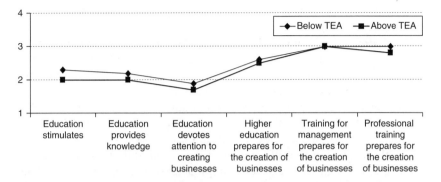

Figure 6.3   Education and training

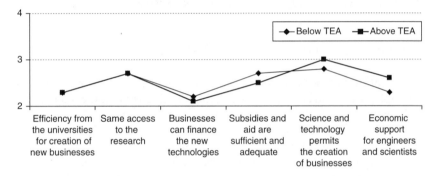

Figure 6.4   R&D transfer

The same section shows that efficiency of the universities for the creation of businesses, to have the same access to research for the entire population or so that the businesses may themselves meet the cost of implementing new technologies, does not explain significant differences in the TEA Index.

The results obtained for the items that measure the commercial and professional infrastructure factor (Table 6.1) allow us to affirm that none of them explains statistically significant differences regarding a greater or smaller entrepreneurial orientation. Thus the presence of sufficient suppliers, consultants and subcontractors, that the new businesses can assume their costs, that new businesses count on a good advisory service or have good access to the services do not explain differences in the TEA Index of the Spanish autonomous regions.

The only variable within the commercial and professional infrastructure that relates positively with the greater entrepreneurial activity index is that most experts agree that the businesses have easy access to third parties.

Regarding the opening of the domestic market, in the opinion of experts there are no significant differences in the entrepreneurial activity index of Spanish businesses depending on whether the consumer markets or businesses change, nor is it influenced by the difficulty the businesses have to enter new markets, or the difficulties to assume entry costs, among other factors. In short, it does not seem that the variables that explain the opening factor to the domestic market have a significant effect on the TEA.

Lastly, regarding the influence that the social and cultural standards may have on a greater or lesser entrepreneurial orientation, the data set shows that, as in the case of some of the factors analysed, they have no significant effect on a greater or lesser entrepreneurial orientation, as opposed to what would, at least initially, be expected.

6.7   FINAL CONSIDERATIONS

The creation of new businesses is one of the main engines vis-à-vis growth in employment and the continuing economic expansion in the majority of countries and in the Spanish autonomous regions.

The empirical analysis has been performed in the 17 autonomous regions and in the autonomous cities of Ceuta and Melilla, from a sample of 570 experts, 30 for each region, which allows us to conclude that the autonomous regions where there is a below average TEA for Spain are characterized by the following:

- They have a broad range of government aid for the creation and development of new businesses.
- They have more than others, in the opinion of the experts, a single information window, a positive rather than negative feature, designed to facilitate the establishment of entrepreneurial initiatives.
- Regarding education and training, the experts coincide in stating that education stimulates the creation of businesses, provides knowledge, devotes little attention to the creation of businesses at a general level and particularly at university and professional training levels. These are questions that call for quite urgent action.
- The experts consider that subsidies and aid for the creation of new businesses are not sufficient.

It also allows us to see that the autonomous regions where there is an above average TEA for Spain are characterized by:

- Having a greater degree of sufficient financing available from private investors, other than the founders of new and up and coming businesses.
- Counting on a greater financing offer through venture capital for new and growing businesses.
- The scientific parks and firm incubators, which stand out for their clear support in the development of growing businesses.
- Greater importance given to science and technology as determining factors for the emergence of new entrepreneurial initiatives and for the growth of existing ones.
- Giving greater economic support to engineers and scientists.
- Businesses have greater and easier access to the physical infrastructure that provides good support for the new and growing businesses.

NOTES

1. These figures should not be compared directly with those of the official register of companies provided by the DIRCE. GEM measures entrepreneurial activity, a broader concept than that of the annual register of new businesses.
2. The following perspectives can be envisaged: the corporate function as a fourth factor of production, the theory of the entrepreneur's profit, the theory of the choice of career when indecisive, the theory of transactional costs, Schumpeter's theory of economic development and the theory of endogenous regional development.
3. The theories of personality traits, the psychodynamic theory of the entrepreneur's personality and Kirzner's theory of the entrepreneur can be enshrined in this perspective.
4. This perspective envisages Leibenstein's theory of X-efficiency, the theory of the entrepreneur's behaviour, the success models of the new enterprise, and the models for generating and developing new innovator projects 'corporate entrepreneurships'.
5. This perspective envisages the theory of margination, the theory of the role, the theory of networks, the incubator theory, the evolutionist theory, Weber's focus on economic development, Hagen's theory on social change, the theory of population ecology and the institutional theory.

REFERENCES

Ajzen, I. (1991), 'The theory of planned behaviour', *Organizational Behaviour and Human Decision*, **50**, 179–211.

Audrestsch, D.B. (2003), *Entrepreneurship. A Survey of the Literature*, Enterprise Papers no. 14, Enterprise Directorate-General, Luxembourg: European Commission.

Audrestsch, D.B., R. Thurik and I. Verheul (2002), *Entrepreneurship: Determinants and Policy in a European-US Comparison*, Boston, MA: Kluwer Academic Publishers.

Bastida, R.M., A. Correa and E. Hormiga (2007), 'Innovación en las iniciativas empresariales españolas en el marco nacional GEM', *Revista de Empresa*, **20**, 32–50.

Batjargal, B. (2005), 'Entrepreneurial versatility, resources and firm performance in Russia: a panel study', *International Journal of Entrepreneurship and Innovation Management*, special issue, **5**, 284–97.

Brännback, R.H., A. Carsud, J. Elfving, J. Kickul and N. Krueger (2006), 'Why replicate entrepreneurial intentionality studies? Prospects, perils and academic reality', presentation to EDGE Conference 2006, Singapore Management University.

Brockaus, R.H. (1981), 'Risk taking propensity of entrepreneurs', *Academy of Management Journal*, **23**, 509–20.

Burns, J. and K. Nielsen (2006), 'How do embedded agents engage in institutional change?', *Journal of Economic Issues*, **40**, 449–56.

Coduras, A. and R. Justo (2002), 'Análisis de la actividad emprendedora en Iberoamérica', *Revista de Empresa*, **2**, 66–83.

Collins, O.F., D.G. Moore and D.B. Unwalla (1964), *The Organization Makers: A Bevioural Study of Independent Entrepreneurs*, New York: Meredith.

Contín, I., M. Larraza and I. Mas (2007), 'Características distintivas de los emprendedores y los empresarios establecidos: evidencia a partir de los datos REM de Navarra', *Revista de Empresa*, **20**, 10–19.

Cuervo, A. (2007), 'Entrepreneurship: concepts, theory and perspectiva. Introduction', in A. Cuervo García D.R. Soriano and S.R. Dobón (eds), *Entrepreneurship. Concepts, Theory and Perspectivas*, Berlín: Springer, pp. 1–23.

De Castro, J., R. Justo and A.M. Olivares (2008), *La naturaleza del proceso emprendedor en España en el contexto internacional*, Bilbao: Fundación BBVA.

De Carolis, D. and P. Saparito (2006), 'Social capital, cognition and entrepreneurial opportunities: a theoretical framework', *Entrepreneurship Theory and Practice*, **30**, 41–56.

Delmar, F. and P. Davidsson (2000), 'Where do they come from? Prevalence and characteristics of nascent entrepreneurs', *Entrepreneurship and Regional Development*, **12**, 1–23.

Druker, P.F. (1985), *Innovation and Entrepreneurship*, New York: Harper and Row.

Gao, Y.Q. (2007), *Gaining Competitive Advantage Through Strategic Use of Government Within Mainland China*, proceedings of the International Conference on Public Administration, 3rd ICPA, University of Electronic Science and Technology of China, Chengdu, China, 21-22 October, pp. 397–403.

Gao, Y.Q. (2008), 'Institutional change driven by corporate political entrepreneurship in transitional China: a process model', *International Management Review*, **4**, 22–35.

Gartner, W.B. (1985), 'A conceptual framework for describing the phenomenon of new venture creation', *Academy of Management Review*, **10**, 696–706.

Gartner, W.B. (1988), 'Who is the entrepreneur? is the wrong question', *American Journal of Small Business*, **12**, 11–32.

Gartner, W.B. and N.M. Carter (2003), 'Entrepreneurial behaviour and firm organizing processes', in Z.J. Acs and D.B. Audretsch (eds), *Handbook of Entrepreneurship Research: An Interdisciplinary Survey and Introduction*, Boston, MA: Kluwer Academic Publishers, pp. 195–221.

Gartner, W.B., T.R. Mitchell and K. Vesper (1989), 'A taxonomy of new business ventures'. *Journal of Business Venturing,* **4**, 169–86.

Gartner, W.B., K.G. Shaver, N.M. Carter and P.D. Reynolds (2004), 'Foreword', in W.B. Gartner, K.G. Shave, N.M. Carter and P.D. Reynolds (eds), *Handbook of Entrepreneurial Dynamics: The Process of Business Creation,* Thousand Oaks, CA: Sage, pp. 9–23.

Gnyawali, D.R. and D.S. Fogel (1994), 'Environments for entrepreneurship development: key dimensions and research implications', *Entrepreneurship Theory and Practice,* **18** (4), Summer, 43–62.

Gómez, J.M, I. Mira and J.M. Mateo (2007), 'Condiciones de la actividad emprendedora e instituciones de apoyo desde el ámbito local: el caso de la provincia de Alicante', *Revista de Empresa,* **20**, 20–31.

Herbert, R.F. and A.N. Link (1989), 'In search of the meaning of entrepreneurship', *Small Business Economics,* **1**, 39–49.

Johnson, P., S.C. Parker and F.H. Wijbenga (2006), 'Nascent entrepreneurship research: achievements and opportunities', *Small Business Economics,* **27**, 1–4.

Katz, J.A. (1990), 'Longitudinal analysis of self-employment follow-through', *Entrepreneurship and Regional Development,* **2**, 15–25.

Katz, J.A. (1992), 'A psychosocial cognitive model of employment status choice', *Entrepreneurship, Theory and Practice,* **17**, 29–38.

Kirzner, I. (1973), *Competition and Entrepreneurship,* Chicago, IL. University of Chicago Press.

Koppl, R. and M. Minniti (2003), 'Market process and entrepreneurial studies', in Z.J. Acs and D.B. Audretsch (eds), *Handbook of Entrepreneurship Research: An Interdisciplinary Survey and Introduction,* Boston, MA: Kluwer Academic Publishers, pp. 81–102.

Krueger, N.F. and D.V. Brazeal (1994), 'Entrepreneurial potential and potential entrepreneurs', *Entrepreneurship: Theory and Practice,* **18**, 91–104.

Levie, J. and E. Autio (2008), 'A theoretical grounding and test of GEM model', *Small Business Economics,* **31**, 235–63.

Li, D., D.J. Feng and H. Jiang (2006), 'Institutional entrepreneurs', *American Economic Review,* **96**, 358–62.

Low, M.B. and I. MacMillan (1988), 'Entrepreneurship: past research and future challenges', *Journal of Management,* **14**, 139–61.

McClelland, D.C. (1961), *The Achieving Society,* Princeton, NJ: D. Van Nostrand.

Mira, I. (2006), 'La creación de empresas por titulados universitarios. Una aproximación a los factores de influenciadle ámbito de la Universidad', doctoral thesis, Universidad Miguel Hernández de Elche.

Mira, I. (2007), 'Condicionantes de la actividad emprendedora e instituciones de apoyo desde el ámbito local: el caso de la provincia de Alicante', *Revista de Empresa,* **20**, 20–31.

Morris, M.H. (1998), *Entrepreneurial Intensity: Sustainable Advantages for Individuals, Organizations and Societies,* Westport, CT: Quorum.

North, D.C. (1993), *Instituciones, cambio institucional y desempeño económico,* Mexico City: Fondo de Cultura Económica.

Parto, S. (2005), 'Economic activity and institutions: taking stock', *Journal of Economic Issues,* **39**, 70–82.

Pistrui, J. (2004), 'Conducta emprendedora: Como fomentar la creación de riqueza familiar generación tras generación', *Revista de Empresa,* **7**, 70–82.

Reynolds, P.D., M. Hay and R.M. Camp (1999), *Global Entrepreneurship Monitor, 1999. Executive Report*, London: London Business School.

Reynolds, P.D., W.D. Bygrave, E. Autio, L.W. Cox and M. Hay (2002), *Global Entrepreneurship Monitor, 2002. Executive Report*, Kansas City, MO: Kauffman Foundation.

Reynolds, P.D., N. Bosma, E. Autio et al. (2005), 'Global entrepreneurship monitor: data collection design and implementation 1998–2003', *Small Business Economics*, **24**, 443–56.

Rumelt, R.P. (1987), 'Theory, strategy and entrepreneurship', in D.J. Teece (ed.), *The Competitive Challenge*, Cambridge, MA: Ballinger, pp. 137–58.

Schumpeter, J. (1934), *Theory of Economic Development*, Cambridge, MA: Harvard University Press.

Shane, S. (2003), *A General Theory of Entrepreneurship: The Individual-opportunity Nexus*, Cheltenham, UK and Northampton, MA, USA: Edward Elgar.

Shane, S. and S. Venkataraman (2000), 'The promise of entrepreneurship as a field of research', *Academy of Management Review*, **25**, 217–26.

Shapero, A. and L. Sokol (1982), 'The social dimension entrepreneurship', in C.A. Kent, D.L. Sexton and E. Vesper (eds), *Encyclopaedia of Entrepreneurship*, Englewood Cliffs, NJ: Prentice-Hall, pp. 72–90

Sharma, P. and J.J. Chrisman (1999), 'Toward a reconciliation of the definitional issues in the field of corporate entrepreneurship', *Entrepreneurship Theory and Practice*, **24**, 11–27.

Sternberg, R. and S. Wennekers (2005), 'Determinants and effects of new business creation using Global Entrepreneurship Monitor data', *Small Business Economics*, **24**, 193–203.

Urbano, D. (2006), 'Factores condicionantes de la creación de empresas en Catalunya: un enfoque institucional', *Estudios de Economía Aplicada*, **24**, 24–37.

Veciana, J.M. (1988), 'Empresari i procés de creació d´empreses', *Revista Económica de Catalunya*, **8**, 53–67.

Veciana, J.M. (1999), 'Creación de empresas de investigación científica'. *Revista Europea de Dirección y Economía de la Empresa*, **8**, 11–35.

Veciana, J.M. (2005), *La creación de empresas. Un enfoque gerencial*, Barcelona: Servicio de Estudios. Caja de Ahorros y Pensiones de Barcelona.

Venkatamaran, S. (1997), 'The distinctive domain of entrepreneurship research: an editor's perspective', in J. Katz and J. Brockhaus (eds), *Advances in Entrepreneurship, Firm Emergence, and Growth*, Greenwich, CT: JAI Press, vol. 3, pp. 119–38.

Verheul, I., D. Wennekers, D.B. Audretsch and R. Thurik (2001), 'An eclectic theory of entrepreneurship: policies, institutions and culture', Economics of Science, Technology and Innovation Economic Commission for Europe discussion paper, pp. 11–81.

Verheul, I., D. Wennekers, D.B. Audretsch and R. Thurik (2002), *An Eclectic Theory of Entrepreneurship: Policies, Institutions and Culture*, Boston, MA: Kluwer Academic Publishers.

7. Differences in financial and legal systems and contribution of private equity funds to transfers of shares in Europe

Rafik Abdesselam, Sylvie Cieply and Anne-Laure Le Nadant

INTRODUCTION

Private equity provides capital to companies that are not publicly traded on a stock exchange. This capital can be used to finance new firms, to develop new products and technologies, or to expand working capital. Most academic articles on private equity finance deal with the funding of these activities, that is, with venture capital only. Venture capital can be defined as a subset of private equity investment, which provides capital to companies in the early stages of the life cycle, particularly in innovative sectors.

Private equity, however, is also used to finance acquisitions and to resolve ownership and management issues. Successions in family-owned companies or buy-outs of businesses by experienced managers can be achieved using private equity funding. Private equity is thus a way of stimulating entrepreneurship and of energizing small and medium-sized enterprises (SMEs), which are caught between the difficulty of accessing the financial markets and the reluctance of banks to expose themselves to risk. Understanding the financial and legal factors that help private equity to flourish and to contribute to transfers of shares is therefore an important question for research.

Following Glachant et al. (2008), who stress the common features of the private equity segments rather than highlighting their differences, we focus, in this study, on the role played by private equity firms in the financing of all types of transfers of ownership rights in order to advance the understanding of private equity investing as a whole. The organization around funds that obey common rules is the first factor that unites the private equity industry, but the nature of the relationship between investor and entrepreneur is the most important thing that distinguishes private equity from other forms of funding.

The role of private equity firms is deeply influenced by the nature of financial systems (Black and Gilson, 1998; Gompers and Lerner, 1998, 2001; Jeng and Wells, 2000). The principal proposition established in the literature is that private equity flourishes in countries with deep and liquid stock markets. But financial systems still remain different among European countries, despite the process of the European integration (Schmidt et al., 2002). In our study we first identify the expected effects of differences in financial systems on private equity activity. Second, we study, with individual data, similarities and dissimilarities between five European countries (France, Germany, Italy, Spain and the UK) in the contribution of private equity firms to transfers of ownership rights.

We retain these five countries because they are the five largest European countries in terms of gross domestic product, their private equity markets are relatively well developed and their governance systems still remain different (La Porta et al., 1998, Caby, 2007). We use data from Zephyr, a database from Bureau Van Dijk, which contains information on deals involving transfers of ownership rights. These deals include mergers (business combinations in which the number of companies decreases after the transaction), acquisitions of majority interests (all cases in which the acquirer ends up with 50 per cent or more of the votes of the target), transfers of minority stakes (below 50 per cent), leveraged buy-outs (LBOs), and initial public offerings (IPOs), which involve targets (companies being sold, or companies in which a stake is being sold) from France, Germany, Italy, Spain and the UK. Transfers of ownership can be supported by private equity firms but this feature is not compulsory. The information used in this study is thus very different from the data gathered by surveys which only concern deals financed by venture capital (Cumming et al., 2009; Manigart et al., 2002).

We structure the chapter as follows. Section 7.1 identifies expected relationships between the nature of governance systems and the role of private equity firms in transfers of ownership rights. Section 7.2 describes the sample and the data. In section 7.3 we present the results of the tests of the expected relationships between target nationality and the financing of transfers of ownership rights by private equity firms. We conclude by underlining the specific case of France.

7.1   LITERATURE REVIEW

For Cumming et al. (2009), the nature of the legal system can justify differences of venture capital funds' practices around the world. These authors apply to venture capital the lessons of the classification of legal systems introduced by La Porta et al. (1998). These authors justify differences in financing structures between 49 members of the OECD with legal arguments. This approach, which links 'Law' and 'Finance' topics, has deeply renewed the comparative study of financing systems which, hitherto, was only based on financing means and on a dual classification of countries, which are either market centred or bank oriented. Some authors complete these two approaches by taking into account the structure of shareholdings. In this section we use these three approaches to analyse the role of private equity firms in the five countries studied. For each approach, we describe the countries studied and then we identify the consequences of their characteristics on the role of private equity.

7.1.1.   Role of Private Equity Firms and Financing Systems

Classification of financing systems and position of countries studied
Traditionally, the distinction between Anglo-Saxon countries and continental European countries has been expressed in terms of dominant providers of financing resources. Two systems are opposed: one is centred on financial markets whereas the other is centred on banks (Allen and Gale, 2000; Levine, 2002). In bank-centred systems, such as Germany and Japan during the 1970s and 1980s, banks play a major role in the collection of financial resources, the allowance of capital and the definition of firms' investment plans. In market-based systems, such as the Anglo-Saxon countries, securities markets play an important role besides banks in the collection of resources and their assignment, which makes investment less sensitive to banking debt (Demirgüç-Kunt and Levine, 2001).

This classification has been called into question by Mayer (1988) and Corbett and Jenkinson (1996). Using net financial data (new debt minus reimbursement of existing debt and banking deposits), these authors do not find any significant difference in the way companies of the most developed countries are financed. Self-financing is the most important financing source everywhere, and then, among external financial resources, debt, in particular from banks, is the most used financing source (except for Canada). Schmidt et al. (1998, 2002) disputed these results. According to them, Mayer's results and those of Corbett and Jenkinson are mainly due to a statistical artefact related to the use of net data. When gross data from national accounts are used, Mayer's results are not confirmed and significant differences still exist in financing structures across the world: on the one hand, Germany is still very centred on banking debt and, on the other hand, the UK still relies on financial markets for external financing.

For France, results are less clear but show a radical transformation of the financing system, which could converge towards the British system.

Demirgüç-Kunt and Levine (2001) also find significant differences in financial structures for a sample of 150 countries during the 1990s. They compute an index of financial development[1] and show the segmentation of countries into two classes, which corresponds to the traditional classification between bank-centred and market-based countries. According to this research, France, Germany, Italy and Spain belong to bank-centred economies whereas the UK belongs to market-based ones. Paillard and Amable (2002), using net data on six European countries (Germany, France, Italy, the Netherlands, Sweden and the UK), also find an opposition between two types of economies: one is characterized by a high level of internal financing and the other one by an important use of banking loans.

To sum up, various financing systems still remain in Europe. However, results by country are not always homogeneous. The British case is an exception; this country still remains a market-based country, with a high level of external financing. For the other countries, the situation is less clear.

For Germany, Demirgüç-Kunt and Levine (2001) and Schmidt et al. (1998) assert that this country is still a bank-centred economy. On the contrary, Friderichs and Paranque (2001) and Paillard and Amable (2002) show that only small and medium-sized firms are related to this financing system. The largest German firms are less and less financed by banks, and their financing tends to get closer to the Anglo-Saxon model.

For France, Demirgüç-Kunt and Levine (2001) show that this country is a bank-centred economy. Schmidt et al. (1998) underline, nevertheless, that the recent transformation of this economy makes its situation confused. According to the authors, in the middle of the 1990s the French economy was difficult to classify. Paillard and Amable (2002) also underline the evolution of the French financing system. They show the high increase in the internal financing of French firms during the 1990s and their important degearing. Moreover, Caby (2007) shows that the role of financial markets has sharply increased in France so that it tends to approach the British and US levels. In 2001 the ratio stock exchange capitalization to GNP was equal to 103 per cent (against 49 per cent in 1997), whereas the same ratio was equal to 152 per cent in the USA (against 132 per cent in 1997) and 166 per cent in the UK (against 161 per cent in 1997).

For Italy, Demirgüç-Kunt and Levine (2001) and Paillard and Amable (2002) classify this country as a bank-centred economy. Paillard and Amable (2002), however, underline the relative importance of securities in Italy, a fact that the traditional classification between bank-centred and market-based economies cannot take into account.

For Spain, very few studies exist on the financial system. Demirgüç-Kunt and Levine (2001) classify this country as a bank-centred economy. Artola et al. (2002) analyse the Spanish financing system and confirm this conclusion.

To conclude, this traditional typology of financial systems must be used carefully. We can retain the clear opposition between the British case, a pure market-based economy, and the Italian and Spanish cases, which are still bank-centred economies. The German case is dual; the situation of large firms is very different from the situation of small firms. Insofar as the activity of private equity firms is concentrated on unquoted firms which are, for the most part, small or medium-sized firms, we retain, for Germany, the model of a bank-centred economy. The French case is more difficult to characterize and deserves further research.

Financing systems and activity of private equity firms
Levels of private equity investment vary both across time and countries (Gompers and Lerner, 1999; Jeng and Wells, 2000; Mayer, 2001), closely tracking business cycles in the economy generally. Theory and evidence also indicate a strong link between the size and liquidity of a nation's stock markets and the extent of its private equity investment market (Black and Gilson, 1998; Gompers and Lerner, 1999, 2001; Jeng and Wells, 2000; Mayer et al., 2005).

As private equity funds need financial markets where shares can be sold, a more active role of private equity funds can be expected in market-based economies, such as the UK, or, in a more restrictive way, in countries where the securities market is particularly active, such as France and Italy. On the contrary, as private equity firms are financial intermediaries, some of them being subsidiaries of banks, they should be more active in countries which are centred on financial institutions such as, traditionally, Germany, Italy, Spain and, to a lesser extent, France. In fact, taking into account the role of private equity funds underlines the limits of the traditional classification of financing systems based on the opposition between markets and banks. Financial intermediation and financial markets are indeed complementary tools rather than substitutes. More recently, another classification based on differences in legal systems has been introduced. It brings other elements to explain the differentiation of governance systems and the role of private equity firms.

7.1.2 Role of Private Equity Firms and Legal Systems

Typology of legal systems and position of countries studied
The classical analysis of financial systems has been recently amended. On the one hand, the development of banking activities on financial markets

shows some limits to the efficiency of this approach, which opposes banks to markets. On the other hand, according to many authors (Beck et al., 2003; La Porta et al., 1998; Levine, 1997, 1999; Paillard and Amable, 2002), this classification is indeed no longer effective to distinguish between financial systems. A new approach, developed by La Porta et al. (1998), takes into account the nature of the legal regimes, which offer a legal and regulatory framework for financial activities, to discriminate between countries. As financing is a matter of contracts and transfer of information, the nature of the legal regime is crucial. In particular, the ability of the legal system to protect creditors and shareholders and its enforcement power are essential criteria for the development of financial activities.

More precisely, La Porta et al. (1998) oppose two types of legal systems. The regime of common law, based on the Anglo-Saxon tradition, ensures a very strong protection to both shareholders and creditors, whereas the regime of French civil law, which derives from the Roman law, offers a low degree of protection to external investors as the power of enforcement of contracts[2] and the quality of information are low. The regimes of German and Scandinavian civil law are intermediate. In these two legal systems the power of enforcement of contracts is higher than in common law countries. For the quality of information, it is better in Scandinavia than in common law countries or in German civil law countries.

Using this typology, La Porta et al. (1998) studied 49 countries, members of the OECD, during the 1990s. According to their results, Italy and Spain belong, like France, to French civil law systems. On the contrary, the UK has a pure common law system. The German legal system is close to the French one but it is closer to the British system than Italy and Spain.

Legal systems and activity of private equity firms
The influence of legal systems on private equity firms has already been studied in the literature. According to Armour and Cumming (2006), the legal environment matters as much as the strength of stock markets. Studies often examine the impact of new regulations on venture capital. For example, Gompers and Lerner (1999) study the influence of new taxes and new processes of initial public offerings on venture capital in the USA. Other studies analyse the impact of differences in legal systems between countries on venture capital firms. Cumming et al. (2009) show, on a sample of 3848 portfolios of venture capital firms from 39 countries during the period 1971–2003, that differences in legal systems have a significant impact on the way venture capital firms screen and monitor businesses. More precisely, countries where shareholders are more protected are those where deals are originated the most quickly, with the strongest rate of

syndication and the highest frequency of private equity firms among the members of the boards.

A number of studies have used a range of 'legal' indices drawn from the work of La Porta et al. (1998) as independent variables to investigate whether legal rules affect venture capital financing (Jeng and Wells, 2000; Lerner and Schoar, 2005). Such factors seem to have little impact on venture capital investment activity, as the rights of private equity firms derive largely from their investment contracts, as opposed to general corporate law (Gompers and Lerner, 1999).

We can formulate two assumptions about the influence of legal systems on the contribution of private equity firms to transfers of ownership rights. On the one hand, the microeconomic approach of private equity firms justifies the existence of these institutions given they use sophisticated contracts which make it possible to limit the consequences of imperfection of information. As, in the French civil law system, information transparency is weak and the power of enforcement of contracts limited, we expect significant advantages of private equity firms in these countries and a more significant role of these institutions in the financing of transfers of ownership rights than in common law countries. On the other hand, as private equity firms are shareholders, we can expect their activity to be more developed in legal systems that protect shareholders the most. Their activity being based on complex contracts, it can be supposed easier in countries where the power of enforcement of contracts is higher. Lastly, as screening and monitoring rely on accounting and financial data, their practices are easier in countries where the quality of information is the best. Consequently, we can expect a more important activity of private equity firms in common law countries and, to a lesser extent, in Germany than in French civil law countries (France, Spain and Italy).

7.1.3 Role of Private Equity Firms and Ownership Structure

Classification of ownership structures and position of the countries studied
Differences in legal systems induce different firms' behaviours in terms of ownership and control, which are, according to Franks and Mayer (2001), the main distinguishing factors between corporate governance models. The ownership structure has been examined in many researches for many years so that we can differentiate the five countries studied.

According to La Porta et al. (1998), the concentration of shareholdings could be indeed a rational response to the lack of protection of investors in a given country. If the law does not protect owners against controllers, owners will seek to be controllers. The authors indicate that, in this situation, agency conflicts between managers and shareholders are not significant because large shareholders have at the same time the incentive and the ability to control the management. La Porta et al. (1998), however, point out that a high concentration of shareholdings leads to an agency problem between the majority shareholders and the minority ones.

Studies show that the structure of ownership is characterized in the UK by a dispersed ownership (Faccio and Lang, 2002). On the contrary, they find a higher concentration of shareholdings in Germany (Franks and Mayer, 2001), in France (Bloch and Kremp, 2003), in Italy (Barca, 1995) and in Spain (Crespí-Cladera and García-Cestona, 2003).

For the UK, ownership structure is characterized, historically, as for the USA, by a great number of quoted firms, the majority of them having a dispersed shareholding.

For Germany, the concentration of shareholdings is historically high because banks have played an active part in the German industrialization and they still hold large stakes in the largest companies (Roe, 1994). Important reforms, however, have been launched during the second half of the 1990s and they may call into question this situation. According to Nowak (2001), the observed increase in hostile takeovers and initial public offerings in Germany can be associated with the changes in German law which improve the situation of shareholders[3]. Wojcik (2003) studied the evolution of the ownership structure of large German firms between 1997 and 2001. He found a decrease in the level of ownership concentration but it remained nevertheless very high. Cross-holdings have become less important and financial sector institutions, including the most powerful ones, have lost their position as blockholders. These financial institutions have adopted behaviours of portfolio investors which are very different from the traditional bank-industry model. Wojcik (2003) documented a quick step of Germany towards the parameters of the Anglo-US corporate governance, but at the same time he identified areas of strong persistence.

For France, the distinctive characteristics of ownership structure are a high concentration, family shareholdings and the important role played by holding companies, the two last characteristics being closely dependent. Concentration of shareholdings is high for both private companies and public companies in the CAC 40 index. Family shareholdings are significant, whereas stakes held by banks, insurance companies and other financial institutions are relatively low, except for CAC 40 firms. Caby (2007) underlines that the percentage of shares held by foreign investors, mainly Anglo-Saxon institutional investors, has become very important: 36 per cent in 2000 (against 6 per cent in the USA, 9 per cent in the UK, 11 per cent in Japan, and 15 per cent in Germany). France is now the most internationalized Western country (by far) as regards to the shareholdings structure.

For Spain, concentration of ownership is high. Non-financial companies are the largest investors. Banks' shareholdings, historically high, have decreased but still remain significant in some sectors as banking and communication. State's shareholdings, that were significant in some sectors and many large companies until 1995, have almost disappeared since 1998 because of the process of privatization.

For Italy, traditionally, ownership structure is characterized by a high concentration with a small number of powerful industrial families holding large stakes in large companies. However, since the end of the 1990s new laws have been introduced in order to modify corporate governance. In particular, thanks to the Draghi law, investors' protection has improved, the development of the Italian financial market has accelerated and concentration of ownership has decreased.

La Porta et al. (1998) show that concentration of ownership varies according to the legal origin of a country (49 countries, measure of ownership structure in 1994). The highest concentration of ownership is observed in countries with a French civil law, with an average stake for the three main shareholders of about 54 per cent for the ten largest privately-held companies. The lowest concentration is observed in the countries with a German legal origin (German civil law), with an average of 34 per cent. Countries with a common law system are intermediate cases, with an average of 43 per cent. Results, however, differ somewhat within legal families. If we consider the average percentages per country, then the UK is characterized by a low concentration of ownership (19 per cent), France by an average concentration (34 per cent), and Germany, Italy and Spain by a high concentration (respectively, 48 per cent, 51 per cent and 58 per cent). The differences in the degree of ownership concentration between all the countries of German civil law and Germany is explained by the very weak concentration of ownership in the Eastern Asian countries where business law has been more influenced by the USA than by Germany, Austria or Switzerland (La Porta et al., 1998, p.1146). Pedersen and Thomsen's results (1997) are similar to 1990 data. Less than 10 per cent of the 100 largest German, Spanish and Italian companies are characterized by a dispersed ownership. This proportion is 61 per cent for the largest British companies. The position of France is intermediate: for 16 per cent of firms, ownership structure is dispersed.

Ownership structure and activity of private equity firms
How could differences in ownership structures influence the activity of private equity firms? To answer this question, we can formulate two alternative answers again.

Private equity funds are often minority investors. Indeed, only larger

LBOs lead private equity firms to become majority shareholders and the number of large LBOs remains limited (number of deals) in Europe. La Porta et al. (1999) show that an agency conflict exists between majority shareholders, those who have control, and minority ones in countries with a high concentration of ownership. The expropriation of minority shareholders appears all the easier since the concentration of ownership is larger in countries with poorer investors' protection. The activity of private equity firms, as minority shareholders, can be more difficult in these countries. Moreover, pyramidal structures and reciprocal stakes are more frequent in countries with poorer shareholders protection. These characteristics of the ownership structure, in particular its complexity, can dissuade private equity firms from investing in some firms because of expected agency costs. As a consequence, we expect a lower contribution of private equity firms to transfers of ownership rights in countries with a high concentration of ownership, except within the framework of larger LBOs.

An argument can contradict this hypothesis. Indeed, in order to support the development of their firms, owners are often constrained to raise equity and to sell shares to external investors. In this situation, the financing by private equity firms, except the case of larger LBOs, is a solution both to find external finance and to keep the control. Private equity firms provide capital to firms, many of them being family-owned businesses, to develop new projects by opening equity to only one investor, for a short period of time (between three and seven years). Moreover, thanks to the introduction of covenants, as the pre-emption one, in the shareholders' agreement, the initial owners can plan to buy the shares held by the private equity firm once the firm's development is achieved. Since maintaining the firm's control is an issue which is common to owners in all countries, we can expect an important contribution of private equity firms in all the countries studied, including those which are characterized by a high concentration of ownership.

Our analysis of the determinants of the contribution of private equity firms to transfers of ownership rights leads, for each group of determinants, to several alternative propositions. Our empirical study will make it possible to identify, for each group of arguments, the proposition which is corroborated.

7.2   DESCRIPTION OF DATA AND VARIABLES

We use a sample that contains deals, corresponding to sales of shares, completed between 1996 and 2004 in France, Germany, Italy, Spain and the UK, and reported by Zephyr, a database from Bureau Van Dijk. Descriptive statistics show the diversity of deals in the sample. The variables used allow us to examine the role played by private equity firms in the financing of transfers of ownership rights.

7.2.1 Population and Sample Selection

The Zephyr database from Bureau Van Dijk contains information on various types of deals including mergers and acquisitions, IPOs, joint ventures and private equity deals, with no minimum deal value. Over 260 000 transactions are included since 1996.[4] We select all deals corresponding to transfers of ownership rights, completed during the period 1 January 1996 to 5 May 2004. These deals are mergers (business combinations in which the number of companies decreases after the transaction), acquisitions of majority interests (all cases in which the acquirer ends up with 50 per cent or more of the votes of the target), transfers of minority stakes (below 50 per cent), LBOs and IPOs, which involve targets (companies being sold, or companies in which a stake is being sold) from France, Germany, Italy, Spain and the UK.

We thus obtain 47 942 deals. The availability of targets' turnover before the deal limits our sample size to 21 155 deals. Moreover, data on deal financing are available for only 7441 deals. In interpreting the results, we note that it is important to be aware that the availability and the quality of data may be better in the UK because of broader Zephyr coverage. Moreover, the coverage of a country seems to improve over time. The sample is redressed so that it is representative of the total population in Zephyr according to the target's country before the filters are applied to select the sample.

7.2.2 Description of Sample

The sample gathers 7441 deals for which data on deal financing are available. For each deal, we retain only the main target company, its first branch of industry and the most significant financing mode. In the sample 27.35 per cent of the deals retained are acquisitions of majority interests (above 50 per cent) whereas 30.47 per cent are mergers, 19.72 per cent transfers of minority stakes (below 50 per cent), 13.24 per cent LBOs (MBOs, MBIs and IBOs) and 9.21 per cent IPOs.

More than half the deals involve British targets (61.41 per cent), 14.45 per cent French targets, 13.13 per cent German targets, 6.47 per cent Spanish targets and less than 5 per cent Italian targets (4.54 per cent). Deals occur in several industries. Among them, the sector of computer, information technology and internet services is the most represented one (23.12 per cent), followed by personal, leisure and business services (14.96 per cent) and industrial, electric and electronic machinery (8.13 per cent). Of these deals 65.55 per cent involve unquoted targets. More than half the deals are mainly financed by capital increase, almost 40 per cent by private equity firms and less than 7 per cent by debt.

7.2.3   Description of Variables

We retain only the main answer for the variables that allow multiple answers. For instance, if a deal is financed by both capital increase and debt, then we retain only the main financing resource.

The deal financing variable aims to identify the presence of private equity firms in deals. It has three modalities:

- 'Presence of a private equity firm' when the deal financing contains an element of private equity activity either as development capital, an MBO, an MBI, an IBO or corporate venturing (when a normal company joins a round of development capital financing or when it owns one of the venture firms).
- 'Debt' when the deal is mainly financed through new bank facilities, a syndicated loan, loan notes or mezzanine debt.
- 'Capital increase' that gathers different methods for placing new shares and convertible bonds.

The 'target country' variable has five modalities: France, Germany, Italy, Spain and the UK. 'Quotation of target', 'quotation of acquirer', 'target activity' and 'acquirer country' are used as illustrative (or supplementary) variables. These variables intervene a posteriori in the characterization of the profiles to enrich their interpretation.

7.3   RESULTS

Descriptive analysis has shown the great number of deals involving British targets. On the 7441 deals for which data on deal financing are available, 39.02 per cent are mainly financed by a private equity firm. 49.79 per cent of the interventions carried out by private equity firms involve British targets, 23.92 per cent French targets, 13.73 per cent German targets, 7.61 per cent Spanish targets and 4.95 per cent Italian targets.

To study the link between target country and the deal financing by a

Table 7.1   Contingency table and independence test of target country by deal financing

Target Country		Deal financing			Total
		Private equity	Debt	Capital increase	
Frequency	France	694	24	356	1 075
Row %		64.6%	2.3%	33.2%	100.0%
Column %		23.9%	4.8%	8.8%	14.4%
Frequency	Germany	399	28	551	977
Row %		40.8%	2.9%	56.4%	100.0%
Column %		13.7%	5.5%	13.7%	13.1%
Frequency	Italy	144	15	179	338
Row %		42.6%	4.4%	53.1%	100.0%
Column %		5.0%	2.9%	4.4%	4.5%
Frequency	Spain	221	18	243	482
Row %		45.9%	3.7%	50.5%	100.0%
Column %		7.6%	3.5%	6.0%	6.5%
Frequency	UK	1 446	420	2 704	4 569
Row %		31.6%	9.2%	59.2%	100.0%
Column %		49.8%	83.3%	67.0%	61.4%
Frequency	Total	2 903	504	4 033	7 441
Row %		39.0%	6.8%	54.2%	100.0%
Column %		100.0%	100.0%	100.0%	100.0%

Note: Test Chi-square Value = 466.26 with 8 DF; Prob. (Chi-square > 466.26) = 0.0001; Test value = 99.99.

private equity firm,[5] we apply a factorial correspondence analysis (FCA) on the two-way table of target country by deal financing (Table 7.1). This analysis leads to two factorial axes, which account for 100 per cent of information to be summarized, that is, of the symmetrical association between target country and deal financing. The Pearson's chi-square test allows us to reject the assumption of independence: there is a significant relationship between target country and deal financing.

Figure 7.1 proposes a simultaneous representation on the first factorial plane of the FCA and illustrates the relations between the modalities of the variables. The first axis, which summarizes 93.81 per cent of the relation between these variables, reveals two notable dependences:

- a positive relation between the financing by private equity firms and French targets;
- a negative relation between debt financing and French targets.

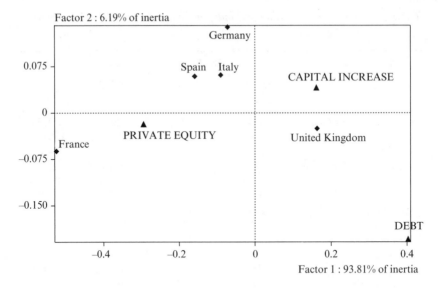

Figure 7.1   Factorial correspondence analysis representation

The second axis, which summarizes 6.19 per cent of information, reveals a negative relation between debt financing and German targets.

After this study of relationships we seek what differentiates and separates these countries according to deal financing. The results from discriminant analysis illustrate the proximities between the countries studied in their methods of financing of transfers of ownership (Figure 7.2 and Table 7.2). They show:

- the strong similarity between Germany, Italy and Spain;
- the notable resemblance between this group and the UK;
- the very specific case of France, which is opposite to other countries.

A ClustanGraphics tree summarizing the final classification of the five target countries studied according to the deal financing is shown in Figure 7.2. This was obtained using an Ascendant Hierarchical Classification (AHC) with Ward's criteria[6] on the results of FCA.

This analysis leads us to split the hierarchical tree into three groups of countries, which are characterized in Table 7.2. The three classes division was strengthened around the centres of gravity for the classes thanks to the k-means method.

The statistical description (using a 5 per cent significance level) of the content of each class of the three classes retained is given in Table 7.2. The

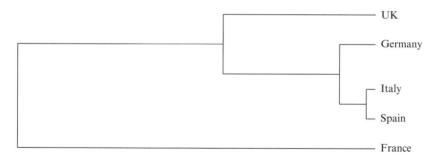

*Figure 7.2   Hierarchical tree of target countries according to deal
financing*

class standard profile is based upon comparisons of percentages of the
modality in the class (per cent of frequency in the class) and of this same
modality out of the class (per cent of frequency in the total sample) taking
into account the degree of inclusion of the class in the modality (per cent of
the class in the frequency). The selection of the most characteristic modalities that come out of each class stems from the gap between the relative
values of the class and the global values. These values are converted into
a test-value criterion (test-value) and are given in a decreasing order with
a lower than 5 per cent error risk (probability) which allows us to classify
the most characteristic modalities for each class.

- The first class corresponds to France. The 1075 deals on French
  targets are distinguished, relative to the whole sample, by a higher
  contribution of private equity financing and a lower use of debt and
  capital increase financing.
- The second class contains three countries (Germany, Italy and
  Spain). The 1797 deals in these countries are distinguished, relative to the whole sample, by a higher contribution of private equity
  financing and a lower use of debt financing.
- The third class corresponds to the UK. The 4569 deals on British
  targets are distinguished, relative to the whole sample, by a larger
  use of debt and capital increase financing and a lower contribution
  of private equity financing. The deals on British targets thus exhibit
  the opposite characteristics of the deals in the first class, that is, of
  those on French targets.

We introduce the target turnover as an illustrative (or supplementary)
variable into the discriminant analysis to specify the nature of the deals
that belong to each class. Results (not presented here) show that the two

Table 7.2   Characterization of classes by discriminant analysis

CLASS 1/3   FRANCE

Characteristic frequencies	% of frequency in total sample	% of frequency in the class	% of the class in the frequency	Test value	Proba-bility	Frequency
Private Equity	39.02	64.59	23.92	18.30	0.000	2903
Debt	6.78	2.25	4.81	−7.14	0.000	504
Capital increase	54.20	33.15	8.84	−15.01	0.000	4033

CLASS 2/3   GERMANY, ITALY AND SPAIN

Characteristic frequencies	% of frequency in total sample	% of frequency in the class	% of the class in the frequency	Test value	Proba-bility	Frequency
Private Equity	39.02	42.48	26.29	3.42	0.000	2903
Debt	6.78	3.35	11.94	−7.06	0.000	504

CLASS 3/3   UK

Characteristic frequencies	% of frequency in total sample	% of frequency in the class	% of the class in the frequency	Test value	Proba-bility	Frequency
Debt	6.78	9.19	83.25	10.91	0.000	504
Capital increase	54.20	59.17	67.03	10.81	0.000	4033
Private Equity	39.02	31.64	49.79	−16.41	0.000	2903

classes of deals involving French targets and German, Italian and Spanish targets are characterized by a higher target turnover than the sample average. On the contrary, the class of deals involving British targets is characterized by a lower target turnover than the sample average. This result may be explained by a broader Zephyr coverage for deals involving small companies in the UK.

The three classes obtained correspond to the traditional classification of the financing systems. We find an opposition between the UK, which is a pure market-based economy, and the other countries, which are rather bank-centred economies. According to our results, private equity firms play a more important role in the financing of transfers of shares in bank-centred economies. Hence, by focusing on all transfers of shares, we do not confirm the results of Black and Gilson (1998) and Jeng and Wells (2000) who focused on venture capital. This unexpected result can be explained by the fact that private equity firms can rely on mergers and acquisitions (M&A) markets (indeed most exits are by trade sales) and not so much on IPO markets. Our results show a radical opposition between the British and the French cases, suggesting that convergence towards the Anglo-American corporate governance system is not completed yet.

The three classes also correspond to the typology based on the origin of legal systems. Results suggest that private equity firms play a more important role in the financing of transfers of shares in civil-law countries. On the contrary, we show the lower contribution of private equity firms in the financing of transfers of shares in the UK. This can be explained by the existence of other modes of financing, in particular thanks to the importance of the financial markets. The role of private equity firms in civil-law countries confirms the need for financial intermediaries providing equity financing in the economies with a lower investor protection, in particular for minority ones, a lower quality of accounting standards and a lower quality of law enforcement.

Finally, the three classes obtained are in accordance with the expected opposition between the countries with a dispersed ownership and those with a higher concentration of ownership. Results show that private equity firms play a more important role in the economies with a higher concentration of ownership. This result validates the interpretation according to which private equity can be used by owners-managers to open the capital of their firms, possibly temporarily, in order to raise external funds while maintaining control.

7.4 CONCLUSION

In this study we consider private equity as a specific category, characterized by its unity (Glachant et al., 2008). We seek to explain the relative importance of private equity in the financing of transfers of ownership rights among five major European countries. We use differences in financial and legal systems to explain the differences in the findings. Based on a large sample of transfers of ownership rights in France, Germany, Italy, Spain and the United Kingdom, completed between 1996 and 2004, we find that the classification of deals matches the traditional classification of financing systems. We find indeed an opposition between the UK, which is a pure market-based economy, and the other countries, which are rather bank-centred economies.

According to our results, private equity firms play a more important role in the financing of transfers of shares in bank-centred economies. Hence, we do not confirm the results of Black and Gilson (1998) and Jeng and Wells (2000). This unexpected result can be explained by the fact that private equity firms can rely on M&A markets and not so much on IPO markets. Results also show that private equity firms play a more important role in the financing of transfers of shares in civil-law countries, which confirms the need for financial intermediaries providing equity financing in the economies with a lower investor protection, a lower quality of accounting standards and a lower quality of law enforcement. Results show that private equity firms play a more important role in the economies with a higher concentration of ownership. This result is in line with the proposition according to which private equity can be used by owners-managers to open the capital of their firms in order to raise external funds while maintaining control.

Interestingly, we find that the French case is very specific in terms of financing of transfers of shares. In France private equity firms play a more important role in the financing of transfers of ownership rights than in the other countries studied, suggesting that France's corporate landscape is particularly well suited to private equity. This result also supports the thesis of the specificity of the French corporate governance system. Moreover, the marked opposition between France and the UK in terms of deals' financing suggests that convergence towards the Anglo-American corporate governance system is not yet completed.

Finally, one suggestion for future research can be added. Our analysis relied on data from the five biggest European countries, where the value of private equity investments is relatively high. Hence future research might compare all European Union countries, with significantly less developed private equity markets.

ACKNOWLEDGEMENTS

We thank the Observatoire de l'Epargne Européenne (OEE – European Savings Institute) for financial support.

NOTES

1. This index is based on the ratios of development of the banking environment relative to financial markets (in terms of size, activity and effectiveness). The countries with the highest ratios of banking structures are centred on banks. The countries where the composite index is lower than the average are centred on markets.
2. In particular, the tax authorities can discuss some agreements and modify them deeply.
3. In 1998 a reform has reinforced the power of boards and made the use of stock-options easier.
4. The availability of data varies with types of deals.
5. We use the SPAD software.
6. Generalized Ward's Criteria: aggregation based on the criterion of the loss of minimal inertia.

REFERENCES

Allen, F. and D. Gale (2000), *Comparing Financial Systems,* Cambridge, MA: MIT Press.

Armour, J. and D.J. Cumming (2006), 'The legislative road to Silicon Valley', *Oxford Economic Papers*, **58**, 596–635.

Artola, C., A. Esteban, I. Hernando, M. Ortega, A. Sauvé, T. Sastre, A. Tiomo and A. Tournier (2002), 'Les entreprises industrielles françaises et espagnoles: étude comparative à partir des données comptables', *Bulletin de la Banque de France*, **106**, October, 51–72.

Barca, F. (1995), 'On corporate governance in Italy: issues, facts and agenda', manuscript, Bank of Italy, accessed 14 September 2009 at http://ssrn.com.

Beck, T., A. Demirgüç-Kunt and R. Levine (2003), 'Law and finance: why does legal origin matter?', *Journal of Comparative Economics*, **31** (4), 653–75.

Black, B.S. and R.J. Gilson (1998), 'Venture capital and the structure of capital markets: banks versus stock markets', *Journal of Financial Economics*, **47**, 243–77.

Bloch, L. and E.M. Kremp (2003), 'Ownership and voting power in France' in M. Becht (ed.), *The Control of Corporate Europe*, New York: Oxford University Press, pp. 106–27.

Caby, J. (2007), 'La convergence internationale des systèmes de gouvernance', in *Comités exécutifs: Voyage au cœur de la dirigeance*, Paris: Eyrolles.

Corbett, J. and J. Jenkinson (1996), 'The financing of industry, 1970–1989. An international comparison', *Journal of the Japanese and International Economics*, **10**, 71–96.

Crespí-Cladera, R. and M.A. García-Cestona (2003), 'Ownership and control of Spanish listed firms' in M. Becht (ed.), *The Control of Corporate Europe*, New York: Oxford University Press, pp. 207–27.

Cumming, D., D. Schmidt and U. Walz (forthcoming), 'Legality and venture governance around the world', *Journal of Business Venturing*.

Demirgüç-Kunt, A. and R. Levine (2001), 'Bank-based and market-based financial systems-cross-country comparisons', in *Financial Structure and Economic Growth: A Cross-country Comparison of Banks, Markets, and Development*, Cambridge, MA: MIT Press, pp. 81–140.

Faccio, M. and L. Lang (2002), 'The ultimate ownership of Western European corporations, *Journal of Financial Economics,* **65** (3), 365–95.

Franks, J. and C. Mayer (2001), 'Ownership and control of German corporations', *Review of Financial Studies*, **14** (4), 943–77.

Friderichs, H. and B. Paranque (2001), 'Structures of corporate finance in Germany and France', *Jahrbücher für Nationalökonomie und Statistik'*, Stuttgart, **221** (5–6), October, 648–7.

Glachant, J., J-H. Lorenzi and P. Trainar (2008), *Private equity et capitalisme français*, report of the Conseil d'Analyse Economique, La Documentation Française.

Gompers, P. and J. Lerner (1998), 'What drives venture fundraising?', *Brookings Papers on Economic Activity*, July, 149–92.

Gompers, P. and J. Lerner (1999), 'An analysis of compensation in the US venture capital partnership', *Journal of Financial Economics*, **51**, 3–44.

Gompers, P.A. and J. Lerner (2001), 'The venture capital revolution', *Journal of Economic Perspectives*, **15**, 145–68.

Jeng, L.A. and P. Wells (2000), 'The determinants of venture capital funding: evidence across countries', *Journal of Corporate Finance*, **6**, 241–89.

La Porta, R., F. Lopez-de-Silanes, A. Shleifer and R. Vishny (1998), 'Law and finance', *Journal of Political Economy*, **101**, 678–709.

La Porta, R., F. Lopez-de-Silanes and A. Shleifer (1999), 'Corporate ownership around the world', *Journal of Finance*, **54**, 471–517.

Lerner, J. and A. Schoar (2005), 'Does legal enforcement affect financial transactions? The contractual channel in private equity', *Quarterly Journal of Economics*, **120**, 223–46.

Levine, R. (1997), 'Financial development and economic growth: views and agenda', *Journal of Economic Literature*, **35**, 688–726.

Levine, R. (1999), 'Law, finance and economic growth', *Journal of Financial Intermediation*, **8** (1), 8–35.

Levine, R. (2002), 'Bank-based or market-based financial systems: which is better?', *Journal of Financial Intermediation*, **11** (4), 398–428.

Manigart, S., K. De Waele, M. Wright, K. Robbie, P. Desbrières, H. Sapienza and A. Beekman (2002), 'The determinants of the required returns in venture capital investments: a five-country study', *Journal of Business Venturing*, **17**, 291–312.

Mayer, C. (1988), 'New issues in corporate finance', *European Economic Review*, **32**, 1167–88.

Mayer, C. (2001), 'Institutional investment and private equity in the UK', Oxford Financial Research Centre working paper no. 2001fe10, Oxford.

Mayer, C., K. Schoors and Y. Yafeh (2005), 'Sources of funds and investment activities of venture capital funds: evidence from Germany, Israel, Japan and the UK', *Journal of Corporate Finance*, **11**, 586–608.

Nowak, E. (2001), 'Recent developments in German capital markets and corporate governance', *Journal of Applied Corporate Finance,* **14** (3), 35–48.

Paillard, S. and B. Amable (2002), 'Intégration européenne et systèmes financiers: y a-t-il convergence vers le système anglo-saxon?', in *Intégration européenne et institutions économiques*, Brussels: De Boeck Université, pp. 43–68.

Pedersen, T. and S. Thomsen (1997), 'European patterns of corporate ownership: a twelve-country study', *Journal of International Business Studies*, **28** (4), 759–78.

Roe, M.J. (1994), 'Some differences in corporate governance in Germany, Japan, and America', in T. Baum, T. Bauxbaum and K.J. Hope (eds), *Institutional Investors and Corporate Governance*, Berlin: De Gruyter.

Schmidt, R.H., A. Hackethal and M. Tyrell (1998), 'Disintermediation and the role of banks in Europe: an international comparison', *Journal of Financial Intermediation*, **8**, 36–67.

Schmidt, R.H., A. Hackethal and M. Tyrell (2002), 'The convergence of financial systems in Europe', *Schmalenbach Business Review*, special issue, **1**, 7–53.

Wojcik, D. (2003), 'Change in the German model of corporate governance: evidence from Blockholdings, 1997–2001', *Environment and Planning A*, **35** (8), 1431–58.

PART III

Accounting for the interplay between the individual and the organizational levels and the firm's behaviour and performance

'The analysis of post-entry strategies by start-ups is rather rare in the literature' (Fosfuri and Giarrantana, 2004, p. 2). Yet the behaviour of the entrepreneur may be just as important as the founding conditions (the firm performance being the product of various combinations of individual characteristics of the entrepreneur and organizational or environmental factors (Lumpkin and Dess, 1996, 2001)) when regarding the survival of the firm (Covin and Slevin, 1991). Recent firm studies focus on entrepreneurial orientation (proactiveness, innovativeness, risk taking propensity) and show that this behaviour increases the financial performance (Keh et al., 2007; Stam and Elfring, 2008; Wiklund and Shepherd, 2005) or the growth of the firm (Moreno and Casillas, 2008).

In the first contribution, Domingo García Pérez de Lema and Antonio Duréndez (Chapter 8) identify organizational culture and assess the relationship between organizational culture, particularly regarding innovative culture, management control systems (MCS) use, and their effects on performance. Using a sample of 89 young Spanish SMEs they find that innovative culture and use of management control systems have a positive effect on firm performance.

Jean Bonnet and Nicolas Le Pape (Chapter 9) show the link between the post-entry strategies of new entrepreneurs and the duration of the firm in the population of new French firms during 1995–7. Using a Cox model (proportional hazard model) it is shown that firms which adopt an entrepreneurial behaviour are more likely to survive, so a proactive posture constitutes an efficient strategy for the development of the firm.

Csaba Deák and Stephania Testa (Chapter 10) use the concept of intellectual capital in two dimensions, regional and organizational, to examine the food industries in Northwest Italy and North Hungary. Their research confirms that different behaviours exist and that heterogeneity depends on individual-level entrepreneurial characteristics, and not only on a firm's knowledge bases or position within networks.

Franck Bailly and Karine Chapelle (Chapter 11) explore the non-profit entrepreneurship in the French region of High-Normandy. This type of entrepreneurship is based more on social motivation and does not seem to be more constrained than for-profit organizations. However non-profit organizations seem to attract entrepreneurs who are less endowed with personal financial resources. These entrepreneurs are able to establish their organizations through their managerial and high social qualities (Chapelle, 2008).

REFERENCES

Chapelle, K. (2008), 'Non-profit and for-profit entrepreneurship: a trade-off under liquidity constraint', *International Entrepreneurship and Management Journal Online,* 22 March.

Covin, J.G. and D.P. Slevin (1991), 'A conceptual model of entrepreneurship as firm behaviour', *Entrepreneurship Theory and Practice,* **16** (1), Fall, 7–25.

Fosfuri, A. and M.S. Giarratana (2004), '"Product strategies and startups". Survival in turbulent industries: evidence from the security software industry', Universidad Carlos III. Departamento de Economía de la Empresa business economics working papers no. wb044816.

Keh, H.T, T.T.M. Nguyen and H.P. Ng (2007), 'The effects of entrepreneurial orientation and marketing information on the performance of SMEs', *Journal of Business Venturing,* **22**, 592–611.

Lumpkin, G.T. and G.G. Dess (1996), 'Clarifying the entrepreneurial orientation construct and linking it to performance', *Academy of Management Review,* **21**, 135–72.

Lumpkin, G.T. and G.G. Dess (2001), 'Linking two dimensions of entrepreneurial orientation to firm performance: the moderating role of environment and industry life cycle', *Journal of Business Venturing,* **16**, 429–51.

Moreno, A.M. and J.C. Casillas (2008), 'Entrepreneurial orientation and growth of SMEs: a causal model', *Entrepreneurship Theory and Practice,* **32**, 507–28.

Stam, W. and T. Elfring (2008), 'Entrepreneurial orientation and new venture performance: the moderating role of intra- and extraindustry social capital', *Academy of Management Journal,* **51**, 97–111.

Wiklund, J. and D. Shepherd (2005), 'Entrepreneurial orientation and small business performance: a configurational approach', *Journal of Business Venturing,* **20**, 71–91.

8. Innovative culture, management control systems and performance in young SMEs

Domingo García Pérez De Lema and Antonio Duréndez

8.1 INTRODUCTION

Research focus on young firms within the field of entrepreneurship is a common topic, due to the relevance and potential for growth, innovation and economic force (Biga et al., 2008). The analysis of young firms' performance, principally growth, has received substantial empirical and theoretical attention (Steffens et al., 2006). Usually, young firms should be inside the period of expansion, so these firms are characterized by their ability to identify new business opportunities (Penrose, 1959). According to the knowledge-based view of the firm young firms accumulate knowledge through a learning process which constitutes the driving force for growth in order to achieve a sustainable competitive advantage. This is seen as the source of change and dynamism in society and the economy (McQuaid, 2002; Spender and Grant, 1996). Furthermore, young firms have cognitive learning advantages in entirely new markets because of fewer systemic rigidities (Autio et al., 2000). Another characteristic of young firms is they have several objectives, such us: maintaining autonomy, high-quality innovation, new opportunity detection and solid growth (Fischer and Reuber, 2004).

Analysing young firms is particularly relevant due to the high level of failure this kind of firm shows (Brown et al., 1990; Philips and Kirchhoff, 1989). Previous economic research literature confirms that bankruptcy is inversely related to the age of the company (Audretsch and Mahmood, 1994; Dunne et al., 1988; Mata and Portugal, 1994; Philips and Kirchhoff, 1989). According to Henderson (1999) there are different approaches to analyse the relationship between business age and failure: (1) liability of newness approach, failure is higher at the start-up stage; (2) liability of adolescence approach, failure reaches the maximum some years after the business foundation and decreases subsequently; and (3) liability of obsolescence, failure is expected to increase in accordance with the growth of the firm. Thus it is relevant that young firms are aware of the importance to develop an organizational culture to innovate, in order to get a competitive advantage and to survive. Innovation lets companies achieve sustainable advantages (Vermeulen, 2004) and represents a key factor for economic growth (Cheng and Tao, 1999). Organizational culture stands for a collection of beliefs, expectations and values shared by the people in a company (Leal Millan, 1991). These beliefs and expectations generate behavioural rules which make the company different. The culture encompasses values and preferences about the goals the company must achieve (De Long and Fahey, 2000). The most studied hypothesis by academics is that broadly established cultures strengthen business performance (Rosenthal and Masarech, 2003). This hypothesis is based on the idea that organizations benefit from having motivated employees with common goals (Kotter and Heskett, 1992).

Management control systems (MCS) are crucial elements in the decision-making process. According to Henri (2006), an extensive literature argues that organizational culture has an important effect on MCS. In addition, a well-developed and structured information system is a sustainable competitive advantage (Barney, 1991; Morikawa, 2004). As management decisions should be based on unbiased information, managerial techniques such us financial planning, cost accounting and financial diagnosis should be common tools in the decision-making process. Nevertheless, several studies show that management accounting systems are not broadly used in small and medium sized enterprises (SMEs) (Chenhall and Langfield-Smith, 1998a; Choe, 1996).

This study analyses the influence of innovative culture and management control systems on the performance of young SMEs. The research shows the results of an empirical study on a sample of 89 Spanish young SMEs. The main questions this work aims to answer are the following: what is the culture of the young SMEs? How does organizational culture influence young SMEs' performance?, Do MCS help young SMEs to achieve competitive success? Does innovative culture improve firm performance?

The chapter is organized as follows. First, we determine the theoretical framework. We make a review of the empirical literature, and then we define our hypotheses. Second, we explain the methodology used in the empirical study: sample description and variables definition. Third, we carry out the analysis of results and finally, we include the main conclusions.

8.2   THEORETICAL FRAMEWORK AND EMPIRICAL EVIDENCE

8.2.1   Organizational Culture and Performance

The organizational culture is a key factor that can help companies to achieve the planned goals. If managers change the values, rules and customs of the company, they could modify employees' behaviour and attitude, leading to an improvement in the firm performance (Rosenthal and Masarech, 2003). The central issue associated with organizational culture is its linkage with organizational performance. An increasing body of evidence supports a relationship between an organization's culture and the firm performance. Considering the process of economic globalization, firms cannot provide sustainable performance unless an organization's culture and people are fully prepared and aligned to support changes. Culture is what distinguishes truly high-performing organizations from the pack (Jeuchter et al., 1998).

In this sense, organizational culture is becoming a key managerial instrument to enhance performance. On the one hand, companies constantly look for a sustainable competitive advantage. Moreover, organizations depend on innovation to grow and to obtain a high performance. The most studied hypothesis in the literature is that broadly established cultures strengthen organizational performance. In support of this argument, some empirical studies show that companies with well-established cultures achieve higher performance than those characterized by weak cultures (Gordon and Di Tomaso, 1992; Kotter and Heskett, 1992). Indeed, Kotter and Heskett (1992) reveal that during a ten-year period companies that deliberately designed their cultures, obtained higher performance than those that did not have a well-developed culture.

Sonrensen (2002) shows that companies with strong cultures face a trade-off regarding their adaptation skills to the changing environment. The well-developed organizational cultures facilitate the stability of the performance in uncertainty environments. However, as the volatility increases, these benefits dramatically decrease. This pattern is consistent with the main trade-off between exploration and exploitation observed by March (1991). This author suggests that companies with strong cultures are extremely good at taking advantage of established competences, but they find difficulties in discovering new competences that best fit with the changing environment conditions. These results suggest that the best strategy for companies would be to develop cultures clearly based on an exploratory learning attitude and innovation (Gordon and Di Tomaso, 1992).

The innovative culture is based on values that enhance a shared view of the organization. Managers and employees feel part of a unique project, where benefits and individual improvements bear directly on benefits and improvements of the team and, in short, on the organization as a whole. Nemeth (1997) considers that innovative culture strengthens the cohesion, the loyalty and some clear rules of attitudes and appropriate behaviours. Furthermore, innovative culture promotes the autonomy of working teams, the managers' support to research projects, departmental relationships, trust, sincerity and consideration, as well as recompense and recognition (Shirivastava and Souder, 1987). This type of culture decreases the resistance to change and facilitates the introduction of new technologies. In this framework the managerial leadership is a key factor in the creation of a cultural context and an organizational structure that encourages innovation (Van de Ven, 1986). On the contrary, in a non-innovative culture the feeling of individualism prevails in the team. The employees feel like isolated agents who defend individual goals, thus the consideration of the organization as a whole is lost. The employees are unable to assess the consequences of their individual actions on the rest of the organization. Their rules and customs enhance the organizational routines (Argyris, 1977). The employees wait for somebody to tell them what to do, instead of having the initiative to carry out actions for themselves. In addition, the management stresses the values of stability (even opposing the changes) and rejoicing in past successes.

In the case of young entrepreneurs is broadly recognized the innovative character and the contribution to increase innovation and its effects on business performance (Acs and Audretsch, 1990). Concretely, Johannessen et al. (1999), who developed their study with young (ten years old or less) SMEs, found a trade-off between successful innovations and performance. Yli-Renko et al. (2001) showed a positive relationship between innovation (through new product development) and performance (sales growth) for young English firms that were not more than ten years old.

These arguments lead to the formulation of the following hypothesis:

Hypothesis 1: The innovative culture influences positively the young SME's performance.

8.2.2   Management Control Systems (MCS) and Performance

Once the culture has been defined, the second step implies using the MCS to transmit and reinforce the culture of the firm throughout the organization to manage strategic and operational decisions and actions (Flamholtz, 1983). The relationships between an organization's control system and culture are two-way because once created, they have an impact on the way values are subsequently changed. This means that culture is regarded as something manageable though partly created through the passage of the organization (Herath et al., 2006).

Firms need to establish control tools to help managers make the right decisions. The strong competition due to market globalization and technological change is forcing firms to develop MCS (AECA, 2005). MCS balance the trade-off between creative innovation and predictable goal achievement, thus MCS address the organizational antagonism between control and flexibility (Simons, 1995a). A cost accounting system allows managers to elaborate information regarding inventories assessment, cost control, income-cost-benefit analysis, and products and market performance for the decision-making process. Financial planning lets firms assess their financial requirements in advance. Thus, firms are able to efficiently consider the different financing choices. Finally, financial analysis helps the company to realize what its strengths and weaknesses are, as far as liquidity, solvency, indebtedness and performance are concerned.

Kennedy and Affleck-Graves (2001) show how the implementation of activity based costing systems has a positive effect on performance. These authors compare two matched samples composed of 37 British companies. Those companies that implemented cost systems significantly achieved a 27 per cent higher performance than those without this system. Bright et al. (1992) find a significant relationship between the development of new cost techniques and the improvement of product performance. Chenhall and Langfield-Smith (1998b), on a sample of 140 Australian manufacturing companies, find evidence on the positive relationship between MCS' use and company performance. Adler et al. (2000) show, after analysing 165 New Zealand manufacturing companies, that MCS positively influence product performance. Finally, McMahon and Davies (1994) state a positive correlation between amplitude and frequency of accounting information elaborated by the company and the net profit per employee.

MCS are not only tools used in a planning-and-control cycle, but MCS are also used by firms to foster and control innovation, creativity, change and learning (Henri, 2004). According to Miller and Friesen (1982), apart from getting information by means of MCS, managers correctly assess that this information is essential. For example, if managers ignore relevant information that indicates the need to innovate, then this innovation will not be implemented. Planning and correct information analyses are key aspects for the decision-making process. The greater the analysis made by managers, the greater the tendency to investigate the real roots of the problems and to work on the best alternative solutions. Thus, the chance of discovering and implementing innovation opportunities will increase. Dávila (2000) positively connects MCS with innovation and performance.

Finally, MCS are especially necessary to ensure innovation effectiveness (Simons, 1995b). Using data from a sample of 120 Spanish companies, Bisbe and Otley (2004) show that the greater the use of MCS, the higher the effect of innovation on SME performance. Shields and Young (1994) find, on a sample of 160 US companies, that MCS (budgets and management accounting) increase innovation effectiveness.

Taking into account these premises, this research considers the second hypothesis:

Hypothesis 2: The use of MCS positively influences young SME's performance.

8.3   METHODOLOGY

8.3.1   Sample

Data were obtained from the project 'Introducción de la cultura innovadora en las empresas', funded by the European Union. This database contains qualitative and quantitative information gathered through a self-administered questionnaire that was addressed to the company manager. The fieldwork was developed from May to June 2003. Our target population was composed of companies whose number of employees varies between ten and 250. The distribution of companies in the population has been considered starting from the 'Directorio de Empresas del Instituto Nacional de Estadística' (Business Directory). The sample is composed of 89 young Spanish SMEs up to ten years old. We follow the same criteria of previous research studies that consider firms to be young when not more than ten years old (Beckman et al., 2007; Certo et al., 2001; Covin and Slevin, 1990; Yli-Renko et al., 2001).

To test for non-response bias, we use late respondents as surrogates for non-respondents (Nwachukv et al., 1997). Responses of firms answering to the initial mailing (85 per cent of the sample) were tested with those responding to the follow-up (15 per cent of the sample). No responses were significantly different between the two groups using t and chi-squared tests for all the variables in the models.

8.3.2   Measurement of Variables

Organizational culture
This concept is measured by the 'Organizational Culture Assessment Instrument' (OCAI) proposed by Cameron and Quinn (1999). These

authors identify four cultures: market, hierarchy, clan and adhocracy, in relation to two dimensions. The first dimension shows the company orientation towards control, stability and order. The companies within this dimension fluctuate between, on the one hand, those with high stability, predictable and order emphasis and, on the other hand, those maintaining high flexibility levels, organic structures and adaptation skills. The second dimension concerns the internal versus external business orientation. Considering these two variables, we obtain four types of culture.

The clan culture is typical in companies that look for internal control of the organization but with flexibility, worrying about their employees and showing a special customer concern. The adhocratic culture is related to companies focused on external aspects of the organization, looking for a high degree of flexibility and innovation. The market culture appears in those organizations that stress the external orientation of the business, but consider at the same time the need for control and internal stability. The hierarchical culture pays special attention to internal aspects requiring control and stability. The literature states that in any organization, in spite of sharing values of the four cultures, there is usually one culture prevailing over the others. In the questionnaire managers were asked to distribute 100 points among four possible answers in relation to 'company definition', 'managerial style', 'shared values by personnel' and 'key issues for the business success' (Table 8.1).

The total value of the clan culture is obtained by adding the relative points of the answers 'a' for the four questions; the total value of the adhocratic culture implies the sum of the points associated with the answers to the 'b' questions; the total value of the market culture contains the points to the answers to the 'c' questions; and the total value of the hierarchical culture is the sum of the answers to the 'd' questions:

$$\text{Clan culture value} = (a1 + a2 + a3 + a4) = P_1$$
$$\text{Adhocratic culture value} = (b1 + b2 + b3 + b4) = P_2$$
$$\text{Market culture value} = (c1 + c2 + c3 + c4) = P_3$$
$$\text{Hierarchical culture value} = (d1 + d2 + d3 + d4) = P_4$$

Innovative culture
The values, rules and customs of an innovative culture are in accord with those of the adhocratic and clan cultures. Innovative companies hold a clear and flexible orientation and are prone to changes. For this reason, a new variable, 'innovative culture', has been calculated through a mathematical algorithm. According to the results of a panel of organizational research experts, this algorithm is composed of three components that

Table 8.1   Organizational culture measurement

	Present
Company definition:	**Present**
a.1) It is like a great family. People share a lot of values with the others	
b.1) It is a dynamic and adventurous firm. People defend their ideas and take risks	
c.1) It is managed to obtain results. People are very competitive and focused to accomplish with targets	
d.1) It is a very hierarchical, formalized and structured company. There are procedures and rules for any operation	
TOTAL	**100**
Company managerial style:	**Present**
a.2) To promote working as a team, consensus and participation	
b.2) To promote individual initiatives, risk taking and innovation	
c.2) To promote aggressive competitiveness and the achievement of ambitious goals	
d.2) To promote employment stability and less uncertainty	
TOTAL	**100**
Shared values by personnel:	**Present**
a.3) Loyalty, commitment, trust and team work	
b.3) Commitment to innovation and continuous development	
c.3) Aggressiveness, winner attitude and achievement of planned goals	
d.3) Respect towards established rules and company policies as well as accomplishment with organizational hierarchy	
TOTAL	**100**
Key issues for the business success:	**Present**
a.4) Team work, commitment and employee satisfaction	
b.4) Development of new and innovative products	
c.4) Market entrance and market share. Maintain leadership in the market	
d.4) Efficiency, manufacturing planning and low costs strategy	
TOTAL	**100**

Source: Cameron and Quinn (1999).

measure the value of the innovative culture. This variable ranges between 0 and 1. The more innovative the company, the higher the variable value:

$$\text{Innovative culture} = (Z_1 + Z_2 \times 100 + Z_3 \times 100)/300$$

where:

Z_1 reflects the total importance of clan (P_1) and adhocratic (P_2) cultures. $Z_1 = P_1 + P_2$.

Z_2 measures the importance of adhocratic culture in relation to the sum of cultures that conforms to the innovative culture (adhocratic and clan cultures). This component is needed because the panel of experts consider that the adhocratic culture is more important than the clan culture in the definition of the innovative culture. $Z_2 = P_2/(P_1 + P_2)$.

Z_3 includes the difference between the importance given to both clan and adhocratic cultures. According to the panel of experts, the smaller the difference between adhocratic and clan cultures, the more innovative the company. $Z_3 = 1 - [(|P_2 - P_1|)/(P_1 + P_2)]$.

Management Control Systems (MCS)
In order to analyse the level of MCS' use, we measure the subjective perception of the manager about three items, through a five-point Likert scale. The items considered are management accounting techniques, short-term cash-flow budgets and financial analysis. The variable is the average of those three items, ranging from 1 to 5. This type of measure has been used by Choe (2004) and Hoque and James (2000). The reliability of the scales (Cronbach's Alpha), verifying the consistency of the variable, reaches the value of 0.751. Furthermore, by means of a factorial analysis (explained variance: 67.36; sig. Bartlett: 0.000; KMO: 0.676), we prove that the previous indicators summed up in a single factor, are able to properly reflect the considered measure about the use of MCS.

Performance
We have used the performance variables proposed by Quinn and Rohrbaugh (1983). These authors set a framework for the organizational analysis, distinguishing three dimensions within organizational efficiency. The first dimension relates to the organizational approach, from an internal point of view, based on a 'micro' perspective about good understanding and development of personnel, to an external one, in which emphasis relies on a 'macro' level of business success. The second dimension is focused on the organizational structure, emphasizing on business stability and flexibility. The third dimension is based on organizational means and aims. Four performance models arise from the combination of these three dimensions.

● Model of internal processes: this model is focused on internal control, giving high importance to the communication of information and considering stability and control as the main goals.

- Open system model: this model is laid down on external flexibility, considering growth, resources and external support as the main goals.
- Rational model: this model is related to control from an external point of view, focusing on efficiency and productivity criteria.
- Model of human relations: this model pays attention to flexibility from an internal point of view, with the purpose of human resources development within the firm.

In order to assess these models, 12 items are used (three items per model) through a Likert's scale from 1 to 5. We build a global performance variable, as the average of the 12 items, with a theoretical rank from 1 to 5. Table 8.2 shows the items used as well as the reliability of the scales and the statistic tests.

Table 8.2   Performance variables

Indicate the evolution of the following aspects in your company in the last two years in relation to the competition: (1 = Very unfavourable situation, 5 = Very favourable situation)		Scale Reliability
Model of internal processes	● Product quality improvement ● Internal processes coordination improvement ● Personnel tasks organization improvement	Cronbach α = 0.784 Factorial: 1 factor Explained variance: 70.22 Sig. Bartlett: 0.000 KMO: 0.657
Open system model	● Customer satisfaction increase ● Increase in the ability to adapt to market needs ● Improvement of corporate and products image	Cronbach α = 0.694 Factorial: 1 factor Explained variance: 62.06 Sig. Bartlett: 0.000 KMO: 0.660
Rational model	● Market share increase ● Profitability increase ● Productivity increase	Cronbach α = 0.805 Factorial: 1 factor Explained variance: 72.13 Sig. Bartlett: 0.000 KMO: 0.698
Model of human relations	● Personnel motivation increase ● Staff turnover decrease (voluntary resignation) ● Absenteeism decrease	Cronbach α = 0.775 Factorial: 1 factor Explained variance: 69.34 Sig. Bartlett: 0.000 KMO: 0.605

8.4   RESULTS

Before we start testing the research hypotheses, a primary objective is to determine the prevalent type of culture for the young SMEs. In Table 8.3 we can observe that values coming from the clan culture are predominant (reaching a mean value of 34.99 over a maximum of 100). This type of culture is characterized by having a managerial style which promotes working as a team, consensus and participation, followed by a hierarchical culture (respect towards established rules and company policies as well as accomplishment with organizational hierarchy) reaching a mean value of 24.78. Nevertheless, market culture (aggressive competitiveness and the achievement of ambitious goals) and adhocratic culture (individual initiatives, risk taking and innovation) maintain a less significant influence on the behaviour of young SMEs.

To verify the effect of organizational culture (hypothesis 1) and MCS' use (hypothesis 2) on young SMEs' performance, we use hierarchical regression analysis. This method allows us to introduce the independent variables in different steps, so that the effects of each group of independent variables can be analysed. In our case, first we introduce the culture variables, and later on we introduce the MCS' use variable. The standardized coefficients express the expected change in the dependent variable for each variation unit in the independent variables. The comparison between the two models is carried out through the change in R^2, which indicates if the new variable (MCS's use), incorporated to the second model, has influence on the analysed dependent variables (*Performance*).

Table 8.3   Organizational culture of young SMEs

Culture of young firms (n = 89)	Mean value	Standard deviation
Clan Culture (C)	34.99	15.68
Adhocratic Culture (A)	19.53	9.11
Market Culture (M)	20.66	11.51
Hierarchical Culture (H)	24.78	11.80

Note: *p≤0.1; **p≤0.05; ***p≤0.01.
Wilcoxon rank-sum test:
Difference C−A: ***
Difference C−M: ***
Difference C−H: ***
Difference A−M: n.s.
Difference A−H: **
Difference M−H: ***

$$\text{Model 1: } Performance_i = b_0 + b_1 \cdot culture_i + \varepsilon_i$$
$$\text{Model 2: } Performance_i = b'_0 + b'_1 \cdot culture_i + b_2 MCS + \varepsilon'_i$$

Where *Performance_i* corresponds to five types of performance considered (internal process approach; open systems approach; rational goal approach; human relations and global performance). *Culture_i* identifies the five types of culture considered (clan, adhocratic, hierarchical, market and innovative cultures).

We estimate one model for each type of culture (Table 8.4). We note in all the models independent variables have a variance inflation factor (VIF) below 1.106, so we discard the presence of multicollinearity. The test of White (1980) has not rejected homoskedasticity in all the models. Therefore, coefficients show consistent standard error, which ensures the relevance and reliability of our estimations.

With regard to hypothesis 1, relating to the global performance measure, results show that adhocratic ($p < 0.1$) and innovative culture (as a mix of adhocratic and clan cultures) ($p < 0.05$) have a positive influence on global performance. We cannot obtain significant evidence regarding the relationship between clan, market and hierarchical culture and global performance. Therefore, we can accept our hypothesis that considers that those young companies with more innovative cultures achieve a higher performance.

If we analyse in detail the different kinds of performance, we can observe that the major effects of innovative and adhocratic cultures appear within the internal processes and open system performance models. These results are shown in Table 8.4 for each Model 1, where the standardized coefficients associated with the adhocratic culture variable are positive and significant for the Model 1 of internal processes ($p < 0.01$); and open system ($p < 0.05$). The same behaviour occurs in relation to the coefficients associated with the innovative culture variable (internal processes 0.339***; open system 0.261**).

Additionally, we find a negative and significant relationship between hierarchical culture and performance of internal processes. Where the standardized coefficients related to the hierarchical culture variable are negative and significant for the Model 1 estimations (internal processes −0.337***). Our results are in line with those of Bhaskaran (2006), Hsueh and Tu (2004), Rosenau et al. (1996), Morcillo (1997), DiBella and Nevis (1998) and Tushman and O'Reilly (2002), who support the thesis that innovative firms perform better.

Model 2 reveals the results of the regressions to test the use of MCS (Table 8.4). These results validate the positive and significant effect of MCS' use on performance, once the influence of culture has been taken

Table 8.4   *Culture and MCS' use influences on firm performance*

Model of Performance

	Internal processes		Open system		Rational		Human relations		Global performance	
	Model 1	Model 2	Model 1	Model 2	Model 1	Model 2	Model 1	Model 2	Model 1	Model 2
Clan	0.123	0.083	0.079	0.043	0.001	−0.032	0.021	−0.013	0.068	0.020
Culture	(1.155)	(0.821)	(0.737)	(0.417)	(0.009)	(−0.310)	(0.195)	(−0.121)	(0.640)	(0.207)
MCS		0.341***		0.307***		0.285***		0.288***		0.412***
		(3.365)		(2.976)		(2.735)		(2.766)		(4.166)
Highest VIF		1.014		1.014		1.014		1.014		1.014
F	1.333	6.406***	0.543	4.724**	0.000	3.741**	0.038	3.845**	0.410	8.920***
R^2	0.015	0.130	−0.005	0.078	−0.11	0.059	−0.011	0.061	−0.007	0.153
Change R^2		0.115***		0.093***		0.080***		0.082***		0.167***

Model of Performance

	Internal processes		Open system		Rational		Human relations		Global performance	
	Model 1	Model 2	Model 1	Model 2	Model 1	Model 2	Model 1	Model 2	Model 1	Model 2
Adhocratic	0.293***	0.277***	0.261**	0.247**	0.056	0.043	−0.014	−0.027	0.185*	0.166*
Culture	(2.860)	(2.871)	(2.521)	(2.491)	(0.523)	(0.414)	(−0.127)	(−0.262)	(1.758)	(1.720)
MCS		0.337***		0.300***		0.279***		0.287***		0.406***
		(3.494)		(3.030)		(2.697)		(2.781)		(4.204)
Highest VIF		1.002		1.002		1.002		1.002		1.002
F	8.180***	10.722***	6.354**	8.065***	0.274	3.783**	0.016	3.875**	3.092*	10.680***
R^2	0.075	0.181	0.057	0.138	−0.008	0.059	−0.011	0.061	0.023	0.180
Change R^2		0.114***		0.090***		0.078***		0.082***		0.165***

Table 8.4 (continued)

Model of Performance

	Internal processes		Open system		Rational		Human relations		Global performance	
	Model 1	Model 2	Model 1	Model 2	Model 1	Model 2	Model 1	Model 2	Model 1	Model 2
Market Culture	-0.050	-0.095	-0.152	-0.194*	-0.005	-0.041	-0.002	-0.039	-0.63	-0.116
	(-0.464)	(-0.936)	(-1.432)	(-1.914)	(-0.047)	(-0.391)	(-0.023)	(-0.372)	(-0.586)	(-1.183)
MCS		0.362***		0.336***		0.286***		0.291***		0.428***
		(3.578)		(3.321)		(2.746)		(2.297)		(4.366)
Highest VIF		1.016		1.016		1.016		1.016		1.016
F	0.215	6.522***	2.051	6.657***	0.002	3.772**	0.001	3.912**	0.343	9.738***
R^2	-0.009	0.112	0.012	0.114	-0.011	0.059	-0.11	0.062	-0.088	0.166
Change R^2		0.129***		0.111***		0.081***		0.083***		0.181***

Model of Performance

	Internal processes		Open system		Rational		Human relations		Global performance	
	Model 1	Model 2	Model 1	Model 2	Model 1	Model 2	Model 1	Model 2	Model 1	Model 2
Hierarchical Culture	-0.337***	-0.253**	-0.154	-0.62	-0.040	0.052	-0.015	-0.081	-0.171	-0.047
	(-3.342)	(-2.467)	(-1.454)	(-0.593)	(-0.375)	(0.475)	(-0.144)	(0.746)	(-1.617)	(-0.460)
MCS		0.272***		0.292***		0.297***		0.311***		0.399***
		(2.653)		(2.716)		(2.734)		(2.874)		(3.874)
Highest VIF		1.106		1.106		1.106		1.106		1.106
F	11.168***	9.491***	2.113	4.822***	0.141	3.812**	0.021	4.140**	2.616	9.022***
R^2	0.104	0.162	0.012	0.080	-0.10	0.060	-011	0.067	0.018	0.154
Change R^2		0.067***		0.077***		0.080***		0.088***		0.144***

Model of Performance

	Internal processes		Open system		Rational		Human relations		Global performance	
	Model 1	Model 2	Model 1	Model 2	Model 1	Model 2	Model 1	Model 2	Model 1	Model 2
Innovative	0.339***	0.316***	0.261**	0.240**	0.049	0.029	0.027	0.008	0.212**	0.184*
	(3.356)	(3.310)	(2.520)	(2.417)	(0.453)	(0.280)	(0.257)	(0.073)	(2.020)	(1.905)
Culture										
MCS		0.328***		0.295***		0.279***		0.286***		0.401***
		(3.345)		(2.967)		(2.691)		(2.758)		(4.162)
Highest VIF		1.005		1.005		1.005		1.028		1.005
F	11.263**	12.268***	6.351**	7.862***	0.205	3.732***	0.066	3.840**	4.080**	11.084***
R^2	0.104	0.204	0.057	0.135	−0.009	0.058	−0.11	0.061	0.034	0.186
Change R^2		0.107***		0.087***		0.078***		0.081***		0.160***

Notes: Since White's test for heteroskedasticity has not been rejected in any regression, homoskedasticity is assumed in all of them. Associated t-student statistic (between brackets) below each standardized coefficient.
*$p \leq 0.1$; **$p \leq 0.05$; ***$p \leq 0.01$.

into account. This is so because the change in R^2 is significant for each type of estimation, as F statistic values disclose. In models 2 MCS' use has a significant and a positive coefficient for all the different performance models analysed. Therefore, hypothesis 2 is confirmed according to previous literature results (Adler et al., 2000; Bright et al., 1992; Chenhall and Langfield-Smith, 1998b; Kennedy and Affleck-Graves, 2001).

8.5   CONCLUSIONS

According to Steffens et al. (2006), the development and evolution of young firms is a central issue in entrepreneurship research. The outcome in terms of firm performance, particularly growth, has received considerable empirical and theoretical consideration. Nevertheless, the simultaneous pattern of growth and profit performance evolution of young firms has received relatively little empirical attention. In order to contribute with new evidence, this research analyses the relationship between organizational culture, management control systems and performance of young SMEs, using a sample of 89 firms from 'Región de Murcia', Spain. In order to measure culture, we base our research on the 'Organizational Culture Assessment Instrument' proposed by Cameron and Quinn (1999), in which four cultures can be identified: market, hierarchical, clan and adhocratic. This model has been improved by building a new type of culture called 'innovative culture'. Besides, in order to measure performance we use the methodology proposed by Quinn and Rohrbaugh (1983) which identifies four qualitative performance models: internal processes, open system, rational and human relations.

Organizational culture can become a definitive factor to assure the survival of young firms. In that sense, implementing a culture that promotes innovation could help young SMEs to gain a competitive advantage. However, our results show that these firms' culture is predominantly a clan culture characterized by having a managerial style which promotes working as a team, consensus and participation, while adhocratic culture (more innovative) is less important. The cause of these results should be associated with the specific industry characteristics of 'Región de Murcia' since low-technology businesses prevail.

In contrast, organizational culture has influence on young SMEs' performance, though our results are not conclusive for the different performance models. The empirical evidence proves that an innovative culture (a mixture of clan and adhocracy positively) affects a young firm's global performance, while a hierarchical culture negatively influences an internal process model of performance.

Additionally, our findings show that management control systems allow the young firms to achieve higher organizational performance. Thus, we verify that management control systems become an essential factor for young firms, since they provide essential information for decision-making processes.

We expect our results to be useful for young entrepreneurs in the sense that they should be aware of the benefits from the implementation of an innovative culture and the use of management control systems. They should understand that an innovative attitude implies the adoption of new ideas and values that are not threats but strengths, in order to gain competitiveness and assure the future of the firm. The best strategy could be to focus on exploratory learning and innovation. We also expect that the results of the study will help policy makers to drive their efforts in continually facilitating the progress of young SMEs, knowing they are the main contributors to the welfare and well-being of developed economies.

REFERENCES

Acs, Z.J. and D.B. Audretsch (1990), *Innovation and Small Firms*, Cambridge, MA: MIT Press.

Adler, R., A.M. Everett and M. Waldron (2000), 'Advanced management accounting techniques in manufacturing: utilization, benefits, and barriers to implementation', *Accounting Forum*, **24** (2), 131–50.

Argyris, Ch. (1977), 'Double loop learning in organizations', *Harvard Business Review*, **55** (5), September–October, 115–25.

Asociación Española de Contabilidad y Administración de Empresas (AECA) (2005), *Estrategia e innovación de la Pyme industrial en España*, Madrid: AECA.

Audretsch, D.B. and T. Mahmood (1994), 'The rate of hazard confronting new firms and plants in US manufacturing', *Review of Industrial Organization*, **9** (1), 41–56.

Autio, E., H.J. Sapienza and J. Almeida (2000), 'Effects of age at entry, knowledge intensity and imitability on international growth', *Academy of Management Journal*, **43**, 909–24.

Barney, J.B. (1991), 'Firm resources and sustained competitive advantage', *Journal of Management*, **17**, 199–220.

Beckman, C.M., M.D. Burton and C. O'Reilly (2007), 'Early teams: the impact of team demography on VC financing and going public', *Journal of Business Venturing*, **22**, 147–73.

Bhaskaran, S. (2006), 'Incremental innovation and business performance: small and medium-size food enterprises in a concentrated industry environment', *Journal of Small Business Management*, **44** (1), 64–80.

Biga, D.H., D. Francois, B. Gailly, M. Verleysen and V. Wertz (2008), 'An empirical taxonomy of start-up firm growth trajectories', in A. Fayolle and P. Kyrö (eds), *The Dynamics Between Entrepreneurship, Environment and Education*, Cheltenham, UK and Northampton, MA, USA: Edward Elgar, pp. 193–219.

Bisbe, J. and D. Otley (2004), 'The effects of the interactive use of management control systems on product innovation', *Accounting, Organizations and Society*, **29**, 709–37.

Bright, J., R.E. Davies, C.A. Downes and R.C. Sweeting (1992), 'The deployment of costing techniques and practices: a UK study', *Management Accounting Research*, **3**, 201–11.

Brown, C., J. Connor, S. Heeringa and J. Jackson (1990), 'Studying small businesses with the Michigan Employment Security Commission longitudinal data base', *Small Business Economics*, **2**, 261–77.

Cameron, K.S. and R.E. Quinn (1999), *Diagnosing and Changing Organizational Culture. Base on the Competing Values Framework*, Reading, MA: Addison-Wesley.

Certo, S.T., J.G. Covin, C.M. Daily and D.R. Dalton (2001), 'Wealth and the effects of founder management among IPO-stage new ventures', *Strategic Management Journal*, **22**, 641–58.

Cheng, L.K. and Z. Tao (1999), 'The impact of public policies on innovation and imitation: the role of R and D technology in growth models', *International Economic Review*, **40** (1), 187–207.

Chenhall, R.H. and K. Langfield-Smith (1998a), 'Adoption and benefits of management accounting practices: an Australian study', *Management Accounting Research*, **9**, 1–19.

Chenhall, R.H. and K. Langfield-Smith (1998b), 'The relationship between strategic priorities, management techniques and management accounting: an empirical investigation using a systems approach', *Accounting, Organizations and Society*, **23** (3), 243–64.

Choe, J.M. (1996), 'The relationships among performance of accounting information systems, influence factors, and evolution level of information systems', *Journal of Management Information Systems*, **12** (4), 215–39.

Choe, J.M. (2004), 'The relationships among management accounting information, organizational learning and production performance', *Journal of Strategic Information Systems*, **13**, 61–85.

Covin, J.G. and D.P. Slevin (1990), 'New venture strategic posture, structure, and performance: an industry life cycle analysis', *Journal of Business Venturing*, **5**, 123–35.

Dávila, A. (2000), 'An empirical study on the drivers of management control systems design in new product development', *Accounting, Organizations and Society*, **25**, 383–410.

De Long, D. and L. Fahey (2000), 'Diagnóstico de las barreras culturales frente a la gestión del conocimiento', *Academy of Management Executive*, **14** (4), 113–27.

Dibella, A. and E.C. Nevis (1998), *How Organizations Learn: An Integrated Strategy for Building Learning Capability*, San Francisco, CA: Jossey-Bass.

Dunne, T., M.J. Roberts and L. Samuelson (1988), 'Patterns of firm entry and exit in US manufacturing industries', *Rand Journal of Economics*, **19**, 495–515.

Fischer, E. and R. Reuber (2004), 'Contextual antecedents and consequences of relationships between young firms and distinct types of dominant exchange partners', *Journal of Business Venturing*, **19**, 681–706.

Flamhottz, E.G. (1983), 'Accounting, budgeting and control systems, in their organizational context: theoretical and empirical perspectives', *Accounting Organizations and Society*, **8** (2–3), 153–69.

Gordon, G.G. and N. Di Tomaso (1992), 'Predicting corporate performance from organizational culture', *Journal of Management Studies*, **29**, 783–99.

Henderson, A.D. (1999), 'Firm strategy and age dependence: a contingent view of the liabilities of newness, adolescence, and obsolescence', *Administrative Science Quarterly*, **44** (2), 281–314.

Henri, J.F. (2004), 'Performance measurement and organizational effectiveness: bridging the gap', *Managerial Finance*, **30** (6), 93–123.

Henri, J.F. (2006), 'Organizational culture and performance measurement systems', *Accounting, Organizations and Society*, **31**, 77–103.

Herath, S.K., A. Herath and A. Abdul Azeez (2006), 'Fancy firms and corporate culture: a case study for a Less Developed Country (LCD)', *International Journal of Management and Enterprise Development*, **3** (3), 227–43.

Hoque, Z. and W. James (2000), 'Linking balanced scorecard measures to size and market factors: impact on organizational performance', *Journal of Management Accounting Research*, **12**, 1–17.

Hsueh, L. and Y. Tu (2004), 'Innovation and the operational performance of newly established small and medium enterprises in Taiwan', *Small Business Economics*, **23**, 99–113.

Jeuchter, W.H., C. Fisher and R.J. Alford (1998), 'Five conditions for high performance cultures', *Training and Development*, **52** (5), 63–7.

Johannessen, J., J. Olaisen and B. Olsen (1999), 'Strategic use of information technology for increased innovation and performance', *Information Management and Computer Security*, **7** (1), 5–22.

Kennedy, T. and J. Affleck-Graves (2001), 'The impact of activity-based costing techniques on firm performance', *Journal of Management Accounting Research*, **13**, 19–45.

Kotter, J.R. and J.L. Heskett (1992), *Corporate Culture and Performance*, New York: Free Press.

Leal Millan, A. (1991), *Conocer la cultura de las organizaciones. Una base para la estrategia y el cambio*, Madrid: Actualidad Editorial.

March, J.G. (1991), 'Exploration and exploitation in organizational learning', *Annual Review of Sociology*, **14**, 319–40.

Mata, J. and P. Portugal (1994), 'Life duration of new firms', *Journal of Industrial Economics*, **42** (3), 227–46.

McMahon, R. and L. Davies (1994), 'Financial reporting and analysis practices in small enterprises: their association with growth rate and financial performance', *Journal of Small Business Management*, **32** (1), 9–17.

McQuaid, R.W. (2002), 'Entrepreneurship and ICT industries: support from regional and local policies', *Regional Studies*, **36** (8), 909–19.

Miller, D. and P.H. Friesen (1982), 'Innovation in conservative and entrepreneurial firms', *Strategic Management Journal*, **3**, 1–27.

Morcillo, P. (1997), *Dirección estratégica de la tecnología e innovación. Un enfoque de competencias*, Madrid: Civitas.

Morikawa, H. (2004), 'Information technology and the performance of Japanese SMEs', *Small Business Economics*, **23**, 171–7.

Nemeth, C.J. (1997), 'Managing innovation: when less is more', *California Management Review*, **40** (1), 59–74.

Nwachuku, S.S., F. Vitell and J. Barnes (1997), 'Ethics and social responsibility in marketing: an examination of the ethics evaluation and advertising strategies', *Journal of Business Research*, **39** (2), 107–18.

Penrose, E. (1959), *The Theory of the Growth of the Firm*, Oxford: Oxford University Press.

Philips, B.D. and B.A. Kirchhoff (1989), 'Formation, growth and survival: small firm dynamics in the US economy', *Small Business Economics,* **1**, 65–74.

Quinn, R.E. and J.A. Rohrbaugh (1983), 'Spatial model of effectiveness criteria: towards a competing values approach to organizational analysis', *Management Science*, **29** (3), 363–77.

Rosenau, M.D., A. Griffin, G. Castellion and N. Anschuetz (1996), *The PDMA Handbook of New Product Development*, New York: John Wiley and Sons.

Rosenthal, J. and M. Masarech (2003), 'High performance cultures: how values can drive business results', *Journal of Organizational Excellence*, **22** (2), 3–18.

Shields, M. and S.M. Young (1994), 'Managing innovation costs: a study of cost conscious behaviour by R&D professionals', *Journal of Management Accounting Research*, **6**, 175–96.

Shirivastava, P. and W.E. Souder (1987), 'The strategic management of technological innovations: a review and a model', *Journal of Management Studies*, **24** (1), 25–41.

Simons, R. (1995a), *Levers of Control: How Managers Use Innovative Control Systems to Drive Strategic Renewal,* Boston, MA: Harvard Business School Press.

Simons, R. (1995b), 'Control in an age of empowerment', *Harvard Business Review*, **73** (2), 80–8.

Sonrensen, J. (2002), 'The strength of corporate culture and the reliability of firm performance', *Administrative Science Quarterly*, **47** (1), 70–91.

Spender, J.C. and R.M. Grant (1996), 'Knowledge and the firm: overview', *Strategic Management Journal*, **17**, 5–9.

Steffens, P.R. P. Davidsson and J.R. Fitzsimmons (2006), 'The performance of young firms: patterns of evolution in the growth-profitability space', paper presented at the Academy of Management Conference, Hawaii, 5 August.

Tushman, M.L. and Ch.A. O'Reilly III (2002), *Winning Through Innovation. A Practical Guide to Leading Organizational Change and Renewal,* Boston, MA: Harvard Business School Press.

Van de Ven, A.H. (1986), 'Central problems in the management of innovation', *Management Science*, **32**, 590–607.

Vermeulen, P. (2004), 'Managing product innovation in financial service firms', *European Management Journal*, **22** (1), 43–50.

White, H.A. (1980), 'Heteroscedasticity-consistent covariance matrix and a direct test for heteroscedasticity', *Econometrica*, **48**, 817–38.

Yli-Renko, H., E. Autio and H.J. Sapienza (2001), 'Social capital, knowledge acquisition, and knowledge exploitation in young technology-based firms', *Strategic Management Journal,* **22**, 587–613.

9. Successful post-entry strategies of new entrepreneurs

Jean Bonnet and Nicolas Le Pape

9.1 INTRODUCTION

Numerous empirical studies have focused on the relationship between business failure of new firms and industry growth (Audretsch and Mahmood, 1995; Honjo, 2000; Mata et al., 1995). The results are mixed because two opposite conclusions can be drawn: a direct effect when the industry growth creates new opportunities or an increasing demand; an indirect effect when the growing industry generates more instability in the market structure due to stronger competition between established firms and new firms.

Few studies have been conducted at the individual level on the behavior of the new entrepreneur and their relationship to the success of the firm. In fact, when dealing with new firms, qualitative information on firms' strategies is rare and difficult to collect: 'the analysis of post-entry strategies by start-ups is rather rare in the literature' (Fosfuri and Giarrantana, 2004, p. 2).

This chapter is based on the SINE (information system on new firms) survey which documents the conditions under which 30 778 French firms were founded in 1994 (SINE 94-1). In 1997, 15 550 firms were still running and replied to a second survey (SINE 94-2). The survey collected qualitative information on the real behavior of the firm during the period 1996–7. Then, using duration analysis (Cox model) (Cox, 1972), we determine to what extent the strategic orientation of the firm affects the probability of exit during the period 1997–9 (SINE 94-3).

We consider the real behavior of the firm in its product market, and we identify the impact of post-entry product market strategies on the firm's durability. Within the set of different post-entry strategies we focus on the firm's competitive behavior or its willingness to overcome competitors to gain market shares. This competitive entrepreneurial behavior includes all activities or attitudes aimed at overcoming rivals: willingness to increase activity, willingness to subcontract and commercial aggressiveness (concerning prices, new customers and advertising strategy). Employing these aggressive product market strategies is also a way to obtain additional liquidities if such strategies generate more sales. In this case, aggressive behavior alleviates the financial constraints suffered by young firms and positively affects the longevity of the firm. Yet aggressive product market behavior is a risky strategy. Such entrepreneurial behavior carries its own costs that could have a detrimental effect on a firm's survival.

Globally, the relationship between entrepreneurial behavior and survival is a priori unknown. Therefore, it would be interesting to investigate the effect of the development of an entrepreneurial strategy on the firm's survival. We show that a proactive market strategy improves the firm's survival. This result suggests that a forceful strategy does not necessarily increase the risk of the firm exiting the market. Yet when firms are confronted with a problem of constrained production,[1] an entrepreneurial strategy based on advertising decreases the life span. In the case of small and new firms, the behavior is strongly shaped by the human capital of the entrepreneur. It is well known that human capital is typically found to have a major positive impact on survival (Bates, 1990). Our results show that for firms with unconstrained production, having an entrepreneur with an advanced educational background significantly improves the longevity of a new firm when conducting an entrepreneurial policy. On the other hand, specific human capital related to work experience is valued in leading less entrepreneurial oriented policies.

The chapter is organized as follows. Section 9.2 relates this study to relevant literature on survival of new firms. Section 9.3 presents the database, explains the construction of the index of entrepreneurial strategy and the methodology used. The results of duration models are stated in Section 9.4. Section 9.5 concludes.

9.2 FOUNDING CONDITIONS, POST-ENTRY STRATEGIES AND LONGEVITY OF NEW FIRMS

It is well known that the longevity of a firm depends on the conditions under which it was founded (Abdesselam et al., 2004). Previous research distinguishes between the impact of firm characteristics (start-up/takeover, initial size, legal status, financial constraints, branch of industry and so on) and individual characteristics (age, gender, human capital and so on). In particular, the previous occupation of the entrepreneur and the industry branch in which their previous experience was acquired play a major role in determining the probability of success of the firm (Bhattacharjee et al., 2008). If we consider the firm's characteristics, the most significant variables are the initial size of the firm and the origin of the firm (firms that have been taken over are more prone to survive because of the pre-existence of a market).

Firm performance results in various combinations of individual characteristics of the entrepreneur and organizational or environmental factors (Lumpkin and Dess, 1996, 2001). Then the behavior of the entrepreneur may be just as important as the founding conditions when regarding the survival of the firm (Covin and Slevin, 1991). Recent studies focus on entrepreneurial orientation (proactiveness, innovativeness, risk taking propensity) and show that this behavior increases the financial performance (Keh et al., 2007; Stam and Elfring, 2008; Wiklund and Shepherd, 2005) or the growth of the firm (Moreno and Casillas, 2008).

According to Mata and Portugal (1994) and Agarwall (1997), there is a direct relationship between the growth rate of the firm and its survival. Empirical studies on the growth of the firm very often refer to Gibrat's law (the law of proportionate effect) which states that the growth of firms is independent of their initial size. Yet in the case of small new firms it is well known that the variability of the growth is higher than for larger, older ones.[2] Yet firm growth may not affect the survival of small firms as long as they are able to occupy strategic niches in their market (Caves and Porter, 1977). Therefore, the link between growth and survival is altered by the strategic orientation of the firm. According to Hannan and Freeman (1984), the selection process favors inertia. Firms that tend to maintain the same strategies have a lower probability of exit. In contrast, Levinthal (1997) underlines the positive impact of firm strategy upon survival. In such a case, strategic orientations allow the firm to adapt to a changing environment. The actions or decisions taken after entry towards competitors or customers can create competitive advantages and exert a positive impact on survival. In the case of new firms, strategic orientation (advertising policy, capacity to reduce prices and so on) conveys information to competitors and customers, allows them to build a reputation, and has an effect on the survival.

Therefore, the strategic orientation of the firm allows a trade-off between growing fast in a competitive environment and establishing a market niche in order to ease the constraint of strong growth. Firm growth can be seen as a function of rivalry conditions and the competitive behavior of the firm on its product market. Smith et al. (2001) have shown that aggressive behavior spread amongst several firms in the same industry increases the degree of competition, and then deteriorates the global profitability of the branch of industry. Yet these behaviors still remain beneficial for the firms that initiate them. Moreover, it is better to be the most aggressive in order to gain or maintain status as a market leader (Ferrier, 2001; Ferrier et al., 1999). The proactive attitude of the entrepreneur identified as the willingness to seize initiatives in the market can be viewed, in industrial organization literature, in terms of first mover advantages in a Stackelberg game (Lieberman and Montgomery, 1998). Firms attempt to capture market opportunities before rivals through the introduction of new products (Dess et al., 2003).

Covin and Covin (1990) defined aggressiveness with respect to firm behavior in terms of three basic strategies: initiating action, introducing new products and adopting a very competitive stance. They have also defined a type of very competitive, hostile environment dominated by several big firms. In this environment small firms have to adopt weak aggressive behavior. Nevertheless in the group of newly created firms, the more aggressive they are, the better they perform. Thus it is interesting to delve deeper into the link between growth and survival, and to research the existence of different kinds of entrepreneurial strategies which improve the longevity of the firm.

9.3   DATA, VARIABLES AND METHOD

We rely on the SINE database to empirically test the link between the use of an entrepreneurial strategy and the durability of the new French firms during the period 1997–9. The database contains information about the real behavior of the new firm, which allows us to characterize the different types of post-entry strategies and to build an index representing the level of the entrepreneurial strategy of the firm.

9.3.1   The Database

The first survey (SINE 94-1) was conducted by the French National Institute of Statistical and Economic Studies[3] in 1994 and takes into account 30 778 firms which had been set up or taken over during the first half of 1994. The sample[4] originally represents the total population of 96 407 new French entrepreneurs. In this survey new firms are identified on the basis of their registration in the 'Système d'Informations et de Répertoire des Entreprises et des Etablissements' (SIRENE repertory[5]). The surveyed firms belong to the private sector in the fields of industry, building, trade and services. This first survey identifies qualitative data surrounding the conditions under which the firm was founded. It contains variables related to the attributes of the entrepreneur, and the context and the environment of the entrepreneurship. In order to take into account the heterogeneity of the sample, these variables are taken as covariates in the duration analysis.

A second survey, carried out in 1997 (SINE 94-2), contains information about the status of the 30 778 firms surveyed in 1994, closed down[6] or still running. In 1997, 15 550 firms were still running. The transformation of firms from sole proprietorship to partnership is excluded. Subsidiaries and firms created by several individuals (team projects) have been removed. Finally, after such an adjustment, we obtain 9927 firms.[7] This survey explores the real behavior of the firm on its product market and its strategy against competitors between 1996–7. This information allows us to construct an index representing the level of entrepreneurial behavior of the firm.

A third survey conducted in 1999 (SINE 94–3) identifies the firms which are still running and those that closed down over the period 1997–9. Therefore, we calculate the life span of the firm in months. We consider firms that exited to be entrepreneurial failures (voluntary or involuntary). Takeovers are included in the category of firms still running. A duration model measures the impact of the variables representing the nature and the level of entrepreneurial behavior on the life span of the firm.

9.3.2 Methodology

We use a Cox model (proportional hazard model) in order to examine the impact of post-entry strategy on survival. The basic hazard function is not specified here, since the results of the non-parametric estimation (Kaplan-Meier) of the duration show that none of the known statistical laws can be adapted to our data.

Consider a firm sample of size n. The rate of discontinuation at date t is measured by the hazard rate function $h(t)$. For each firm i, the data provide information on its life span t_i measured in months,[8] its individual characteristics (x_i), and also whether the firm was still alive at the end of the period covered by the study (1999). The latter information may be summarized by defining a binary variable (a_i) that indicates the right censor as follows.

$$a_i = \begin{cases} 0: \text{if the firm } i \text{ is still active at the time of the third survey in 1999} \\ 1: \text{if the firm } i \text{ ceased its activity between 1997 and 1999} \end{cases}$$

The proportional hazard rate expression is given by:

$$h(t; x\beta) = h_0(t)\exp(x\beta)$$

Where $h_0(t)$ is an unspecified function of t called the baseline hazard and β is a vector of the estimated parameters.

Estimators are obtained by maximizing the following partial likelihood expression:

$$PL = \prod_{i=1}^{n}\left[\frac{\exp(x_i\beta)}{\sum_{j=1}^{n} Y_{ij}\exp(x_j\beta)}\right]^{a_i}$$

Where $Y_{ij} = 1$ if $t_j \geq t_i$; and $Y_{ij} = 0$ if $t_j < t_i$. The Ys are a convenient method to exclude from the denominator those individuals who have already experienced the event and are, thus, not part of the risk set. The population concerned in the denominator has not ceased its activity before t_i. For censored individuals the exit time is not observed so that no probability of exit may be included in the partial likelihood. This is why $a_i = 0$ for such individuals. The log of the partial likelihood is written as follows:

$$\text{Log } PL = \sum_{i=1}^{n} a_i\left\{x_i\beta - \log\left[\sum_{j=1}^{n} Y_{ij}\exp(x_j\beta)\right]\right\}$$

This expression is maximized with respect to β so as to obtain the maximum partial likelihood estimators $\hat{\beta}$. The estimation has been carried out using the 'PHREG' procedure in SAS (see Allison, 1995).

9.3.3 Measure of Entrepreneurial Behavior and Descriptive Statistics

The aggressiveness of a firm in its market is naturally expressed by a decrease in price or an increase of the production level. It also refers to several modes of winning market shares in the context of non-price competition: attracting new clients (personal connection), advertising efforts or subcontracting. Subcontracting is a way to either alleviate capacity constraints or outsource procedures that cannot be accomplished by the firm itself (specialty subcontracting).

A variable is constructed so as to express the firm's entrepreneurial behavior on its market. It is identified by evaluating five criteria, which represent five main dimensions of the entrepreneurial behavior. An entrepreneurial behavior is then assigned to each criterion according to the answer given. The questions which have been retained from the SINE 94-2 survey are as follows.

What has been your global approach towards your firm over the last two years (1995–7)?

	GL. APPR.
Increasing the activity	1
Maintaining the activity at its level	0
Attempting to safeguard the activity	0

Have you made advertising efforts over the last two years?

	ADV. EFF.
Yes	1
No	0

Have you made efforts to prospect new clients over the last two years?

	PROS. EFF.
Yes	1
No	0

Have you made any effort on your prices over the last two years?

	PRICE EFF.
Yes	1
No	0

Did you give subcontracting works (to other firms) over the last two years?

	SUB. GIVEN
Yes	1
No	0

By summing up these scores, we construct a global index of entrepreneurial behavior on a scale of $[0; 5]$ – the higher the global index, the higher the entrepreneurial behavior ascribed to the firm.

We split the sample into two sub-populations: those with constrained production and those with unconstrained production (Table 9.1). This division allows us to determine if entrepreneurial behavior is a good way for a firm to overcome a difficult position on its market. In addition, it allows avoiding any criticism regarding the fact that our definition of entrepreneurial behavior does not include the conduct of the entrepreneur but rather the growth or growth potential that differ according to the branch of industry.

Less entrepreneurial firms (that is, firms for which the index equals zero or one) represent about half of the population of firms with constrained production but only a third of the population of firms with unconstrained production. This gap indicates that entrepreneurial behavior is not a

Table 9.1   Distribution of firms according to the entrepreneurial behavior index

Entrepreneurial behavior index: EB	Unconstrained production		Constrained production	
	Numbers	**Percentage (%)**	**Numbers**	**Percentage (%)**
EB5: Very high (score=5)	162 (12)	0.61 (1.47)	74 (0)	0.75 (0.00)
EB4: High (score=4)	1459 (101)	5.52 (12.33)	974 (43)	9.81 (11.38)
EB3: Medium (score=3)	4156 (204)	15.74 (24.91)	2442 (148)	24.60 (39.15)
EB2: Low (score=2)	8224 (229)	31.14 (27.96)	3360 (93)	33.85 (24.60)
EB1: Very low (score=1)	8429 (188)	31.92 (22.95)	2373 (55)	23.90 (14.55)
EB0: No entrepreneurial behavior (score=0)	3980 (85)	15.07 (10.38)	704 (39)	7.09 (10.32)
Total	26410 (819)	100 (100)	9927 (378)	100 1(00)

Note: Numbers refer to the total population of new firms; number within parentheses refer to the sub-population of innovative firms.

consequence of a growing sectorial demand but instead constitutes a specific approach of entrepreneurs in an effort to circumvent difficulties related to production outflow caused by a low level of the demand.

Innovative firms are more entrepreneurial than non-innovative firms: 42 percent have an index greater than or equal to three compared with only 25 percent in the second population. This observation is also true in the sub-populations of firms with and without constrained production. The sub-population of innovative firms that evolve in markets with constrained production falls in the category of most entrepreneurial firms.

9.4   EMPIRICAL RESULTS

The purpose of this section is to investigate to what extent a firm's placement in one of the five classes of entrepreneurial behavior or its practice of a specific entrepreneurial behavior alters the firm's survival, while controlling the heterogeneity of our population by the addition of variables relevant in the explanation of survival. As control variables, we include seven representing the firm and the context of its foundation and five characterizing the entrepreneur.

9.4.1   Post-entry strategy and firms' duration

Too low a level of entrepreneurial behavior (that is, no contact made with customers or no advertising effort) can expose the firm to the risk of losing its customers to its competitors. However, too high a level of entrepreneurial behavior is also ineffective since it generates a cost which weakens the firm.

We obtain results for two populations: firms with constrained production and firms with unconstrained production. We consider two models with the entrepreneurial behavior variable measured according to its intensity and nature (Table 9.2).

Entrepreneurial behavior improves the durability of new firms in the two sub-populations. We can distinguish a small difference in the survival rates between firms with constrained production and firms with unconstrained production. This surprising result could be explained by the fact that firms with constrained production are more entrepreneurial (see Table 9.1). Concerning the impact of aggressive behavior on survival, modalities *global approach* and *subcontracting works given* have a positive impact. Advertising efforts improve durability in the population of firms with unconstrained production but deteriorate the survival in the other sub-population. In the population of firms with unconstrained production, efforts made to attract new customers or efforts on prices negatively affect the survival but they do not have an effect on the population with constrained production.

One possible explanation of these results is that some proactive attitudes (for example willingness to respond to the demand by the delegation of subcontracting works) do not generate costs (or sunk costs) even when the state of the market is unfavorable. The other kinds of proactive behaviors (prices cut, advertising expenses, prospective potential customers) generate costs, specifically when the product market conjuncture is low. The existence of problems on production outflows could be explained by the fact that the product fails to satisfy consumer tastes. Consequently, advertising or pricing policies have little effect on survival. For firms with unconstrained production, a price decrease or efforts to attract new customers that deteriorate the survival may reflect a miscontrolled growth.

Two types of entrepreneurial behavior exert a positive effect on the durability of the firm: the global approach of the entrepreneur towards the development of the firm and the amount of subcontracted work delegated to other firms. Firms that reduced prices had an inclination to fail over the two year period.

Second, after splitting the sample according to the level of entrepreneurial behavior (in three classes: high – score in [4,5]; medium – score in [2,3];

Table 9.2 Duration of the new firm according to the intensity and type of entrepreneurial behavior

	Unconstrained production			Constrained production	
	Risk ratio: exp(β)	(Pr > χ²)		Risk ratio: exp(β)	(Pr > χ²)
Variables: Intensity of entrepreneurial behavior			**Variables: Intensity of entrepreneurial behavior**		
EB5	0.935	(0.7646)	EB5	0.445*	(0.0797)
EB4	0.617***	(< 0.0001)	EB4	0.707***	(0.0092)
EB3	0.763***	(< 0.0001)	EB3	0.709***	(0.0033)
EB2	0.662***	(< 0.0001)	EB2	0.644***	(< 0.0001)
EB1	0.971	(0.5844)	EB1	0.950	(0.6436)
EB0	Ref.		EB0	Ref.	
−2LogL	58889		−2LogL	22441	
LR statistic	735.84***		LR statistic	501.38***	
Variables: Type of entrepreneurial behaviour			**Variables: Type of entrepreneurial behavior**		
GL.APPR.	0.515***	(< 0.0001)	GL.APPR.	0.741***	(< 0.0001)
ADV.EFF.	0.928*	(0.0792)	ADV.EFF.	1.113*	(0.0839)
PROS.EFF.	1.336***	(< 0.0001)	PROS.EFF.	0.957	(0.4714)
PRICE EFF.	1.091**	(0.0295)	PRICE EFF.	0.919	(0.1622)
SUBGIVEN	0.887**	(0.0138)	SUBGIVEN	0.714***	(0.0001)
−2LogL	58642		−2LogL	22427	
LR statistic	982.93***		LR statistic	515.42***	
Number of firms	26410		Number of firms	9927	
Percent censored	88.85		Percent censored	87.36	

Notes: According to the referential class of each variable, if exp(β) > 1 and if Pr > χ² is inferior to 10 percent the variable contributes significantly to decrease the life span of the firm.
***, ** and * indicate significance at the 1 percent, 5 percent and 10 percent level, respectively.

low – score in [0,1]), we examine which type of entrepreneurial behavior affects the survival of the firm (Table 9.3).

The comparison of survival rates shows that firms with the lower level of the index exhibit the lowest survival rates. Nevertheless, a positive relationship between entrepreneurial behavior and survival is only observed for the category of firms with unconstrained production.

When we consider the type of aggressiveness/survival relationship, it is worth noting that the positive impact of the different types of proactive behaviors on survival is more pronounced for firms with constrained production. In particular, customer and pricing strategies which positively impacted survival for firms with constrained production had the opposite effect on firms with unconstrained production, regardless of the level of entrepreneurial behavior.

9.4.2   Founding Conditions and Survival: How Does the Entrepreneurial Behavior Matter?

We now try to determine if the effect of various variables (Table 9.4) that characterize the firm and the entrepreneur for each entrepreneurial behavior class changes the impact of post-entry strategies on the survival (Table 9.5).

In the population of aggressive firms, firms under limited liability status are more prone to survive. The opposite is true for the category of non-aggressive firms. We can notice that takeovers are more prone to survive – whatever the level of aggressiveness – for firms with unconstrained production, which is in line with Audrestch (1995). In the population of firms with constrained production, there does not exist such a differentiation and for the medium class of aggressiveness, being a takeover even deteriorates the life span of the firm.

If the start-up size is greater than one salaried employee, this constitutes a handicap for moderately to highly aggressive firms in the population of firms with unconstrained production. This result is also true for the medium class in the population with constrained production. Regarding the financial dimension of projects, a sizeable initial level of investment is a guarantee of durability for firms with constrained production regardless of the level of aggressiveness. For firms with unconstrained production, undertaking a small project is preferable when sustaining a policy of low level of entrepreneurial behavior. Obtaining public aid improves the durability of firms in both populations except for highly aggressive firms with unconstrained production. However, for weakly aggressive firms within the population with constrained production, public aid decreases the life span of the firm. Application and approval for a bank loan (DEM. AND OBTAINED) increases longevity. Firms with constrained production that

Table 9.3 Duration of the new firm crossing the intensity and the type of entrepreneurial behavior

	Unconstrained production					
	Intensity of entrepreneurial behavior					
	Low		Medium		High	
	Risk ratio: exp(β)	(Pr > χ²)	Risk ratio: exp(β)	(Pr > χ²)	Risk ratio: exp(β)	(Pr > χ²)
GL.APPR.	0.510***	(< 0.0001)	0.699***	(< 0.0001)	1.227	(0.6694)
ADV.EFF.	1.130	(0.1687)	1.233***	(0.0065)	0.467***	(0.0072)
PROS.EFF.	1.845***	(< 0.0001)	1.440***	(< 0.0001)	8.937***	(< 0.0001)
PRICE EFF.	1.163**	(0.0387)	1.234***	(0.0087)	4.362***	(< 0.0001)
SUBGIVEN	0.789**	(0.0190)	1.023	(0.7965)	3.617***	(0.0003)
−2LogL	29350		21856		1954	
LR statistic	702.07		423.18		264.65	
Number of firms	12409		12380		1621	
Percent censored	87.07		90.40		90.68	

Constrained production

| | Intensity of entrepreneurial behavior | | | | | |
| | Low | | Medium | | High | |
	Risk ratio: exp(β)	(Pr > χ^2)	Risk ratio: exp(β)	(Pr > χ^2)	Risk ratio: exp(β)	(Pr > χ^2)
GL.APPR.	0.563***	(0.0098)	1.051	(0.6720)	2.226	(0.4240)
ADV.EFF.	1.023	(0.8951)	1.391***	(0.0018)	1.089	(0.9268)
PROS.EFF.	0.957	(0.7384)	1.134	(0.2567)	0.172**	(0.012)
PRICE EFF.	0.836	(0.2136)	1.267**	(0.0428)	0.217**	(0.0133)
SUBGIVEN	0.713	(0.2017)	0.852	(0.1958)	0.172***	(0.0044)
−2LogL	7425		10396		1767	
LR statistic	274.13		404.26		216.41	
Number of firms	3077		5802		1048	
Percent censored	84.27		89.19		86.26	

Note: According to the referential class of each variable, if exp(β) > 1 and if Pr > χ^2 is inferior to 10 percent the variable contributes significantly to decrease the life span of the firm.
***, ** and * indicate significance at the 1 percent, 5 percent and 10 percent level, respectively.

Table 9.4   Explanation of control variables

Variables	Modalities	Abbreviations
Legal status	Limited liability Unlimited liability	LIM. LIABILITY UNLIM. LIABILITY*
Origin of the firm	Start up Take over	START UP* TAKE OVER
Branch of industry	Food industry Industry Transport Construction Catering Household services Services for enterprises Trade	FOOD INDUSTRY INDUSTRY TRANSPORT CONSTRUCTION CATERING HOUSE. SERVICES SERVICES ENT. TRADE*
Initial size of the enterprise	One salaried and more No salaried	SALARIED >=1 SALARIED =0*
Amount of money invested to set up the firm	Less than 7623 euros Between 7623 euros and 15245 euros Between 15245 euros and 38112 euros More than 38112 euros	INVEST. <7623 €* 7623 €.<INVEST. <15245 € 15245 €. <INVEST. <38112 € INVEST.> 38112 €
Obtaining a public financial aid in 1994	Public financial aid obtained Public financial aid none obtained	PU. FI. AID OBTAINED PU. FI. AID NONE OBTAINED*
Asking for bank loans and obtained them in 1994	Demand and refusal Demand and obtained No demand	DEM. AND REFUSAL* DEM. AND OBTAINED NO DEMAND
Gender	Man Woman	MAN WOMAN*
Age of the entrepreneur	Less than 25 years old Between 25 and 35 years old Between 35 and 45 years old More than 45 years old	AGE <25 25 < AGE < 35* 35 < AGE < 45 AGE >45
Human capital of the entrepreneur	Skills acquired in a different branch of activity and no diploma Skills acquired in a different branch of activity and diploma Skills acquired in the same branch of activity and no diploma	NO EXP. AND NO DIPLOMA* NO EXP. AND DIPLOMA EXP. AND NO DIPLOMA

Table 9.4 (*continued*)

Variables	Modalities	Abbreviations
	Skills acquired in the same branch of activity and diploma	EXP. AND DIPLOMA
Occupation before the setting up of the new firm	Unemployed None working population Working population	UNEMPLOYED NONE WORK. POP. WORK. POP.*
Main motivation when the entrepreneur sets up its firm	New idea Opportunity Without employ Entourage example Taste for entrepreneurship	NEW IDEA OPPORTUNITY WI. EMPLOY ENT. EXAMPLE TASTE ENTREP.*

Note: * reference class in the estimates.

have been refused a loan (those financially constrained at start-up) do not fare as well compared to those who did not apply for a loan at all.

For firms with constrained production, the effect of the age of the entrepreneur, usually a limiting factor, disappears for highly aggressive firms. Compared to entrepreneurs aged 25 to 35, an older entrepreneur (over 45) does not constitute a handicap for strongly aggressive firms whereas it is a limiting factor for firms with a medium or a low aggressiveness.

In the category of firms with unconstrained production, the combination of a diploma and experience acquired in the same branch of activity (EXP. AND DIPLOMA) improves survival. For highly aggressive firms, it is the diploma that contributes to a better survival but it is experience for middle aggressive firms. An aggressive post-entry strategy is then all the more efficient if the individual has general human capital that allows them to better deal with uncertainty (inherent to an aggressive behavior) than specific human capital. Human capital is an important variable in entrepreneurship and observed human capital is typically found to have a large impact on survival (Bates, 1990). Nevertheless, it is evident that to conduct a successful entrepreneurial behavior having a diploma is preferable to having branch experience. General human capital is then more valued in leading entrepreneurial policies that are complex and require some abilities to deal with uncertainty. On the other hand, specific human capital related to experience is more valued in leading non-entrepreneurial policies, which suggests that know-how and mastery of a job is all the more important since the firm does not want to sustain strong competition.

Table 9.5 Control variables

	Unconstrained production					
	Level of the index of entrepreneurial behavior					
	Low		Medium		High	
	Risk ratio: exp(β)	(Pr > χ^2)	Risk ratio: exp(β)	(Pr > χ^2)	Risk ratio: exp(β)	(Pr > χ^2)
LIM. LIABILITY	1.145**	(0.0272)	0.902	(0.1338)	0.514***	(0.0011)
TAKEOVER	0.892*	(0.0670)	0.745***	(< 0.0001)	0.553*	(0.0523)
FOOD INDUSTRY	0.654**	(0.0225)	0.988	(0.9461)	1.354	(0.6087)
INDUSTRY	0.830*	(0.0765)	1.014	(0.9011)	0.467***	(0.0048)
CONSTRUCTION	0.498***	(< 0.0001)	0.707***	(0.0010)	0.179***	(0.0005)
TRANSPORT	0.691***	(0.0068)	0.771	(0.1137)	0	(0.9767)
CATERING	1.219**	(0.0102)	1.159	(0.1679)	0.888	(0.7936)
HOUSE. SERVICES	0.457***	(< 0.0001)	0.720***	(0.0029)	0.434**	(0.0202)
SERVICES ENT.	0.857*	(0.0616)	0.634***	(< 0.0001)	0.511**	(0.0125)
TRADE	Ref.		Ref.		Ref.	
SALARIED >= 1	0.915	(0.1700)	1.458***	(< 0.0001)	2.282***	(0.0009)
7623 €.<INVEST.< 15245 €.	1.176**	(0.0255)	0.926	(0.3608)	1.319	(0.2429)
15245 €. <INVEST.< 38112 €.	1.183***	(0.0325)	1.267***	(0.0067)	0.558*	(0.0634)
INVEST.> 38112 €.	1.148*	(0.0887)	1.151	(0.1281)	0.320***	(0.0085)
INVEST. < 7623 €.	Ref.		Ref.		Ref.	

	Estimate	(p)	Estimate	(p)	Estimate	(p)
PU. FI. AID OBTAINED	0.621***	(< 0.0001)	0.748***	(0.0003)	0.710	(0.1674)
DEM. AND OBTAINED	0.705***	(0.0117)	0.691***	(0.0074)	ns	ns
NO DEMAND	0.963	(< 0.7865)	0.778**	(0.0507)	ns	ns
DEM. AND REFUSAL	Ref.		Ref.		Ref.	
MAN	1.032	(0.5842)	0.928	(0.2888)	1.689**	(0.0187)
AGE < 25	0.734**	(0.0151)	1.224*	(0.0790)	2.731***	(0.0080)
35 < AGE < 45	1.108	(0.1133)	1.016	(0.8287)	1.338	(0.1549)
AGE > 45	1.475***	(< 0.0001)	1.409	(< 0.0001)	1.676*	(0.0830)
25 < AGE < 35	Ref.		Ref.		Ref.	
NO EXP. AND DIPLOMA	1.038	(0.6609)	0.966	(0.6980)	0.365**	(0.0129)
EXP. AND NO DIPLOMA	1.057	(0.4063)	0.592***	(< 0.0001)	1.211	(0.3780)
EXP. AND DIPLOMA	0.768***	(0.0024)	0.767***	(0.0022)	0.346***	(0.0031)
NO EXP. AND NO DIPLOMA	Ref.		Ref.		Ref.	
UNEMPLOYED	1.779***	(< 0.0001)	1.497***	(< 0.0001)	2.132***	(0.0051)
NON-WORK. POP.	1.391***	(0.0001)	1.444***	(0.0003)	1.969*	(0.0658)
WORK. POP.	Ref.		Ref.		Ref.	
NEW IDEA	1.086	(0.3800)	1.147	(0.1809)	0.690	(0.1781)
OPPORTUNITY	0.796***	(0.0005)	0.848**	(0.0365)	1.998***	(0.0070)
WI. EMPLOY	0.819**	(0.0149)	0.989	(0.9096)	1.656	(0.1531)
ENT. EXAMPLE	0.959	(0.7438)	2.035	(< 0.0001)	0.163*	(0.0796)
TASTE ENTREP.	Ref.		Ref.		Ref.	

Table 9.5 (*continued*)

Constrained production

	Level of the index of entrepreneurial behavior					
	Low		Medium		High	
	Risk ratio: exp(β)	(Pr > χ^2)	Risk ratio: exp(β)	(Pr > χ^2)	Risk ratio: exp(β)	(Pr > χ^2)
LIM. LIABILITY	2.310***	(< 0.0001)	1.590***	(< 0.0001)	0.570**	(0.0305)
TAKEOVER	1.109	(0.3628)	1.401***	(0.0007)	0.935	(0.7840)
FOOD INDUSTRY	0.348**	(0.0216)	1.067	(0.8266)	6.805**	(0.0305)
INDUSTRY	0.838	(0.2585)	1.205	(0.2332)	1.759	(0.2377)
CONSTRUCTION	0.771	(0.1415)	1.414***	(0.0085)	0	(0.9791)
TRANSPORT	0.576**	(0.0378)	1.1	(0.6843)	0.876	(0.6769)
CATERING	0.785	(0.1600)	1.427**	(0.0185)	1.910**	(0.0431)
HOUSE. SERVICES	0.615***	(0.0053)	1.095	(0.5403)	1.753	(0.2848)
SERVICES ENT.	0.255***	(< 0.0001)	0.487***	(< 0.0001)	2.309**	(0.0197)
TRADE	Ref.		Ref.		Ref.	
SALARIED >= 1	0.834	(0.1238)	1.945***	(< 0.0001)	1.308	(0.2842)
7623 €.<INVEST.< 15245 €.	0.869	(0.2752)	0.798**	(0.0352)	1.094	(0.7141)
15245 €. <INVEST.< 38112 €.	0.518***	(< 0.0001)	0.374***	(< 0.0001)	0.206***	(0.0035)
INVEST.> 38112 €.	0.492***	(< 0.0001)	0.574***	(< 0.0001)	0.817	(0.5330)
INVEST. < 7623 €.	Ref.		Ref.		Ref.	

PU. FI. AID OBTAINED	2.269***	(< 0.0001)	0.752***	(0.0098)	0.187***	(< 0.0001)
DEM. AND OBTAINED	0.475***	(< 0.0003)	0.286***	(< 0.0001)	0.256***	(< 0.0001)
NO DEMAND	0.382***	(< 0.0001)	0.288***	(< 0.0001)	0.207***	(< 0.0001)
DEM. AND REFUSAL	Ref.		Ref.		Ref.	
MAN	0.879	(0.2456)	0.987	(0.8914)	1.159	(0.5562)
AGE < 25	0.533**	(0.0235)	0.891	(0.5503)	0.443**	(0.0473)
35 < AGE < 45	1.796***	(< 0.0001)	0.887	(0.2290)	0.609*	(0.0555)
AGE > 45	1.762***	(< 0.0001)	0.841	(0.1234)	0.381***	(0.0003)
25 < AGE < 35	Ref.		Ref.		Ref.	
NO EXP. AND DIPLOMA	0.830	(0.2146)	1.106	(0.4547)	1.599	(0.1792)
EXP. AND NO DIPLOMA	0.615***	(0.0002)	0.802**	(0.0456)	1.845**	(0.0238)
EXP. AND DIPLOMA	0.817	(0.1645)	0.826	(0.1178)	2.374***	(0.0031)
NO EXP. AND NO DIPLOMA	Ref.		Ref.		Ref.	
UNEMPLOYED	0.652***	(0.0036)	1.983***	(< 0.0001)	1.579*	(0.0934)
NON WORK. POP.	1.117	(0.4578)	0.874	(0.4051)	1.453	(0.3401)
WORK. POP.	Ref.		Ref.		Ref.	
NEW IDEA	0.889	(0.5446)	2.066***	(< 0.0001)	0.185***	(0.0005)
OPPORTUNITY	0.850	(0.1681)	1.164	(0.1497)	0.876	(0.6316)
WI. EMPLOY	0.884	(0.4077)	0.727**	(0.0340)	2.558***	(0.0007)
ENT. EXAMPLE	1.893**	(0.0107)	1.113	(0.6070)	0	(0.9932)
TASTE ENTREP.	Ref.		Ref.		Ref.	

Abdesselam et al. (2004) showed that firms set up by unemployed people are more prone to exit. We find also that setting up a firm for a 'push' motive negatively impacts the durability of the new firm, except for firms with constrained production in the low entrepreneurial behavior category. In the population of firms with unconstrained production, firms set up by individuals out of the labor force (NON-WORK. POP.) are more prone to exit than those set up by those already in the labor force. One explanation could be that being in the labor force is favorable to integration into networks and facilitates successful entrepreneurship (better ability to grasp opportunities on the market, to acquire technical knowledge and so on).

9.5   CONCLUSION

In this chapter we investigated the complex relationships between entrepreneurial post-entry behavior and firm survival. We show that some interesting results can be drawn from the actual real behavior of new French firms, results that go beyond the usual explanations of survival based on the initial conditions under which new firms are founded. The duration of the firm is not only dependent on the willingness but also the ability of the entrepreneur to conduct entrepreneurial policies aiming at increasing the firm's market share.

Firms which adopt an entrepreneurial behavior are more likely to survive. For sure entrepreneurs who promote proactive strategies are themselves resolute individuals. Proactiveness could result from a specific entrepreneurial spirit, from a lower aversion to risk on the part of some entrepreneurs or from entrepreneurial abilities that some individuals are endowed with. Even if entrepreneurial behavior contributes to increased competition or branch dynamism, it could be the intensity of competition that explains the propensity to be proactive.

Further research needs to be undertaken concerning the determinants of the entrepreneurial behavior. What is the main driver: 'entrepreneurial human capital' or the level of competition in the product market? It is clear that the intriguing connections between this 'entrepreneurial human capital' and the implementation of successful aggressive policies must be explored in further detail.

NOTES

1. In the database we identify this population of firms as they answer: the main problem they faced (during 1996–7) is related to difficulties to sell their products (either it could be

due to a lack of industry demand or to an inadequate product market). The firms which answer they did not encounter difficulties to sell their products are identified as unconstrained firms.

2. The relationship between the survival rate and the current size of the firm shows that smaller firms are generally more prone to exit the market (Doms et al., 1995; Evans, 1987; Hall, 1987) and that the effect of current size (on post-entry survival) is more pronounced than initial size. The survival probability of a firm is also positively related to its initial size (Audretsch and Mahmood, 1995; Mata and Portugal, 1994) and this effect persists some years after entry (Geroski et al., 2002).

3. INSEE (Institut National des Statistiques et des Etudes Economiques).

4. The sample was built by randomly drawing out samples from the 416 (2 × 8 × 26) elementary strata. These strata are classified according to origin (start-up or takeover: two modalities), branch (eight modalities) and location (22 French regions plus four overseas departments). The database must then be used with the correction of a weight variable (the reverse of the draw rate per branch, per region and per origin). Firms which had survived less than one month have been removed. It is a compulsory survey which obtained a 98.8 percent rate of reply.

5. However economic 'activations' and 'reactivations' are excluded from the surveyed sample. Economic 'activations' correspond to units which do not have any activity and which decide to exercise one. Economic 'reactivations' correspond to units which had stopped their activity and which start up again. They only deal with individual entrepreneurs – craftsmen or shopkeepers. Financial and agricultural activities and the French units established abroad are set aside as well.

6. Closed down firms correspond to a cancellation of the registration of the firm from the SIRENE repertory (Information and Registration System of Firms and Plants). They may be voluntary or involuntary (failures) in the proportion of around 4/5 to 1/5. Some of these firms may be taken over so we included them in the group of survival firms even though their Sirene number changed. So, by giving greater place to the continuation of the economic activity, rates of cessation correspond to an entrepreneurial failure (voluntary cessation or cessation following a compulsory liquidation).

7. After correction by a weight variable they represent 36 337 firms.

8. t_i is the difference between the date of cessation of activity and the date of setting up of the i firm.

REFERENCES

Abdesselam, R., J. Bonnet and N. Le Pape (2004), 'An explanation of the life span of new French firms', *Small Business Economics*, **23**, 237–54.

Agarwal, R. (1997), 'Survival of firms over the product life cycle', *Southern Economic Journal*, **63** (3), 571–83.

Allison, P.D. (1995), *Survival Analyses Using the SAS Système: A Practical Guide*, Cary, NC: SAS Institute.

Audretsch, D. (1995), *Innovation and Industry Evolution*, Cambridge, MA: MIT Press.

Audretsch, D. and T. Mahmood (1995), 'New firm survival: new results using a hazard function', *Review of Economics and Statistics*, **77**, 97–103.

Bates, T. (1990), 'Entrepreneur human capital inputs and small business longevity', *Review of Economics and Statistics*, **72**, 551–9.

Bhattacharjee, A., J. Bonnet, N. Le Pape and R. Renault (2008), 'Entrepreneurial motives and performance: why might better educated entrepreneurs be less successful?', working paper.

Caves, R. and M.E. Porter (1977), 'From entry barriers to mobility barriers: conjectural decisions and contrived deterrence to new competition', *Quarterly Journal of Economics*, **91**, 241–61.

Covin, J.G. and T.J. Covin (1990), 'Competitive aggressiveness, environmental context and small firm performance', *Entrepreneurship Theory and Practice*, **15** (2), Summer, 35–50.

Covin, J.G. and D.P. Slevin (1991), 'A conceptual model of entrepreneurship as firm behavior', *Entrepreneurship Theory and Practice*, **16** (1), Fall, 7–25.

Cox, D.R. (1972), 'Regression models and life tables', with discussion, *Journal of the Royal Statistical Society*, **B34**, 187–220.

Dess, G.G., R.D. Ireland, S.A. Zahra, S.W. Floyd, J.J. Janney and P.J. Lane (2003), 'Emerging issues in corporate entrepreneurship', *Journal of Management*, **29**, 351–78.

Doms, M., T. Dunne and M.J. Roberts (1995), 'The role of technology use in the survival and growth of manufacturing plants', *International Journal of Industrial Organization*, **13**, 523–42.

Evans, D. (1987), 'The relationship between firm growth, size and age: estimates for 100 manufacturing industries', *Journal of Industrial Economics*, **35**, 657–74.

Ferrier, W.J. (2001), 'Navigating the competitive landscape: the drivers and consequences of competitive aggressiveness', *Academy of Management Journal*, **44** (4), 858–77.

Ferrier, W.J., K.G. Smith and C.M. Grimm (1999), 'The role of competitive action in market share erosion and industry dethronement: a study of industry leaders and challengers', *Academy of Management Journal*, **42** (4), 372–88.

Fosfuri, A. and M.S. Giarratana (2004), '"Product strategies and startups". Survival in turbulent industries: evidence from the security software industry', Universidad Carlos III Departamento de Economía de la Empresa business economics working papers no. wb044816.

Geroski, P.A., J. Mata and P. Portugal (2003), 'Founding conditions and the survival of new firms', Banco de Portugal working paper no. 1-03.

Hall, B.H. (1987), 'The relationship between firm size and firm growth in the US manufacturing sector', *Journal of Industrial Economics*, **35** (4), 583–606.

Hannan, M.T. and J. Freeman (1984), 'Structural inertia and organizational change', *American Sociological Review*, **49** (2), 149–64.

Honjo, Y. (2000), 'Business failure of new firms: an empirical analysis using a multiplicative hazards model', *International Journal of Industrial Organization*, **18**, 557–74.

Keh, H.T., T.T.M. Nguyen and H.P. Ng (2007), 'The effects of entrepreneurial orientation and marketing information on the performance of SMEs', *Journal of Business Venturing*, **22**, 592–611.

Lieberman, M.B. and D.B. Montgomery (1998), 'First-mover (dis)advantages: retrospective and link with the resource-based view', *Strategic Management Journal*, **19**, 1111–25.

Levinthal, D. (1997), 'Adaptation on rugged landscapes', *Management Science*, **43**, 934–50.

Lumpkin, G.T. and G.G. Dess (1996), 'Clarifying the entrepreneurial orientation construct and linking it to performance', *Academy of Management Review*, **21**, 135–72.

Lumpkin, G.T. and G.G. Dess (2001), 'Linking two dimensions of entrepreneurial orientation to firm performance: the moderating role of environment and industry life cycle', *Journal of Business Venturing*, **16**, 429–51.

Mata, J. and P. Portugal (1994), 'Life duration of new firms', *Journal of Industrial Economics*, **42**, 227–45.

Mata, J., P. Portugal and P. Guimaraes (1995), 'The survival of new plants: start-up conditions and post-entry evolution', *International Journal of Industrial Organization*, **13**, 459–81.

Moreno, A.M., and J.C. Casillas (2008), 'Entrepreneurial orientation and growth of SMEs: a causal model', *Entrepreneurship Theory and Practice*, **32**, 507–28.

Smith, K.G., W.J. Ferrier and C.M. Grimm (2001), 'King of the hill: dethroning the industry leader', *Academy of Management Executive*, **15** (2), 59–70.

Stam, W. and T. Elfring (2008), 'Entrepreneurial orientation and new venture performance: the moderating role of intra- and extraindustry social capital', *Academy of Management Journal*, **51**, 97–111.

Wiklund, J. and D. Shepherd (2005), 'Entrepreneurial orientation and small business performance: a configurational approach', *Journal of Business Venturing*, **20**, 71–91.

10. Interaction between regional intellectual capital and organizational intellectual capital: the mediating roles of entrepreneurial characteristics

Csaba Deák and Stefania Testa

10.1 INTRODUCTION AND OBJECTIVE

Intellectual capital (IC), or the ability to utilize knowledge resources, is largely recognized by scholars and practitioners as the fundamental source and driver of an organization's competitive advantage (for example, Sullivan, 1998). Recently several researchers have begun to speak about IC not only in reference to business organizations but also to other contexts (Bounfour and Edvinsson, 2005). For example, Smedlund and Poyhonen (2005) deal with IC at cluster and regional levels while Malhotra (2001) deals with IC at a national level. When facing regions and nations, the same fundamental components used for organizations are mentioned, while adopting extended and refined definitions. According to Stewart (2001), within the field of strategic management IC includes three main components: human capital, structural capital and relational capital. Human capital is embodied in the skills, knowledge and expertise that individuals have; structural capital comprises the general system and procedures of the organization as well as physical infrastructures; and relational capital is made up of the relationships that an organization has with the environment in which it operates.

The concept of regional cognitive and intangible resources is particularly relevant when facing small and medium-sized enterprises (SMEs). SMEs are often limited by resource availability and must heavily rely on external knowledge and skills, which are often embedded in their local area. Thus the issue of how SMEs exploit the elements of regional IC, combined with their own organizational IC, in order to gain a competitive advantage has been addressed by numerous studies. Such a combination of and interaction between regional and organizational IC and, more generally, the knowledge exchange phenomenon are usually described by means of two main yet opposing explanatory approaches (Giuliani, 2005). The one describes the phenomenon as a quasi-automatic mechanism (for example, the economists' perspective on 'localized knowledge spillover') based on geographical proximity, the other points to the necessity to include specific features of the firms and of firm-level learning. As an example, Giuliani and Bell (2005) claim that such an interaction is characterized by a pronounced heterogeneity deriving from differences in the companies' knowledge bases. In the same vein, Steiner and Ploder (2008) introduce the position of firms within networks as another determinant in the nature and intensity of knowledge exchange. Nevertheless, such authors claim the need to take other aspects into consideration, such as those related to the organizational context. Stimulated by such considerations and on the basis of evidence collected in previous research (Massa and Testa, 2008, 2009, 2010), further investigation has started to add new insights on the topic. In the above-mentioned research the authors found evidence that aligns with that of both Giuliani and Bell (2005) and Steiner and Ploder (2008). Results showed that some companies actively contribute to the development of local IC. This is because the firms' boundaries are porous and they let inside knowledge out, while others remain cognitively isolated or just act as knowledge takers. The present research aims at investigating the possible determinants of such heterogeneity by both enlarging the observation to a wider sample and deepening the analysis. The possible determinants have been searched for in the personal characteristics of the business owners.

The focus of researchers investigating issues of knowledge resources is often on knowledge-intensive sectors (Smith, 2002) since knowledge is assumed to be more critical in those sectors due to the necessity to be more innovative (Ruiz Mercader et al., 2006). Thus a lack of investigations into non-knowledge-intensive sectors is claimed. Indeed Cooke (2002, p. 3) underlines that 'all human economic activity depends upon knowledge, so in a trivial sense, all economies are knowledge economies'.

For the present research, two food industries have been selected and compared: the food industry in Northwest Italy and the food industry in North Hungary. There are multiple reasons that lead to this choice. First, the food industry is included in the low-technology manufacturing category by the OECD (1999) classification of knowledge-based industries, even though some authors speak about misplacement (see, for example, Cooke, 2002). Second, the food industry is a mature industry and faces an increasingly heightened competitive environment due to a variety of reasons such as globalization, mature markets, need of cost reduction and so on (Puliafito et al., 2008). Companies in this industry are forced into change to avoid decline, ever more often than in the context of emerging industries, thus supplying the potential for a renewed role for entrepreneurship (Cassia et al., 2006). Third, the food industry is mainly a knowledge-using rather than knowledge-creating industry but it has become recently more scientifically knowledge embedded. The food industry mainly relies on a synthetic knowledge base which, according to Asheim and Gertler (2005), refers to activities where innovation mainly takes place through the application of existing knowledge or through the new combination of knowledge. This often occurs in response to the need to solve specific problems that arise during interaction with clients and suppliers. Novel knowledge is mainly created by an inductive process of testing and experimenting or through practical work. Such knowledge is mainly tacit due to the fact that it often results from experience gained at the workplace and through learning by doing, using and interacting. The need for concrete know-how, craft and practical skills in the knowledge creation process makes the regional dimension and spatial proximity more important than in other kinds of industries which, in turn, make regional IC very central. Fourth, both geographical areas examined in this research have a high regional IC as regards the chosen industry (that is, the selected companies operate in areas where their knowledge is the dominant knowledge and it has been accumulated over many years), as will be highlighted in the following sections. Fifth, both Italy and Hungary are ranked low by several international evaluations (for example, the World Economic Forum for the 2007–08 period) in terms of competitiveness (respectively 46th and 47th position) and innovation ability. As a result, they urgently need national and regional strategies that can help overcome such weaknesses. Lastly, the food industry is among the three most important sectors both in Italy and Hungary and it has a significantly positive foreign trade balance in both countries.

This chapter is organized as follows. In Section 10.2, the investigation framework is provided. In Section 10.3, some details on the methodology used are presented. In Section 10.4, the research setting is described with reference to the IC of the areas under consideration. In Section 10.5, empirical evidence from the cases is discussed and lastly, in Section 10.6, some conclusions are drawn.

10.2   INVESTIGATION FRAMEWORK

Without undertaking an extensive review of works devoted to SME behaviour, it is clear that a rather broad consensus exists on the fact that the organizational dimensions of SMEs often overlap with their entrepreneurial dimensions (Kickul and Gundry, 2002) and that owners play a preponderant role in shaping SME behaviour. Variables taken into consideration include owners' personality traits, motivations and competencies as well as personal demographic variables. Cardon et al. (2005) even speak about identification between an entrepreneur and his or her venture and Chapman (2000) emphasizes this aspect in the title of her article 'When the entrepreneur sneezes, the organization catches a cold'. Thus, when discussing SMEs' organizational IC it is not surprising that authors often measure the human capital dimension as the education, experience and level of motivation of the entrepreneur his or herself (Peña, 2002). Examples of indicators usually measured to assess regional IC which have been customized to the food sector can be found in Massa and Testa (2008). They range from the number of companies operating in the agro-food sector to the number of sector fairs hosted in the local area and so on.

In order to reach a complete understanding of SME behaviour, contextual and external factors also have to be taken into consideration; however, for the purpose of the present research, the focus is on entrepreneurial characteristics only, adopting the so-called personality-dominated approach (Gibb and Davies, 1990). Following this approach, several contributions to the literature exist that focus on a SME propensity to knowledge exchange. For example, Baron and Markman (2000) identify social skills, among individual competencies, as a factor predisposing companies to effective interaction with others.

The insights gained by the considerations put forth here allow the formulation of the following tentative hypothesis and serve as guiding principles for the ensuing analysis.

Hypothesis: Depending on the characteristics of the founders/owners, not all SMEs participate in equal intensity in regional and organizational IC exchange. Some of them play an essential role in knowledge generation and diffusion, others operate in egoistic terms and others remain totally isolated.

10.3   METHODOLOGY

The research methodology employed is based on the analysis of several business cases. Data collection was based on an average of three to four semi-structured interviews per case with the entrepreneurs and other informants. Informants included marketing or commercial managers, among others. Individual interviews lasted from one to two hours and whenever possible they ended with group discussions involving all the previously interviewed informants. A special effort was devoted to identifying the personal characteristics of the business owners, in terms of traits, competencies and motivations.

Archival documents have also been collected, in accordance with the distinct tradition in the literature on social science research methods that advocates different sources of data (and methods) be used to validate one another (Jick, 1979). Data collection was conducted over a period of six months and standard techniques for case studies were followed (Yin, 2003). After transcribing the interviews data was coded to identify themes, recurring comments and parameters that could be analysed with regard to the research issue.

Due to limitations of space, only four cases out of the complete dataset are presented in the present chapter. The cases have been purposely selected in order to effectively represent the findings of the research. They come from a set of 20 cases in the Italian food industry, all of which concern SMEs located in Northwest Italy and 12 cases from the food industry in North Hungary. The authors are aware that SME behaviours are highly differentiated across sectors, regions and countries but the focus here is on entrepreneurial characteristics at an individual level.

10.4   RESEARCH SETTING

10.4.1   Northwest Italy and the Food Sector

Northwest Italy is one of the historical cradles of the Italian food industry, where the main multinationals of the sector are located alongside small and medium artisan firms that promote traditional local foods. Northwest Italy alone covers 30–35 per cent of total Italian agro-food exports (22 billion euros per year). The Northwest represents the Italian food industry's most advanced region where hi-tech research, industrial production and creativity in food production coexist with the preservation of that special quality of food as a synthesis of culture and centuries-old traditions. Moreover, this area, which was recently recognized as the 'Italian Food Valley', is becoming a national and international reference point for critical reflection on food production and consumption, as well as for the excellence of its gastronomic specialties.

The region hosts prestigious international events such as Salone del Gusto (Taste Show) in Turin and will host Expo 2015, entitled 'Feeding the planet, energy for life' in Milan. Moreover, many science parks and research centres in the agro-food sector are located in this area. The Slow Food Association, established to interpret the emerging need of food consumers linked to the ethical and social dimensions of eating habits, was founded in this region in 1986 as a non-profit association. The region also boasts a large number of Protected Designation of Origin/Protected Geographical Indication (PDO/PGIs)[1].

10.4.2 North Hungary and the Food Sector

The food industry is an important sector of the Hungarian national economy, although its importance – due to the forging ahead of other progressive sectors – has gradually decreased in the last ten to 12 years. Amongst the processing industry sectors, the food industry is in third place, accounting for output of about 11.4 per cent (2005) of the total. In Hungary the food industry is the only sector that has a significantly positive foreign trade balance. Its activity directly affects other sectors since the Hungarian food industry uses most of the country's agricultural product and a considerable quantity of packaging products. It provides stocks for the catering industry and it is an important consumer of logistical and educational services. The food industry is a major user of energy and other natural resources, such as water and its permanent improvement is therefore one of the important factors of sustainable development. Currently 46 per cent of the Hungarian food industry's production is derived from SMEs. The Hungarian food industry has time-honoured traditions in producing high-quality products. Traditionally North Hungary has been the country's leading food exporting area. Due to its favourable production site and climate conditions, as well as food culture, several excellent Hungarian products are produced there.

Concerning the economic structure of North Hungary, the food industry seems to play an important role in the region. Wine growing has specific importance in the region's food industry. Both Tokaji and Eger local wines are internationally well known. For the most part, the region's companies are small-sized businesses. Seventy per cent of firms make under 80000 euros turnover, 13 per cent reach 80000 to 200000 euros and 11.1 per cent make under 1200000 euros a year. In addition, several industrial bakeries are located in the region. They range from small bakeries to large bake houses. With spreading hypermarkets, in-house bakeries brought an increased selection, resulting in losses for large capacity, in-town bakeries. Recently the meat industry also underwent a serious transformation. The capacities of Hungarian slaughterhouses are larger than they should be and most of them do not comply with European norms. Consequently many were closed down since they could not make the huge investments in technological innovation that were required. However, most of the region's active enterprises provide the technical conditions for hygienic slaughtering, meat and sausage production, factory and personal hygiene and follow public health, epidemic and veterinary health standards.

10.5 EMPIRICAL EVIDENCE AND DISCUSSION

In this section several cases are briefly presented in order to purposely represent differences in the companies' behaviours in terms of exchanging intellectual resources with the local context. Some of them play an essential role in knowledge generation and diffusion (Give&Take subgroup), others operate in egoistic terms (Take subgroup) and others remain totally isolated (No give-No take subgroup). The possible determinants of such heterogeneity have been searched for among the personal characteristics of the business owners.

Table 10.1 summarizes the main features of the selected companies in Italy and Hungary.

10.5.1 Exchanging Intellectual Resources with the Local Context

Company Alpha is a good example of a company that is highly involved in exchanging intellectual resources with the local context. Alpha produces high-quality butter and cheese sold mainly in specialty shops and in selected large retail stores. The founder started up Alpha in 1975 after leaving his activity in the field of electronics and moved by his affection for the local territory and its ancient farming tradition. The entrepreneur rediscovered ancient local cheese recipes and started producing typical cheeses that had almost disappeared, relying on the historical memory of local people and restoring old production processes and devices. He also created new and original cheeses derived from traditional recipes reinterpreted to meet modern taste. Alpha aims at safeguarding local cuisines, traditional products, and vegetable and animal species at risk of extinction. It is actively involved in promoting a new model of agriculture, which is less intensive and healthier. It is founded on the knowledge and know-how of local communities. Several company initiatives aim at defending biodiversity and promoting sustainable regional development. The entrepreneur is directly and passionately involved in promoting producer cooperatives. These cooperatives draw together producers from the local area to share expertise, endogenous knowledge and behavioural codes. Furthermore, with a group of researchers from a local university, the

Table 10.1   Main features of selected companies

Company	Alpha (Italy)	Beta (Italy)	Gamma (Hungary)	Delta (Hungary)
Foundation year	1975	1911	1992	1992
Kind of business	Family business	Family business	Family business	Family business
Main products	High quality butter and cheeses	Olive oil (virgin and extra-virgin) Preserves (vegetables in oil and sauces) Line of cosmetics	Edible snails, snail shell, preserved pickles	Special quality wine
Main distribution channels	Small retailers (food boutiques)	Mail order selling	Food stores/ supermarkets	Wholesalers and web shop
Main markets	National and international (15%)	National (100%)	National and international (70%)	National and international (40%)
Sales [K€]	7.865	107.708	2.690	600
ROE[a]	18.5%	7.41%	–	64% (not including the vineyard)
ROTA[b]	14.7%	4.81%	–	32% (not including the vineyard)
ROS[c]	5.1%	3.5%	–	19%
Employees	20–49	50–249	50–249	20–49

Notes:
[a] Net income/shareholder equity.
[b] Income before interest and tax/(fixed assets + current assets).
[c] Income before interest and tax/sales.

entrepreneur is developing a research programme concerning the presence of particular botanic species in meadows and their influence on the characteristics of the milk. Recently the entrepreneur launched a project aimed at safeguarding an ancient Armenian cheese, bringing the shepherds out of their isolation, fostering collaboration among them, improving cheese making conditions and obtaining the hygienic authorization. This authorization will allow them to sell the cheese in national and international markets. The entrepreneur has also launched and sponsored several initiatives connected to tourism. He recuperated and restored several buildings in an ancient 'cheese hamlet' which are used to refine and mature typical cheeses according to traditional methods. Recently a restaurant offering Alpha's products as well as those of other small local producers opened in such a historical hamlet. A large conference room is also available to host events. In spring the conference room becomes an educational centre for the local University of Gastronomic Sciences. This has a great impact on the promotion of the whole territory and attracts specialized agro-food competencies.

Company Beta (for a detailed description of company Beta see Massa and Testa, 2009) is, on the contrary, a good example of a company that mainly acts as a 'knowledge taker' (that is a company that is more absorbing of regional IC than releasing of organizational IC). Beta produces olive oil and preserves obtained from traditional recipes, as well as a line of cosmetics. It is a family business that started in 1911 as a print shop: oil production started following overproduction in the family olive harvest. The family decided to sell the production surplus directly to consumers and this choice has persisted to the present with mail order selling as the exclusive distribution channel. Aware of the current growing enthusiasm for local food, Beta relies heavily on the concept of 'localness' in its marketing communication and initiatives. Despite that, Beta does not seem to have strong interactions with its territory, local companies or institutions. On the contrary, it seems to be a closed system that does not exchange knowledge with the territory, as it does not invest resources in its promotion and development. The only valuable example in this direction is the Olive Tree Museum which contributes to the structural IC of the region to some extent. Unfortunately the impact of this contribution is severely limited by the location of the museum, which is on the company's premises. This means the choice was made without the need for agreement with local institutions and it assumes the meaning of mere self-promotion.

Company Gamma produces food from edible snails, including the production of preserves in the North Hungarian region. Its range of products include frosted snails, cleaned snail shells and preserved pickles. The company exports snails and also tries to distribute its preserves in the domestic market. The firm was established in 1992 and has operated as a family business until the present. Their preserves are distributed through food stores and supermarkets in Hungary and abroad. However processed snails are sold exclusively abroad, mainly in France and Romania. The organization is not able to cooperate with other companies, experts and/ or institutions in the region due to its activity and the lack of any university, college or research centre linked to the food industry. The firm would willingly share its acquired knowledge with others and would be open to learning, but at present the firm may be viewed as an isolated small to medium-sized organization. Although it produces high-quality products for the food market, its activity is not reliant on regional knowledge and it does not contribute to the region's intellectual capital. The firm believes that 'considering the activities and perspectives of the region, there's no possibility to do that'.

Company Delta, like Alpha, is again a good example of a company highly involved in exchanging intellectual resources locally. The owner is one of the oldest wine-making families in Tokaj and its family tree dates from the sixteenth century. A passionate love for grape growing and wine making has been in the family for generations. The entrepreneur is one of the pioneers of contemporary Tokaj wines and seeks to return to the roots of Tokaj wine making. He continued the family tradition by gaining a degree in the mid-1970s and working as an agronomist at the agricultural cooperative of Mád. In the 1980s, he carried out mass production on 1000 hectares as one of the cooperative's chiefs. During Hungary's days of political and economical unrest (1989–90) he owned a seven hectare territory, but lost everything in 1992 due to a failed investment (his whole area was taken into Royal Tokaj and later sold to an investor). Thus he had to restart again from nearly zero, that is, from a 1.5 hectare piece of land. In 1999, following his 'showman-like' talent, he started buying up territories, adding to ones he already held. Currently his vineyards cover 54 hectares. This measures approximately half of the largest vineyards (there are five larger ones, mainly in French and Spanish ownership), but the area is nearly the largest Hungarian-owned vineyard. In 1992, while other producers struggled to keep their enterprises afloat, he implemented a never before seen drastic yield restriction. He proved that by intelligent decrease in grape quantity, it was possible to obtain a marked increase in quality.

The entrepreneur is actively involved in professional and social organizations. For example, he was a founding member and chairman (1998–2003) of Tokaj Renaissance (established in 1995, with 22 members). He has recently established and manages a local knowledge-sharing association with 15 other local wine makers. He is involved in joint research projects with Debrecen University, Eger Wine Research Institute and other industrial food producers. He supports the post-secondary Tokaj wine-making programme by receiving students on school trips and practical placements. He does this despite the fact that students will ultimately be employed at other companies in the region. Eger, North Hungary's other large wine-growing area, is about 80 km away.

Despite this, he also keeps up good relations with wine makers there. Knowledge exchange occurs through regular visits and discussions. For example, he had less experience with dry wines, but by acquiring the knowledge of others, mainly in the Eger area, he was able to 'take on the rhythm'. Another episode of knowledge exchange sees him teaching local Eger wine makers about the close link between low yield and quality. In the same location he also studied cider acid decomposition and maturation in bottle. His motivations are not limited to the financial realm, but he also feels responsibility for the community. 'It is worthy of a consciously thinking human,' he said, 'to contribute at spreading food knowledge and culture for a passion and a profit too.' If Delta sets about anything, it tends to set the standard: it brought to light a neglected type of wine. The entrepreneur has set out to make Tokaj wine more popular, more liked and more requested around the world. His goal is to create a new and higher profile image for the Tokaj region.

Tables 10.2 and 10.3 summarize how the selected companies mobilize IC by means of give and take processes.

10.5.2   Entrepreneurial Characteristics of the Business Owners

Analysing the individual-level characteristics of the entrepreneurs from the whole set of case studies (from both Italy and Hungary), it is the entrepreneurial passion towards their venture that seems to allow for distinguishing the Give&Take subgroup from the other subgroups (Take; No give-No take). Until recently emotions have not received significant scholarly attention in the entrepreneurship literature (Shane et al., 2003). Indeed, Weick (1999) and Frost (1999) compellingly argued that theories recognizing emotion resonate with our day-to-day experience, while Baum et al. (2001) demonstrated that passion has a direct significant effect on SME growth. In the words of an entrepreneur reported in Chang (2001, p. 106): 'Passion inspires us to work harder and with greater effect. The irony is that we hardly notice our effort. It comes easily and enjoyably.' As noted by Cardon et al. (2005), passion may lead to both functional and dysfunctional consequences. As an example, passion makes non-monetary rewards as important as monetary gratification, thus it may contribute to postponing the achievement of economic results or it may induce 'temporary blindness' to obstacles (Branzei and Zietsma, 2003).

In our cases passion makes a difference in the propensity to exchange intellectual resources with the local context. Passion impacts on the regional/organizational IC combination, mainly in the outbound direction

Table 10.2   IC mobilizing (Italy)

Give		Take	
Beta	**Alpha**	**Beta**	**Alpha**
Olive Tree Museum	Support to biodiversity, producers' Consortia, presidia	Regional reputation in oil production	Regional reputation in food production
	Internationalization of other local producers	Traditional production processes	Traditional production processes and recipes
	Development and diffusion of specialized knowledge in local University of Gastronomic Sciences	History/culture	History/culture
	Restoration of ancient buildings for tourist purposes		Beauties of nature

Source: From Massa and Testa (2008).

Table 10.3   IC mobilizing (Hungary)

Give		Take	
Gamma	**Delta**	**Gamma**	**Delta**
–	Knowledge and experiences to the local enterprises	–	Regional reputation in wine production
	Development and diffusion of specialized knowledge	–	Traditional production processes
–	in local post-secondary education	–	History/culture
–	Common research with local university and research centres	–	Employees with experience
–	Professional awards for increasing the name of the wine region	–	Knowledge and experiences from local enterprises

(the passionate entrepreneur is also a passionate knowledge giver). The passionate entrepreneur makes no distinction between their private life and their enterprise and always speaks about their business and thus contributes to distributing knowledge and creating awareness in the local context regarding big current changes in food values. As an example, entrepreneur Alpha writes and speaks about local food and traditional production systems in prestigious national and international journals, as well as in the local community during informal meetings and specialized or village fairs. Such a passion recalls a sort of romanticism and resonates in his words:

> The secret of my successful butter resides in the alpine meadows, at high altitude, with few weeds and a lot of lactiferous herbs and many brightly-coloured flowers and an intense scent: myosotes, ranunculuses, martagons, daisies, gentians. . . .The different creams, once mixed together, multiply scents and fragrances creating butter that presents a rich and harmonious bouquet. A delight!

This passion also appears in the case of entrepreneur Delta:

> An intuition derived from experience and faith results. The renovation of many specific growing sites and uncultivated vineyards gives such excellent yields. . . . There is a special relationship between plants, soil, climate and myself. . . . I want to produce even more amazing products, with a high quality level!

It is interesting to note that the majority of the passionate entrepreneurs, as in the case of company Alpha, were outsiders to the food industry when they started up their companies as they came from other experiences. This aspect could have helped them to face the industry without preconceptions and approach the sector primarily as enthusiastic consumers and lovers of local territory and tradition. These aspects may contribute to make them 'unconventional individuals' (Steiner, 1995); however this does not mean that they are acting against what is actually in their own best interest – building and maintaining a venture and making it profitable – but that they are not overly concerned with secrecy and protection of their organizational knowledge resources. Nevertheless, it is not surprising that some companies in the food sector are generous in giving knowledge to the local context. If the environment has a good reputation the company itself will also gain a competitive advantage. For example, a customer may not know a specific producer, but may buy the product because of its territorial origin. In fact, it is well known that local food producers can effectively promote themselves by building up strong synergies between their products and places, thus building a tie between company marketing and regional marketing (Belletti, 2002). Such a tie can be a win-win situation, but it implies profound involvement and commitment by local entrepreneurs in creating – and then proactively participating in – an articulated network allowing information flow and knowledge exchange. In the examples reported above Alpha devoted a lot of resources to rediscovering ancient cheeses and to recreating conditions to produce them. It relied on the local population's historical memory, as well as on restoring old production processes and devices. At the same time, localized area science parks and research centres, as well as prestigious international events and specialized locally organized fairs, represent a valuable asset in influencing Alpha's development and all local businesses that are able to take advantage of it. Thus, in the case of the Give&Take subgroup, regional IC can impact upon local firms' success and vice versa.

Market orientation is another of the most observed individual-level characteristics among the entrepreneurs of this set of case studies. However, as in the case of company Beta, market orientation does not seem to impact alone on the propensity to exchange knowledge with the local context. Such entrepreneurs, in virtue of their market orientation, devote special effort in embedding local knowledge in their products, exploiting local history and heritage for commercial gain and making reference to local craft production methods. Notwithstanding this, local knowledge and PDO/PGI certifications are used as marketing levers, but no concrete effort is made to interact with the territory (Take subgroup).

In the case of company Gamma, it is not surprising that the entrepreneur, with the perception of being an 'island' in the business environment, does not exhibit overt passion and remains cognitively isolated (No give-No take subgroup).

10.6   CONCLUSIONS

This research sought to add new insights on regional and organizational IC exchange by adopting the approach that claims the need to include specific features of firms in order to understand the heterogeneity of SME behaviours. Through an examination of 32 cases in two different contexts (Northwest Italy and North Hungary) this research confirms the existence of different behaviours. This study's contribution is that such heterogeneity also seems to depend on individual-level entrepreneurial characteristics and not only on a firm's knowledge base or position within networks, as already demonstrated in other research (Giuliani,

2006; Giuliani and Bell, 2005; Steiner and Ploder, 2008). The search for entrepreneurial characteristics as determinants of heterogeneity in knowledge exchange is rooted in the literature that emphasizes the role of founders/owners in shaping SME behaviour and claims overlapping between organizational and entrepreneurial dimensions (Kickul and Gundry, 2002). What seems to make the difference is passion, thus implicitly answering Krueger's question (2005): 'Where might passion make a difference?'. Companies that can be clustered in the subgroup Give&Take have passionate entrepreneurs in common who do not hesitate to devote time and resources in spreading food culture. They contribute to developing awareness and knowledge exchanges among both consumers and producers, thus influencing the emergence of an enlarged production system where the customer is also part of value creation. The passionate entrepreneurs often act and appear committed to values that are above commercial considerations.

It is worth noting that passion is not necessary to a venture's success. Many companies that lack passionate entrepreneurs and are placed in the Take subgroup are successful nonetheless. This result is obvious (defining a specific psychological profile for successful entrepreneurs/ventures has proven to be a generally fruitless endeavour) (Smilor, 1997)) but policy makers have to be aware that wide-ranging policies aimed at supporting SMEs, without also taking into consideration entrepreneurial individual-level characteristics, may not have the expected impact on broad well-being in the region. Policy makers should avoid feeding knowledge 'black holes'.

Future research could focus on designing an evaluation system to help regional policy developers to segment companies according to their concrete contributions to regional IC. Furthermore, knowledge exchange with actors outside the local context should also be deepened as several companies in the sample are also well connected beyond the local area.

There are pros and cons in adopting a case study approach. Observing what happens in the real business environment helps to better understand phenomena, but, on the contrary, pointing out general implications through study of a limited number of cases is difficult. Therefore conducting quantitative studies in the future, from which generalizations can be derived, may prove useful.

ACKNOWLEDGEMENT

The authors wish to thank Jesper Manniche for informal and stimulating discussions during the preparation of this chapter.

NOTE

1. PDO/PGI certifications were introduced by the European Union by means of regulations 2081/92 (recently substituted by 510/2006) with the aim of pointing out the link between the production process of an agro-food product and its territorial origin. These certifications aim at protecting the reputation of regional foods against unfair competition by non-genuine products which mislead consumers. Thus, in some ways, these laws act to protect regional IC.

REFERENCES

Asheim, B.T. and M.S. Gertler (2005), 'The geography of innovation: regional innovation systems', in J. Fagerberg, D. Mowery and R. Nelson (eds), *The Oxford Handbook of Innovation*, Oxford: Oxford University Press, pp. 291–317.

Baron, R. and G. Markman (2000), 'Beyond social capital: how social skills can enhance entrepreneurs' success', *Academy of Management Executive*, **14** (1), 106–15.

Baum, J., E. Locke and K. Smith (2001), 'A multidimensional model of venture growth', *Academy of Management Journal*, **44** (2), 292–303.

Belletti, G. (2002), 'Sviluppo rurale e prodotti tipici: reputazioni collettive, coordinamento e istituzionalizzazione' ['Rural development and typical products: collective reputations, coordination and institutionalization'], in E. Basile and D. Romano (eds), *Sviluppo Rurale: Societa', Territorio, Impresa [Rural Development: Society, Territory, Enterprise]*, Milan: Franco Angeli, pp. 373–97.

Bounfour, A. and L. Edvinsson (2005), *Intellectual Capital for Communities*, Boston, MA: Elsevier.

Branzei, O. and C. Zietsma (2003), 'Entrepreneurial love: the enabling functions of positive illusions in venturing', paper presented at the Babson-Kauffman Entrepreneurial Research Conference, Babson College, Wellesley, MA.

Cardon, M., C. Zietsma, P. Saparito, B. Matherne and C. Davis (2005), 'A tale of passion: new insights into entrepreneurship from a parenthood metaphor', *Journal of Business Venturing*, **20**, 23–45.

Cassia, L., M. Fattore and S. Paleari (2006), 'Entrepreneurship as renewal in mature industries', University of Bergamo Department of Management and Information Technology economics and management working paper 1/EM.

Chang, R. (2001), 'Turning passion into organizational performance', *Training and Development*, **55** (5), 104–12.

Chapman, M. (2000), 'When the entrepreneur sneezes, the organization catches a cold: a practitioner's perspective on the state of the art in research on the entrepreneurial personality and the entrepreneurial process', *European Journal of Work and Organizational Psychology*, **9** (1), 97–101.

Cooke, P. (2002), *Knowledge Economies: Clusters, Learning and Cooperative Advantage*, London: Routledge.

Frost, P.J. (1999), 'Why compassion counts', paper presented at the meeting of the Academy of Management, San Diego, CA.

Gibb, A. and L. Davies (1990), 'In pursuit of frameworks for the development of growth models of the small business', *International Small Business Journal*, **9** (1), 15–31.

Giuliani, E. (2005), 'The structure of cluster. Knowledge and networks: uneven and selective, not pervasive and collective', Druid Copenhagen working paper 05-11.

Giuliani, E. (2006), 'The selective nature of knowledge networks in clusters: evidence from the wine industry', *Journal of Economic Geography*, 7, 139–68.

Giuliani, E. and M. Bell (2005), 'The micro-determinants of meso-level learning and innovation: evidence from a Chilean wine cluster', *Research Policy*, 34, 47–68.

Jick, T. (1979), 'Mixing qualitative and quantitative methods: triangulation in action', *Administrative Science Quarterly*, 24 (4), 602–11.

Kickul, J. and L.K. Gundry (2002), 'Prospecting for strategic advantage: the proactive entrepreneurial personality and small firm innovation', *Journal of Small Business Management*, 40 (2), 85–97.

Krueger, N. Jr. (2005), '*From Keynes'* "animal spirits" to human spirits. Passion as the missing link in entrepreneurial intentions', Social Science Research Network working paper series, accessed 27 January 2010 at http://ssrn.com/abstract=1162337.

Malhotra, Y. (2001), 'Knowledge assets in the global economy: assessment of national intellectual capital', in Y. Malhotra (ed.), *Knowledge Management and Business Model Innovation*, London: Idea Publishing Group, pp. 232–49.

Massa, S. and S. Testa (2008), "Localness' is good for business? An intellectual capital-based perspective in the Italian food industry', *International Journal of Innovation and Regional Development*, 1 (2), 192–209.

Massa, S. and S. Testa (2009), 'A knowledge management approach to organization competitive advantage: evidences from the food sector', *European Management Journal*, 27, 129–41.

Massa, S. and S. Testa (2010), 'Knowledge management systems, firm innovativeness and knowledge domain: challenges for small and medium enterprises', *International Journal of Learning and Intellectual Capital*, in press.

Organisation for Economic Co-operation and Development (OECD) (1999), *The Knowledge-based Economy: A Set of Facts and Figures*, Paris: OECD.

Peña, I. (2002), 'Intellectual capital and business start-up success', *Journal of Intellectual Capital*, 3 (2), 180–98.

Puliafito, P.P., S. Massa and S. Testa (2008), 'It's no use crying over spilt milk! Innovation paths in the dairy sector', *International Journal of Management Practice*, 3 (3), 277–90.

Ruiz Mercader, J., A. Merono-Cerdan and R. Sabater-Sanchez (2006), 'Information technology and learning: their relationship and impact on organizational performance in small businesses', *International Journal of Information Management*, 26 (1), 16–29.

Shane, S., E. Locke and C. Collins (2003), 'Entrepreneurial motivation', *Human Resource Management Review*, 13 (2), 257–79.

Smedlund, A. and A. Poyhonen (2005), 'Intellectual capital creation in regions: a knowledge system approach, in A. Bounfour and L. Edvinsson (eds), *Intellectual Capital for Communities*, Boston, MA: Elsevier Butterworth-Heinemann, pp. 227–52.

Smilor, R.W. (1997), 'Entrepreneurship: reflections on a subversive activity', *Journal of Business Venturing*, 12, 341–6.

Smith, K. (2002), 'What is knowledge economy? Knowledge intensity and distributed knowledge bases', The United Nations University Institute for New Technologies working paper 2002-2006.

Steiner, C.J. (1995), 'A philosophy of innovation: the role of unconventional individuals in innovation success', *Product Innovation Management*, **12** (5), 431–40.

Steiner, M. and M. Ploder (2008), 'Structure and strategy within heterogeneity: multiple dimensions of regional networking', *Regional Studies*, **42** (6), 793–815.

Stewart, T.A. (2001), *The Wealth of Knowledge: Intellectual Capital and the Twenty-first Century Organization*, London: Nicholas Brealey.

Sullivan, P.H. (eds) (1998), *Profiting from Intellectual Capital: Extracting Value from Innovation*, New York: Wiley.

Weick, K.E. (1999), 'That's moving: theories that matter', *Journal of Management Inquiry*, **8** (2), 134–42.

World Economic Forum (WEF) (2008), *The Global Competitiveness Report 2007-2008*, Geneva: WEF.

Yin, R.K. (2003), *Case Study Research: Design and Methods*, 3rd edn, Applied Social Research Methods Series vol. 5, Thousand Oaks, CA, London and New Delhi: Sage.

11. Is non-profit entrepreneurship different from other forms? A survey data analysis of motivations and access to funds

Franck Bailly and Karine Chapelle

11.1 INTRODUCTION

In social economics non-profit organizations are generally seen as sharing a common social sensibility; in particular, they aim to serve their members' interests and/or those of the wider community. This does not imply that such organizations are not seeking to make profits but rather that priority should be given to beneficiaries or employees of these organizations rather than to shareholders when it comes to distributing any profits that might be made. This social orientation, which strengthens the effects of the legal non-profit-distribution constraint, leads non-profit organizations to redistribute profits on the basis of 'equity' rather than on 'ownership' (Defourny and Monzon Campos, 1992). Because of this characteristic, they have been considered as marginal or residual organizations located on the fringes of the market economy.

In fact, these non-profit organizations account for quite a significant share of both production and employment. Indeed, in most countries, especially in developed countries, they account for up to 3 per cent of GDP and 10 per cent of jobs. If volunteers are taken into account, their share in total employment may be as high as 15 per cent. From a dynamic point of view, they also contribute significantly to job creation. Between 1990 and 1995, employment in non-profit organizations grew significantly, by between 5 per cent and 40 per cent depending on the country. Some countries such as France, the UK and Hungary, which during this period suffered a decline in employment of between 1 per cent and 2 per cent in the economy as a whole, experienced growth of between 20 per cent and 30 per cent in employment in the non-profit sector (see *The Comparative Non-profit Sector Project: Comparative*

Data Table and Non-profit Sector Growth (Johns Hopkins University, 2006).

The importance of these organizations and their dynamism almost naturally lead us to investigate in greater depth the question of their possible specificities. The answer to this question seems to us essential, since the specificity argument is often put forward, in public discourse as well as in the academic literature, to explain the presence of non-profit organizations and to report on some of their behaviour or characteristics. In particular, their social motivation, by virtue of being a token of trust, could be an important determinant of access to certain funds.

In this chapter, we will focus on two important questions. First, do non-profit entrepreneurs have, as is often argued, higher social motivations than for-profit entrepreneurs? And second, do non-profit entrepreneurs have easier access to public as well as to private funding?

We will try to answer these two questions from an empirical point of view by analysing an original survey carried out in the continuing training sector in Haute-Normandie (France). It is worth noting that few studies have focused on social motivations and access to funds when organizations are established (Hansmann et al., 2002; Mendell et al., 2003; Sloan, 1999, 2000; Wedig et al., 1988).

The chapter is organized as follows. Section 11.2 outlines how the economic literature deals with the two issues of social motivation and access to funds. Section 11.3 details the empirical material used. Sections 11.4 and 11.5 present the results relevant to the themes discussed in the theoretical section. Sections 11.6 concludes.

11.2   SPECIFICITY AND PRESENCE OF NON-PROFIT ORGANIZATIONS

11.2.1   Social Motivations

Economists' interest in non-profit organizations emerged quite late in the 1970s (OECD, 2003) with the publication of studies such as those by Weisbrod (1975), Hansmann (1980) and James (1987), which were regarded as pioneering works (cf. Enjolras, 1995; Nyssens, 2000). Most of these works are based on the idea – found in many subsequent analyses – that non-profit organizations are specific, that is, different from other organizations, including for-profit organizations. In particular, this specificity is said to arise from the fact that entrepreneurs or CEOs of non-profit organizations are more sensitive to social and even ideological considerations; as a result, their practices and activities are said to be more 'unselfish' (James, 1989; James and Rose-Ackerman, 1985; Rose-Ackerman, 1996; Young, 1980). Technically, it is expressed by taking into account 'altruistic' considerations disregarded by for-profit organizations in the utility functions (Du Bois et al., 2003).

Other authors are more cautious about the existence of such specificity. At least three sets of arguments are put forward in the literature. First, non-profit organizations may indeed be 'disguised' profit organizations (James, 1998; Weisbrod, 1988) or may 'cheat' while redistributing profits (Bilodeau and Slivinski, 1998). Second, with the decline of public funds and donations, non-profit organizations that have to seek commercial private funding in order to finance their social missions (James, 1983; Schiff and Weisbrod, 1991; Weisbrod, 1998b) might be diverted away from their original social goals (James, 2004; Tuckman, 1998; Weisbrod, 1998a). Third, even if the creators are initially more socially motivated, their environment may compel them to modify their social sympathies, which may well cause them to lose their specificity (DiMaggio and Powell, 1983, 1991; Enjolras, 1996).

The question of the presence or absence of social motivations seems to be crucial, since it lies at the heart of the explanation for the very existence of non-profit organizations and their behaviours.

11.2.2   Access to Funding

Regarding the issue of non-profit organizations' access to funding, there is also an abundant literature showing the possible existence of a positive link between the presence of social motivations and access to funds. Some authors argue that non-profit organizations inspire greater trust than profit organizations by virtue of the enforced non-profit-distribution constraint and their social motivations (James and Rose-Ackerman, 1985; Mendell et al., 2003; Rose-Ackerman, 1996). In particular, Hansmann (1980) argues that non-profit organizations are required to distribute profits in order to improve working conditions or production (in both quantity and quality) and not to distribute profits to the person who exercises control over the organization. The non-profit status would thus reassure consumers about the nature of the product or service and allay donors' fears about the inappropriate use of funds granted (Glaeser and Shleifer, 2001). As a result, they could benefit from public subsidies and the collection of funds from their members through contributions, donations or tax exemptions (Bilodeau and Slivinski, 1998; Lakdawalla and Philipson, 1998; Weisbrod, 1988). Consequently, they would be less constrained in their access to private and public funds, even if some of those funds are not always suitable (Bises, 2000; Hansmann, 1982, 1986). These assumptions spring from the fact that a significant share of non-profit organizations' income comes essentially from subsidies and that non-profit organizations more frequently benefit from tax exemptions (Mendell et al., 2003; Rose-Ackerman, 1996).

These studies of (non)-profit organizations lead us to believe that the non-profit-distribution constraint and social motivations may counter the barriers to entry that the difficulties of access to financial funds represent. Indeed, this token of trust can help non-profit entrepreneurs generate more private and public aid than for-profit entrepreneurs.

However, according to Rose-Ackerman (1996), tax exemption does not seem to be a very significant comparative advantage in terms of access to finance. Moreover, the constraint of non-profit distribution also has its downside. It may limit the personal contribution of partners. Indeed, the impossibility of redistributing dividends prevents non-profit organizations from issuing securities holdings (Auteri, 2003) and reduces incentives for good management because of the weakening of property rights (Alchian and Demsetz, 1972). In addition, the setting up of financial assets by non-profit organizations may be limited by the nature of these assets: public and private donors often set limits on how grants or donations should be invested (Valentinov, 2006). The CEOs themselves may wish to avoid certain financial resources that would prevent them from achieving their social goals. These various external and internal constraints may force non-profit organizations to reduce their dependence vis-à-vis certain sources of funding. Such social incentives could then be seen as leading to higher risks because they cause less attention to be paid to the objectives of profit or profitability and give rise to lower allocative efficiency. This assumption that non-profit organizations are less efficient could encourage financial institutions to be more demanding when granting loans to such organizations. The question of whether the token of trust provided by non-profit status compensates for the lack of trust that financial institutions may have in organizations is a critical one, particularly when an organization is first being established. Indeed, the lack of access to financial funds can be a major obstacle to entrepreneurship. Many studies, albeit of private enterprises, show that most new firms are subject to tougher liquidity constraints than established firms (Blanchflower and Oswald, 1998; Evans and Jovanovic, 1989; Evans and Leighton, 1989; Holtz-Eakin et al, 1994; Hurst and Lusardi, 2004). Entrepreneurs must, therefore, rely mainly on personal savings, loans or donations from friends and family. These are the most important sources of capital for newly established firms. Once the firm is established, institutional investors perceive fewer risks and, all other things being equal, are more inclined to provide capital (Stiglitz and Weiss, 1981). It can then legitimately be asked if for-profit entrepreneurs are indeed social entre-preneurs and, second, to what extent the funds provided by public and private donations may compensate for the greater difficulties non-profit entrepreneurs may experience in accessing funds.

11.3   PRESENTATION OF THE SURVEY

In an attempt to answer these two interconnected questions – the nature of the motivations of non-profit CEOs and non-profit entrepreneurs' access to financial funds – we conducted an original survey in the continuing training sector in the Haute-Normandie region of France.

There were several reasons for choosing this sector. First, the desire to further expand the knowledge-based economy and the emphasis placed on lifelong learning and training, at least in France, have given it a first-order role, even though to date few studies have analysed its modus operandi (Cahuc and Zylberberg, 2006), particularly regarding the place and role of non-profit organizations. Second, the training sector, in general, and the continuing training sector in particular, is one of the sectors where non-profit organizations are strongly represented (Archambault, 1999). Third, organizations of various legal status can be observed, not only non-profit, but also private companies and public organizations. A comparative analysis of these different categories of organizations is therefore possible. Lastly, there is in this sector, for the purpose of government auditing, a database that includes non-profit organizations (Salamon and Wojciech Sokolowski, 2005). This is seldom the case in other sectors. This database is compiled by the Ministry of Employment from information contained in the *bilans pédagogiques et financiers* (pedagogic and financial reports or BFPs), a government document that all organizations providing continu-ing training in France have to complete annually. They include informa-tion on the organizations that can be used to classify them and select a population to be investigated.

The choice of the Haute-Normandie region is justified by the fact the distribution of continuing training organizations in the region is largely identical to that observed nationally. The survey was conducted between March and July 2007 and involved 824 organizations identified in the BPFs submitted in Haute-Normandie. In the absence of more recent data, we used data from 2004. For the survey sample, we proceeded in two stages. First, we divided up the total population, that is, 824 observations, on the basis of three main criteria: legal status, size of organization and location. For the sample selection, we opted for a classification based on five dif-ferent legal statuses, namely non-profit organizations (1901 associations and other associations), for-profit private businesses, professionals, consular bodies and (quasi)-public bodies and other bodies. However, for the study, we had to group these five statuses into three categories: non-profit organizations, profit-making organizations and (quasi)-public and others. As for size, we opted for five categories: no employees, 1 to 5 employees, 6 to 10 employees, 11 to 20 employees and over 20 employees. Finally, we also distinguished between those organizations located in Eure and those in Seine-Maritime, the two departments[1] of the Haute-Normandie region. In the second stage institutions were chosen randomly within these different categories in order to ensure the initial population was as representative as possible. Our aim was to survey around half the total population. Of the 365 organizations contacted, 146 organizations responded to the questionnaire.

Since not all the organizations could be contacted or responded to the questionnaire, for-profit businesses are slightly over-represented, accounting for 72.60 per cent of the organizations surveyed. This compares with a share in the parent population of 65.78 per cent. Similarly, there is a slight under-representation of non-profit organizations and a more significant under-representation of (quasi)-public bodies and other bodies. However, the overall structure by size and legal status has been retained (Table 11.1).

In the following two sections, we will present the initial results of this survey. The objective is to shed light on some hitherto unknown aspects of non-profit entrepreneurship, earlier work in this field notwithstanding (Ben-Ner and Van Hoomissen, 1990; Bielefeld, 1994; Bond et al., 1999; Doumi 2006; Twombly, 2003). Our contribution is divided into two parts. In the first part we attempt to assess the importance of the social motivations of CEOs of non-profit organizations, particularly in the early stages of their organizations' lives, and whether these motivations are one of the specificities of such organizations. The second part seeks to ascertain to what extent the founders of non-profit organizations have benefited, as implied in the social economics literature, from greater access to funding (James and Rose-Ackerman, 1985).

11.4   THE MOTIVATIONS OF CEOs OF (NON)-PROFIT ORGANIZATIONS: THE CRITERIA FOR SELECTING TRAINEES

The motivations of the CEOs of continuing training organizations were investigated by looking at the reasons that were driving them to provide continuing training, both at the time of the survey and when their

Table 11.1   Representativeness and comparative structure of the total sample and surveyed population

Surveyed population/total initial sample	Legal status			
Size	For-profit enterprises (%)	Non-profit organizations (%)	(Quasi)-public bodies and others (%)	Total (%)
0 employees	**9.43**	**36.84**	**0.00**	**16.45**
	15.50	*22.94*	*11.77*	*17.35*
From 1 to 5 employees	**79.25**	**39.47**	**50.00**	**68.49**
	69.37	*33.33*	*11.77*	*55.70*
From 6 to 10 employees	**6.60**	**10.53**	**0.00**	**7.53**
	8.11	*18.18*	*7.84*	*10.92*
From 11 to 20 employees	**0.95**	**10.53**	**0.00**	**3.42**
	3.51	*10.82*	*9.80*	*5.95*
More than 20 employees	**3.77**	**2.63**	**50.00**	**4.11**
	3.51	*14.73*	*58.82*	*10.08*
Total	**100.00**	**100.00**	**100.00**	**100.00**
	100.00	*100.00*	*100.00*	*100.00*
Total	**72.60**	**26.03**	**1.37**	**100.00**
	65.78	*28.03*	*6.19*	*100.00*

Note: In bold are the distribution of organizations from the surveyed population; in italics are the distribution of organizations from the initial sample.

organizations were being set up, with the aim of capturing the social dimension of these motivations which, according to many studies, should be greater for non-profit organizations.

The CEOs' motivations for providing continuing training differ widely depending on their organizations' legal status (Table 11.2). Indeed, at the time the organizations were founded, only 12.42 per cent of for-profit managers were motivated by social considerations, namely the difficulties encountered by the population benefiting from the training. Such motivations are much more prevalent among non-profit providers. Nearly 31.96 per cent of them refer to this kind of motivation. It should be noted that a significant share (27.84 per cent) of CEOs of non-profit organizations engage in training activity because of the availability of public funds. This percentage may initially suggest opportunistic behaviour on the part of some founders who, because of difficulties in obtaining funds, choose non-profit status in order to attract additional funding from public sources.

Table 11.2 The criteria used for selecting trainees

Legal status in 2007 (obs.)	What were the main criteria when choosing the people to train?								
	Availability of public funds (%)	Social vulnerability of trainees (%)	Desire to differentiate themselves from competition (%)	Financial profitability of the training (%)	Ease of training people (%)	Desire to adapt to clients' wishes (%)	Training sold with software (%)	Other (%)	Total obs.
At the start-up of the organization									
For-profit organizations	3.92	12.42	38.56	31.37	9.15	26.47	13.07	18.95	
	(3)	*(9)*	*(31)*	*(23)*	*(8)*	*(22)*	*(10)*	*(10)*	*(75)*
Non-profit organizations	27.84	31.96	11.34	0.00	2.06	21.65	0.00	45.36	
	(5)	*(6)*	*(2)*	*(0)*	*(1)*	*(4)*	*(0)*	*(10)*	*(21)*
Others	0.00	0.00	100.00	0.00	0.00	0.00	0.00	0.00	
	(0)	*(0)*	*(1)*	*(0)*	*(0)*	*(0)*	*(0)*	*(0)*	*(1)*
Total	9.56	16.91	32.84	23.53	7.35	25.00	9.80	25.00	
	(8)	*(15)*	*(34)*	*(23)*	*(9)*	*(26)*	*(10)*	*(20)*	*(97)*
At present									
For-profit organizations	8.18	13.19	41.95	35.09	9.23	26.39	13.98	16.89	
	(5)	*(12)*	*(39)*	*(29)*	*(10)*	*(27)*	*(13)*	*10*	*89*
Non-profit organizations	46.72	57.66	36.50	2.92	2.92	18.25	0.00	23.36	
	(8)	*(12)*	*(5)*	*(1)*	*(2)*	*(5)*	*(0)*	*8*	*26*
Others	0.00	0.00	100.00	0.00	0.00	0.00	0.00	0.00	
	(0)	*(0)*	*(1)*	*(0)*	*(0)*	*(0)*	*(0)*	*0*	*1*
Total	18.38	24.95	40.62	26.50	7.54	24.18	10.25	18.57	
	(13)	*(24)*	*(45)*	*(30)*	*(12)*	*(32)*	*(13)*	*18*	*116*

Note: Multiple choices are possible; the number of observations are in parentheses.

However, we will see in the next section that this advantage is only a partial one. The figure may also be a consequence of funding made available as part of public policies targeting socially and economically deprived populations, particularly job seekers. The availability of such funds may appear to be a sort of precondition for developing and sustaining the commitment of non-profit organizations. Finally, and unsurprisingly, the profitability of training activities was a strong motivation among for-profit providers at the time when their organizations were founded, with 31.37 per cent of them mentioning it. These pecuniary considerations undoubtedly explain why 38.56 per cent and 26.47 per cent of for-profit organizations, respectively, are motivated by the desire to differentiate themselves from competitors and to adapt to the needs of customers, compared with 11.34 per cent and 21.65 per cent of non-profit organizations. It should be noted that 13.07 per cent of for-profit organizations provide training related to sales of software to companies. This is never the case for non-profit organizations. To some extent, the fact that opportunities for training people is a criterion that for-profit organizations mention more frequently than non-profit organizations (9.15 per cent against 2.06 per cent) could probably also be explained in the same way. Finally, 45.36 per cent of non-profit organizations, compared with 18.95 per cent of for-profit organizations, cite reasons other than those previously stated. These other reasons relate mainly to the choice of training, that is, they choose to train people according to the prerequisites needed to monitor the training. This training may be specific and recurrent or a one-off event. On the face of it, these answers seem to match the criterion of 'adaptation to customer needs'. In this case, however, the organizations' decision-making process is reversed, since training courses are provided in response to customers' wishes. Consequently, the training organization must arrange and adapt its courses on the basis of customers' requests. The concept of prerequisite is probably less important, because it is the training that is adapted to customers' wishes. In the case of the 'other reasons' criterion, it seems that the customers are chosen on the basis of the training to be provided. Organizations first choose the type of training they are going to provide; then they look for people who might be interested in or able to take part in such training. While for-profit organizations seem to favour adaptation to customers (26.47 per cent), non-profit organizations tend to choose the people to be trained according to their skills or suitability for specific training programmes.

If we turn to the current motivations of the different providers, the previous contrasts remain. Indeed, 57.66 per cent of non-profit providers are motivated by trainees' social problems, whereas only one in three were so motivated when their organizations were set up. This increase is difficult to interpret. It can probably be seen as a specialization effect. This specialization could, after all, be achieved only after a certain period of time due to the combined effect of experience and the stabilizing influence of public funds. From this point of view, it can be understood why the availability of public funds is mentioned in 46.72 per cent of cases, compared with 27.84 per cent at the time of founding. However, this emphasis may also undoubtedly be explained by the strengthening over time of the labour force's sympathy with people suffering from social and economic deprivation. This leads them positively to prefer this type of target group, especially since France has experienced chronic unemployment for years. The difficulties and the public funding linked to chronic unemployment have undoubtedly heightened this awareness.

The financial return was also very frequently mentioned by for-profit bodies as being important when they were set up and was also frequently mentioned as being significant at the time of the survey. Indeed, it seems to grow in importance over time. Regarding the desire to differentiate themselves from competitors, it should be noted that the frequency of that motivation increases marginally for for-profit providers between the start-up period and that of the survey, and more significantly for non-profit organizations. The latter was at 11.34 per cent at start-up and rose to more than 36 per cent at the time of the survey. Thus non-profit organizations take into account the fact that they are in competition with other providers, which could support the specialization hypothesis previously advanced. Indeed, while the search for financial profitability is not mentioned as a motivation at start-up, at the time of the survey 2.92 per cent of the non-profit organizations alluded to this criterion in order to justify the choice of trainees. The choice of a target group in relation to 'other criteria' is mentioned by 23.36 per cent of non-profit organizations as an important criterion for selecting the target groups for training, compared with 16.89 per cent of for-profit organizations.

11.5   ACCESS TO FINANCING DURING THE ESTABLISHMENT OF (NON)-PROFIT ORGANIZATIONS

The objective of this section is to shed light on access to funding when (non)-profit organizations are established in the continuing training sector. Indeed, while there is almost unanimous acknowledgement in the economic literature of the social motivations of non-profit organization founders, there is no consensus on the comparative advantage of the non-profit status when it comes to accessing funds. Thus we will try to answer two as yet unresolved questions pertaining to the start-up of non-profit organizations. First, what funds did founders use to start up their business? And second, are there any differences in access to public funds and bank loans between different types of organizations?

According to Table 11.3, 29.43 per cent of the organizations surveyed have no authorized capital and more than 50 per cent have authorized capital exceeding 35000 FF (base year 2001). However, there are differences between non-profit and for-profit organizations. That is 71.65 per cent of non-profit organizations have zero authorized capital, compared with 16.67 per cent of for-profit organizations and despite the strong presence of self-employed workers in this category. However, 72.14 per cent of for-profit organizations have authorized capital exceeding 35000 FF, compared with 18.90 per cent of non-profit organizations (base year 2001). Thus non-profit organizations seem to start with lower authorized capital.

Whatever the legal status of the organizations, most of the funds (65.75 per cent) come from the direct contributions of business founders (Table 11.4). This is one of the stylized facts that characterize profit-making enterprises in the manufacturing sector (Blanchflower and Oswald, 1998; Evans and Jovanovic, 1989; Evans and Leighton, 1989; Holtz-Eakin et al., 1994; Hurst and Lusardi, 2004). Loans account for 15.10 per cent of total start-up capital, public subsidies represent 7.32 per cent and the remainder (and other donations) account for 11.84 per cent.

If one considers all organizations, including those whose authorized capital is zero, the benefit of non-profit organizations disappears, since the average authorized capital of non-profit organizations is 64608 FF, compared with 147859 FF (base year 2001) for for-profit organizations (Table 11.4). Moreover, the founders of non-profit organizations start with a personal wealth seven times lower than that of profit-making founders. The same phenomenon can be observed when what we call initial capital[2] is taken into account. Indeed, the initial capital of the profit-making founders is four times greater than that of non-profit founders. These results may be explained primarily by the existence of the legal constraint of non-redistribution of profits, which weakens the founders' right of ownership. Consequently, they will be less inclined to make a personal contribution over which they would have less control. However, it could also be explained by a wealth effect: the founders of the non-profit organizations are likely to be less wealthy on average. Indeed, non-profit organizations, by providing the entrepreneur social satisfaction on top of the quest for profit, may more easily attract people with strong social motivations and considerable managerial effectiveness, but whose personal financial contributions are lower (Chapelle, 2010).

Table 11.3   *The authorized capital structure of the organizations by legal status*

Authorized capital (K) (*Amount in francs, base year 2001*)							
Initial legal status	**NA**	**K = 0**	**0 <K< 10,000**	**10,000 <K< 35,000**	**35,000 <K< 100,000**	**K >100,000**	**Total**
For-profit enterprises	**10.83** *9*	**16.67** *16*	**3.57** *4*	**7.62** *9*	**45.71** *41*	**26.43** *27*	**100.00** *97*
Non-profit organizations	**39.23** *13*	**71.65** *18*	**1.57** *1*	**7.87** *2*	**7.09** *2*	**11.81** *4*	**100.00** *27*
Other	**100.00** *1*	*0*	*0*	*0*	*0*	*0*	*0*
Total	**22.30** *23*	**29.43** *34*	**3.11** *5*	**7.68** *11*	**36.75** *43*	**23.03** *31*	**100.00** *124*

Note: Figures in italics represent the number of observations. Figures in bold are weighted shares (in %).

Table 11.4 Average amounts from the different sources of initial authorized capital (in francs, base year 2001)

Legal status	Number of organizations	Public assets	Personal/ founders' assets	Donations or gifts	Loans from financial institutions	Other	Average capital	Average number of founders
For-profit enterprises	104	7595	91410	3873	18238	4850	147859	2.114
Non-profit organizations	31	4656	12922	2090	5986	10451	64608	4.778
Total	135	7231	66746	3554	14921	8137	128530	2.745

Note: Weighted shares; the amounts were calculated from the average shares and from the average capital for each status. These amounts were not calculated directly because of some missing data on the amount of capital and the distribution thereof.

Moreover, taking the sample as a whole, the average amount of public contributions, donations and loans is lower for non-profit organizations than for profit-making organizations. In contrast, only the average amounts from 'other sources' are smaller for for-profit organizations. However, these 'other sources' are only a very partial advantage for non-profit organizations since they hardly offset the disadvantage associated with more limited personal contributions, public subsidies and loans. More specifically, we find that the public subsidies and loans granted to non-profit organizations are indeed 1.63 and 3 times, respectively, lower than those granted to profit-making organizations. Thus non-profit organizations do not seem to be favoured by easier access to public funds or bank credit if the whole sample is taken into account. The idea often advanced in the economic literature that the constraint of non-profit distribution could be a token of trust for public funding should, from this point of view, undoubtedly be put into perspective. It seems to serve this purpose only for those founders who have managed to have non-zero authorized capital, that is, those who manage to convince several partners, firstly members, then private donors, and finally governments and banks.

11.6 CONCLUSION

The main results of this survey indicate that the social motivations of non-profit organizations are reflected in the choice of target groups and demonstrate a stronger focus on the most disadvantaged groups, such as job seekers.

The survey also shows that, despite social motivations and the presence of the legal constraint on the non-redistribution of profits that restricts the right of ownership and reduces financial incentives, non-profit organizations seem to be more constrained than for-profit organizations. Indeed, non-profit founders have lower access per founder to loans and public funds. However our results are not clear-cut. In particular, the founders of non-profit organizations have lower personal contributions, which could explain lower access to external funds. In addition, the average authorized capital of non-profit organizations is lower than that of private enterprises and the share of non-profit founders with no authorized capital is higher. In conclusion, non-profit organizations seem to attract entrepreneurs, who would therefore be less endowed with personal contributions. It is through their managerial and higher social qualities that entrepreneurs succeed in starting up their organizations (Chapelle, 2010).

NOTES

1. Departments are administrative sub-regions.
2. Initial capital only consists of personal contributions, donations and other sources of funding.

REFERENCES

Alchian, A. and H. Demsetz (1972), 'Production, information costs and economic organisation', *American Economic Review*, **62** (5), 777–95
Archambault, E. (1999), 'Le secteur associatif en France et dans le monde', in F. Bloch-Lainé (ed.), *Faire société. Les associations au cœur du social*, Paris: Syros, pp. 11–37.
Auteri, M. (2003). 'The entrepreneurial establishment of a nonprofit organisation', *Public Organisation Review*, **3**, 171–89.
Ben-Ner, A. and T. Van Hoomissen (1990), 'The growth of the nonprofit sector in the 1980s: facts and interpretation', *Nonprofit Management and Leadership*, **1** (2), 99–116.
Bielefeld, W. (1994), 'What affects nonprofit survival?', *Nonprofit Management and Leadership*, **5** (1), 19–36.
Bilodeau, M. and A. Slivinski (1998), 'Rational nonprofit entrepreneurship', *Journal of Economics and Management Strategy*, **7** (4), 551–71.
Bises, B. (2000). 'Exemption or taxation for profits of non-profits? An answer from a model incorporating managerial discretion', *Public Choice*, **104**, 19–39.
Blanchflower, D.G. and A.J. Oswald (1998), 'What makes an entrepreneur?', *Journal of Labor Economics*, **16** (1), 26–60.
Bond, L., M. Clément, M. Cournoyer and G. Dupont (1999), 'Taux de survie des entreprises coopératives au Québec', Rapport Développement économique, Innovation et exportation, Direction des Coopératives, Gouvernement du Québec Ministère de l'Industrie et du Commerce, accessed 19 January 2010 at www.mdeie.gouv.qc.ca/fileadmin/sites/internet/documents/publications/pdf/Entreprises/cooperatives/TauxSurvie.pdf.
Cahuc, P. and A. Zylberberg (2006), 'La formation professionnelle des adultes: un système à la dérive', Rapport pour le Centre d'Observation Economique de la CCIP.
Chapelle, K. (2010), 'Non-profit and for-profit entrepreneurship: a trade-off under liquidity constraint', *International Entrepreneurship Management Journal,* **6** (1), 55–80. accessed 19 January 2010 at www.springerlink.com/content/48k87mx807k8w313/.
Defourny, J. and J.L. Monzon Campos (eds) (1992), *Economie Sociale: Entre Economie capitaliste et Economie Publique* and The Third Sector: Cooperative, Mutual and Non Profit Organizations, Collection Ouverture Economique, Brusels: De Boek Université.
DiMaggio, P.J. and W.W. Powell (1983), 'The iron cage revisited: institutional isomorphism and collective rationality in organisational fields', *American Journal of Sociology*, **48** (2), 147–60.
Dimaggio, P.J. and W.W. Powell (1991), 'The iron cage revisited: institutional isomorphism and collective rationality', in P.J. DiMaggio and W. Powell (eds),

The New Institutionalism in Organisational Analysis, Chicago, IL: University of Chicago Press, pp. 63–82.

Du Bois, C., M. Jegers, C. Schepers and R. Pepermans (2003), 'Objectives of non-profit organisations: a literature review', Vrije Universiteit Brussel working paper.

Doumi, M. (2006), 'Impact des projets d'économie solidaire sur les territoires', Etudes et Document du CEREA, Université d'Auvergne II, accessed 19 January 2010 at www.inees.org/fileadmin/INEES/FR/Etude_CEREA.pdf.

Enjolras, B. (1995), 'Comment expliquer la présence d'organisations à but non lucratif dans une économie de marché? L'apport de la théorie économique', *Revue Française d'Economie*, **4** (10), 37–66.

Enjolras, B. (1996), 'Associations et isomorphisme institutionnel', *RECMA*, **261**, 68–76.

Evans, D.S. and B. Jovanovic (1989), 'An estimated model of entrepreneurial choice under liquidity constraint', *Journal of Political Economy*, **97** (4), 808–27.

Evans, D. and L. Leighton (1989), 'Some empirical aspects of entrepreneurship', *American Economic Review*, **79** (3), 519–35.

Glaeser, E.L. and A. Shleifer (2001), 'Not-for-profit entrepreneurs', *Journal of Public Economics*, **81**, 99–115.

Hansmann, H. (1980), 'The role of non profit organisation', *Yale Law Journal,* **89**, 835–901.

Hansmann, H. (1982), 'The effect of tax exemption and other factors on competition between nonprofit and for-profit enterprise', POOBNLS working paper no. 65.

Hansmann, H. (1986). 'The role of non profit organisation', in S. Rose-Ackerman (ed.), *The Economics of Nonprofit Institutions*, New York: Oxford University Press, pp. 57–93.

Hansmann, H. (1998), *The Ownership of Enterprise*, Cambridge, MA: Harvard University Press.

Hansmann, H., D. Kessler and M. McClellan (2002), 'Ownership form and capacity choice in the hospital industry', working paper, March, accessed 19 January 2010 at http://w4.stern.nyu.edu/emplibrary/Hansmann02.pdf.

Holtz-Eakin, D., D. Joulfaian and H.S. Rosen (1994), 'Sticking it out: entrepreneurial survival and liquidity constraints', *Journal of Political Economy*, **102** (1), February, 53–75.

Hurst, E. and A. Lusardi (2004), 'Liquidity constraints, household wealth, and entrepreneurship', *Journal of Political Economy*, **112** (2), 319–47.

James, E. (1983), 'How nonprofits grow: a model', *Journal of Policy Analysis and Management*, **2** (3), 350–65.

James, E. (1987), 'The nonprofit sector in comparative perspective', in W. Powell (ed.), *The Nonprofit Sector: A Research Handbook*, New Haven, CT: Yale University Press, pp. 397–415.

James, E. (1989), 'Economic theories and the nonprofit sector', in H.K. Anheier and W. Seibel (eds), *The Nonprofit Sector: International and Comparative Perspectives*, Berlin and New York: Walter de Gruyter & Co, pp. 21–30.

James, E. (1998), 'Commercialism among nonprofits: objectives, opportunities, and constraints', in B. Weisbrod (ed.), *To Profit or Not To Profit: The Commercial Transformation of the Nonprofit Sector*, Cambridge: Cambridge University Press, pp. 271–85.

James, E. (2004), 'Commercialism and the mission of nonprofits', in P. Frumkin and J.B. Imber (eds), *In Search of the Nonprofit Sector*, New Brunswick, NJ and London: Transaction, pp. 73–84.

James, E. and S. Rose-Ackerman (1985), 'The nonprofit enterprise in market economies', POOBNLS working paper no. 95.

Johns Hopkins University (2006), Institute for Policy Studies, Center for Civil Society Studies 'The comparative nonprofit sector project: comparative data table and nonprofit sector growth'. Last update 27 September 2006, accessed 19 January 2010 at www.jhu.edu/cnp.compdata.html.

Lakdawalla, D. and T. Philipson (1998), 'Nonprofit production and competition', National Bureau for Economic Research working paper no. 6377, June.

Mendell, M., B. Levesque and R. Rouzier (2003), 'Nouvelles formes de finance-ment de l'économie sociale au Québec', in OECD (ed.), *The Non-profit Sector in a Changing Economy*, Paris and Washington, DC: OECD pp. 157–90.

Nyssens, M. (2000), 'Les approches économiques du tiers secteur Apports et limites des analyses anglo-saxonnes d'inspiration néo-classique', *Sociologie du travail*, **42** (4), 551–65.

Organisation for Economic Co-operation and Development (OECD) (2003), *The Non-profit Sector in a Changing Economy*, Paris and Washington, DC: OECD.

Rose-Ackerman, S. (1986), *The Economics of Nonprofit Institutions: Studies in Structure and Policy*, New York: Oxford University Press.

Rose-Ackerman, S. (1996). 'Altruism, nonprofits, and economic theory', *Journal of Economic Literature*, **34**, 701–29.

Salamon, L. and S. Wojciech Sokolowski (2005), 'Nonprofit organisations: new insights from QCEW data', *Monthly Labor Review*, **128** (9), September, 19–26.

Schiff, J. and B. Weisbrod (1991), 'Competition between for-profit and non-profit organisations in commercial markets', *Annals of Public and Cooperative Economics*, **62** (4), 619–39.

Sloan, F.A. (2000), *Not-for-profit Ownership and Hospital Behavior*, accessed 19 January 2010 at www.econ.duke.edu/~fsloan/156/articles/Sloan_Article.html.

Sloan, F.A. (2000), Not-for-profit ownership and hospital behavior', in J. Newhouse and A. Culyer (eds), *Handbook of Health Economics*, volume 1, part 2, North Holland: Elsevier, pp. 1141–74.

Stiglitz, J. and A. Weiss (1981), 'Credit rationing in markets of imperfect informa-tion', *American Economic Review*, **71**, June, 393–410.

Tuckman, H. (1998), 'Competition, commercialization, and the evolution of nonprofit organisational structures', in B. Weisbrod (ed.), *To Profit or Not To Profit: The Commercial Transformation of the Nonprofit Sector*, Cambridge: Cambridge University Press, pp. 25–45.

Twombly, E.C. (2003), 'What factors affect the entry and exit of nonprofit human service organisations in metropolitan areas?', *Nonprofit and Voluntary Sector Quarterly*, **32** (2), 211–35.

Valentinov, V. (2006), 'Nondistribution constraint and managerial discretion: dis-entagling the relationship', *Public Organisation Review*, **6** 305–16.

Wedig, G., A.F. Sloan, M. Hassan and M.A. Morrisey (1988), 'Capital structure, ownership and capital payment policy: the case of hospitals', *Journal of Finance*, **43** (1), March, 21–40.

Weisbrod, B. (1975), 'Toward a theory of the voluntary nonprofit sector in a three-sector economy', in E.S. Phelps (ed.), *Altruism, Morality, and Economic Theory*, New York: Russell Sage Foundation, pp. 171–95.

Weisbrod, B.A. (1988), *The Non-profit Economy*, Cambridge: Cambridge University Press.

Weisbrod, B.A. (ed.) (1998b), *To Profit or Not To Profit. The Commercial Transformation of the Nonprofit Sector*, Cambridge: Cambridge University Press.

Weisbrod, B. (1998a), 'Modeling the nonprofit organisation as a multiproduct firm: a framework for choice', in B. Weisbrod (ed.) *To Profit or Not To Profit: The Commercial Transformation of the Nonprofit Sector*. Cambridge: Cambridge University Press, pp. 47–64.

Young, D. (1980), 'Entrepreneurship and the behaviour of the non-profit organisation: elements of a theory', Ponpo working paper no. 4.

Conclusion

Jean Bonnet, Domingo García Pérez De Lema and Howard Van Auken

Empirical studies suggest that the creation and survival of new firms are important for economic growth and employment (Carree and Thurik, 2003), productivity (Holtz-Eakin and Kao, 2003) and the reduction of social inequalities (Fairlie, 2004). Nevertheless the economic crisis of 2008 clearly demonstrates that entrepreneurial economies can be messy. Part of the explanation of the financial crisis is linked to the overdevelopment of the financial sector due partly to a lack of regulation (individual irresponsibility that leads to a collective risk of default). Also elites and talents have been diverted from more socially productive work by high wages in the financial sector according to Philippon and Reshef (2007). Ester Duflo (2008) notices accordingly that one of the good things to result from the crisis is a better allocation of talents. Indeed entrepreneurial firms can provide leadership during the current period of economic crisis. The economic crisis has led to lower consumer demand, employment and government tax revenue. Market benefits of an entrepreneurial economy are evident in the new technology that has been made available to consumers over the past 10-20 years. Entrepreneurial firms can provide the market with innovations that provide new products for the market and, in turn, generate new employment and tax revenue (Schramm, 2009).

Starting up a firm is not only linked to the managerial skills, the wealth or a low aversion to risk an individual is endowed with, it is also linked to the aspiration and sometimes also to the necessity to create ones' own job. All things being equal, the entrepreneurial choice may be considered as a valuation of the individual's human capital.[1] According to Audrestch (1995), the analysis of the innovation capacity of an industry thus should be conducted at the level of the individual bearing the innovative project rather than at the level of the firm. The reason for that lies in the information asymmetry between the innovator-bearer and the firm's executives as to the feasibility and the profitability of a project. Baumol (2004, p. 2) notices that innovative breakthroughs, since the industrial revolution, have been induced 'in overwhelming proportion by independent inventors and small, newly founded enterprises, not by major firms'.[2] Part of the human capital of the individual is observed by employers and is directly valued on the labour market; another part is unobservable and only the entrepreneurial commitment may value it. A society wanting to benefit from entrepreneurial firms must then favour the emergence of this unobservable human capital and allow individuals to value this surplus. The human capital observed by employers is itself made up of an educational human capital measured by the level of qualification and of a professional and cultural human capital which comprises the professional and social trajectory of the individual. As regards the entrepreneurial choice, having previously held entrepreneurial functions (directorship, management, responsible for a profit centre and so on) is an element that favours entrepreneurship and the survival of the new firm. Professional experience in the same branch of activity is also correlated to a longer life span, as is the experience acquired in a small business thanks to the plurality of functions exercised (Bhattacharjee et al., 2008). Kirzner'alertness that allows an individual to seize business opportunities is concerned with this unobservable human capital. To be creative, having an innovative idea, can also be considered as being endowed with an unobservable human capital. According to Kirzner (2009, p. 10, emphasis added) '*All* the price differentials (*both* attributable to Schumpeterian creativity *and* those present in the simplest of arbitrage contexts) can and should be seen as examples of entrepreneurial arbitrage activity. Such activity drives prices systematically in directions tending to eliminate the price differentials (i.e., the opportunities for pure profit) which are, always, the sparks which ignite entrepreneurial attention, drive, and creativity.' All individuals are not equally endowed with such a capital; for those who are, the appropriation of innovation gains may thus constitute a powerful incentive to entrepreneurship (Lazear and Mc Nabb, 2004).

In the case of perfect and complete markets there are no objective reasons for which an individual might want to become an entrepreneur since in such a case their human capital would be valued at its best. But there are reasons to do with personal and cultural explanations. Anglo-Saxons studies have found that historically firms are more prone to be created by entrepreneurs whose locus of control is internal (Rotter, 1966, 1971; Shapero, 1975; Shapero and Sokol, 1982). In that case individuals are driven by the will to be less dependent upon their environment and to better control the future of their firm. Moreover if new entrepreneurs are also sensitive to the 'need of achievement' motive (McClelland, 1961, 1965), they assess risks according to the level of their abilities and they are more apt to survive. For several years psychological traits such as psychological hardiness (Whetten and Cameron, 1998) or tolerance to ambiguity (Smilor, 1997) stress an effect of theses features both on the propensity to set up a firm and on its performances. Of course these personal characteristics are not independent from a cultural background favouring entrepreneurship. Recent research (Fairlie and Robb, 2006) demonstrates that capturing market opportunities is not independent of a kind of entrepreneurial human capital. This latter, linked to family environment, may explain the higher propensity for entrepreneurship among families of business owners. Yet successful entrepreneurship is nevertheless ensured only if these new entrepreneurs have acquired management experience in the family business. This experience probably allows them to adapt and operate in a risky environment more easily.

In the case of innovative new firms, Moreau (2008) shows that there exists a cycle of entrepreneurial exchange during which the success of the entrepreneurial venture is linked to three phases: the acquisition of an entrepreneurial credit based on the product or the process; the transformation of this entrepreneurial credit in resources (new clients, new financial means, location, public subsidies and so on); and the validation given by partners. According to the author the new innovative firm is extremely fragile and it is the repetition of a performance day after day that consolidates its entrepreneurial credit which is essential for the success of the project. Belonging to social networks might also be crucial as is the case in spin-off formation (Agarwal, 2006; Klepper and Sleeper, 2005). Regarding academic entrepreneurship, close ties established with private firms during joint projects, prior entrepreneurial experience, the ownership of a patent and an entrepreneurial culture where the scientist works are the main factors of entrepreneurial involvement finalized in setting up an innovative firm (Krabel and Mueller, 2008). Innovation should not be restricted to a sectorial definition as some European policies have too often done (Albert, 2009). Public authorities through equating innovation with technological innovation and further with the sole R&D expenses in the end only retain high-tech sectors, when in Europe firms with high growth potential are rather found in traditional sectors. Aiming to replicate the story of Silicon Valley, public authorities miss the fact that it is not a straightforward reproducible model, partly due to the existence of some specific legal conditions conducive to greater mobility of labour (Gilson, 1999). Beside these legal conditions an entrepreneurial culture linked to the presence of small businesses is also an important factor of local entrepreneurship dynamism. Florio (1996) has demonstrated how big firms locating in Mezzogiorno have reduced the entrepreneurial potential of the area. A policy of public grants had the effect of bringing in big production units which modified the circumstances of occupational choice for individuals by making available high wages and thus diverting individuals from freelance activities, which in turn affected the potential for endogenous development. Holcombe (2003) stresses that entrepreneurship exerts a positive influence on the economic environment and that far from only capturing opportunities (Kirzner's entrepreneur), it also creates new opportunities in the local economy.

Entrepreneurial firms are crucial to development and growth; they may actually be regarded as playing a critical role in getting through the current crisis. In the last 50 years rises in living standards have been incredibly huge in all industrialized countries. It is the most important change that humanity has experienced, mainly due to discoveries and innovations in all sectors and branches of activity. A great part of this progress has been achieved by the birth and the development of new innovative firms. Evidently progress also has its own drawbacks and limits. Global warming and the ecological footprint – how much of the Earth's resources does your lifestyle require? – are the most important challenges humanity has to deal with in the current period. According to the association Redefining Progress and its latest footprint analysis, 'humanity is exceeding its ecological limits by 39%. Or, put another way, we would need to have over one third more than the present biocapacity of Earth to maintain the same level of prosperity for future generations'.[3]

The path to use resources in a better way and to avoid wasting them certainly lies in changing our way of life, especially in using new green technologies. These new technologies are the result of two confluences:

- Discovery in new energy saving technology that relies on fundamental economies but also on the capability to practically implement these discoveries in the market. For that we need breakthrough innovations and entrepreneurial firms might then contribute greatly to this new challenge of sustainable growth.
- A strong impulsion from public policies that require cooperation, coordination and the willingness to deal with negative externalities. One of the good results of the current world crisis might be to enlarge the vision of states that are usually focused on egoistic short-term preoccupations. Endowed with the experience of 1929, one might expect that the recession will not be so long and not so deep and above all that a more global regulation of economies could hopefully emerge.

The solution lies in changing consumption modes while promoting new green breakthrough innovations. In this respect, the USA could be in a better position than European countries. Baumol (2004) suggests a very compelling explanation about education where later specialization favours creativity and the ability to 'think outside the box', encourage 'unorthodox ideas and breakthrough approaches and results'.

NOTES

1. Relevant variables accounting for this choice encompass the legal and cultural features specific to each developed country and also the institutional features of its labour market.
2. Baumol (2004, p. 5) notices that the routine innovative activities from large corporations have allowed incremental contributions that have also been very substantial. 'Greater user-friendliness, increased reliability, marginal additions to application, expansions of capacity, flexibility in design – these and many other types of improvement have come out of the industrial R&D facilities, with impressive consistency, year after year, and often pre-announced and pre-advertised.'
3. http://www.rprogress.org/ecological_footprint/about_ecological_footprint.htm (accessed 19 January 2010).

REFERENCES

Agarwal, A. (2006), 'Engaging the inventor: exploring licensing strategies for university inventions and the role of latent knowledge', *Strategic Management Journal*, **27** (1), 63–79.
Albert, P. (2009), 'Le High-Tech, grande illusion du décideur', *l'Expansion Entrepreneuriat, Innover, Développer, Grandir*, January, pp. 14–19.
Audretsch, D. (1995), *Innovation and Industry Evolution*, Cambridge, MA: MIT Press.
Baumol, W.J. (2004), 'Education for innovation: breakthroughs vs. corporate incremental improvements', *National Bureau for Economic Research* paper, no. 5, April.
Bhattacharjee, A., J. Bonnet, N. Le Pape and R. Renault (2008), 'Entrepreneurial motives and performance: why might better educated entrepreneurs be less successful?', University of Cergy-Pontoise THema working paper.
Carree, M.A. and A.R. Thurik (2003), 'The impact of entrepreneurship on economic growth', in Z.J. Acs and D.B. Audretsch (eds), *Handbook of Entrepreneurial Research*, Boston, MA: Kluwer Academic Publishers, pp. 437–71.
Duflo, E. (2008), 'Too many bankers?', research-based policy analysis and commentary from leading economists, 8 October, accessed 19 January 2010 at www.voxeu.org.
Fairlie, R.W. (2004), 'Does business ownership provide a source of upward mobility for Blacks and Hispanics?', in D. Holtz-Eakin (ed.), *Entrepreneurship and Public Policy,* Cambridge, MA: MIT Press, pp. 153–80.
Fairlie, R.W. and A. Robb (2006), 'Families, human capital, and small business: evidence from the Characteristics of Business Owners Survey', in M. Van Praag (ed.), *Entrepreneurship and Human Capital*, Amsterdam, Netherlands: Amsterdam Center for Entrepreneurship, Faculty of Economics and Business, University of Amsterdam, July, pp. 5–11.
Florio, M. (1996), 'Large firms, entrepreneurship and regional development

policy: "growth poles" in the Mezzogiorno over 40 years', *Entrepreneurship and Regional Development*, **8**, 263–95.

Gilson, R. (1999), 'The legal infrastructure of high technology industrial district: Silicon Valley, Route 128, and covenants not to compete', *New York University Law Review*, **3**, 575–629.

Holcombe, R.G. (2003), 'The origins of entrepreneurial opportunities', *Review of Austrian Economics*, **16**, 25–43.

Holtz-Eakin, D. and C. Kao (2003), 'Entrepreneurship and economic growth: the proof is in the productivity', Syracuse University Center for Policy Research, Maxwell School working paper no. 50.

Kirzner, I.M. (2009), 'The alert and creative entrepreneur: a clarification', *Small Business Economics*, **32** (2), February, 145–52.

Klepper, S. and S. Sleeper (2005), 'Entry by spinoffs', *Management Science*, **51** (8), 1291–306.

Krabel, S. and P. Mueller (2008), 'Academic entrepreneurship: what drives scientists to start their company', paper presented at the 25th Celebration Conference 2008 Entrepreneurship and Innovation: Organizations, Institutions, Systems and Regions, CBS, Copenhagen, 17-20 June.

Lazear, E.P. and R. McNabb (2004), *Personnel Economics, Concepts*, vol. 1, and *Performance*, vol. 2, The International Library of Critical Writings in Economics, series editor M. Blaug, Cheltenham, UK and Northampton, MA, USA: Edward Elgar Publishing.

McClelland, D.D. (1961), 'Entrepreneurship behavior' and 'Characteristics of entrepreneurs', in *The Achieving Society*, chapters 6 and 7, Princeton, NJ: D Van Nostrand, pp. 205–58, 259–300.

McClelland, D.D. (1965), 'Achievement and entrepreneurship: a longitudinal study', *Journal of Personality and Social Psychology*, **1** (2), 389–92.

Miller, D. (1983), 'The correlates of entrepreneurship in three types of firms', *Management Science*, **29**, 770–91.

Moreau, R. (2008), 'La spirale du succès entrepreneurial', grand prix 2007 de la réflexion impertinente sur le développement durable, l'entrepreneuriat, et le développement des territoires, *revue Population and Avenir*, 687, March-April.

Philippon, T. and A. Reshef (2007), 'Skill biased financial development: education, wages and occupations in the U.S. finance sector', mimeo, NYU Stern Business School, September.

Rotter, J.B. (1966), 'General expectancies for internal versus external control of reinforcement', *Psychology Monographs*, **80**, 609.

Rotter, J.B. (1971), 'External control and internal control', *Psychology Today*, **5** (37-42), 58–9.

Schramm, C. (2009), 'Our role in the evolution of capitalism', in *Kauffman Thoughtbook*, Kansas City, MO: Kaufman Foundation, pp. 8–14.

Shapero, A. (1975), 'The displaced, uncomfortable entrepreneur', *Psychology Today*, **9** (6), 83–8.

Shapero, A. and L. Sokol (1982), 'The social dimensions of entrepreneurship', in C. Kent, D.L. Sexton and K.H. Vesper (eds), *Encyclopedia of Entrepreneurship*, Englewood Cliffs, NJ: Prentice Hall, pp. 72–90.

Smilor, R. (1997), 'Entrepreneurship reflexions on a subversive activity', *Journal of Business Venturing*, **12**, 341–6.

Whetten, D.A. and K.S. Cameron (1998), *Developing Management Skills*, Reading, MA: Addison-Wesley.

Index